East of the Sun

The title of this book is from the Norwegian folk tale *East O' the Sun and West O' the Moon* on page 218.

ODYSSEY An HBJ Literature Program

Sam Leaton Sebesta

Consultants

Elaine M. Aoki	Myra Cohn Livingston
Willard E. Bill	Daphne P. Muse
Sylvia Engdahl	Margaret D. Simpson
Carolyn Horovitz	Barre Toelken

East
of the Sun

HARCOURT BRACE JOVANOVICH, PUBLISHERS
New York Chicago San Francisco Atlanta Dallas *and* London

ISBN 0–15–333356–1

Acknowledgments

For permission to reprint copyrighted material grateful acknowledgment is given to the following sources:

The Ashland Poetry Press: "Today Song" from *A Poetry Ritual for Grammar Schools* by Robert McGovern. The Ashland Poetry Press, 1974.

Atheneum Publishers: "The Return to Egypt" from *The Egypt Game* by Zilpha Keatley Snyder. Copyright © 1967 by Zilpha Keatley Snyder. "Metaphor" from *It Doesn't Always Have to Rhyme* by Eve Merriam. Copyright © 1964 by Eve Merriam. Adapted from pages 3–22 of *Jennifer, Hecate, MacBeth, William McKinley, and Me, Elizabeth* by E. L. Konigsburg. Copyright © 1967 by E. L. Konigsburg. "Wailed a ghost in a graveyard at Kew" from *A Lollygag of Limericks* by Myra Cohn Livingston (A Margaret K. McElderry Book). Copyright © 1978 by Myra Cohn Livingston. First verse from "Hickenthrift and Hickenloop" from *The Phantom Ice Cream Man More Nonsense Verse* by X. J. Kennedy (A Margaret K. McElderry Book). Copyright © 1979 by X. J. Kennedy.

The Bobbs-Merrill Company and Faber and Faber Limited: "My Uncle Dan" and "My Aunt" from *Meet My Folks* by Ted Hughes. Copyright © 1961, 1973 by Ted Hughes.

The Book House for Children, Lake Bluff, Illinois: "East O' the Sun and West O' the Moon" from *The Magic Garden of My Book House* (Vol. 7) by Olive Beaupre Miller, editor.

Coward, McCann & Geoghegan, Inc.: Adapted from *Where Was Patrick Henry on the 29th of May?* by Jean Fritz. Text copyright © 1975 by Jean Fritz.

Thomas Y. Crowell: "The Worst Morning" (retitled) adapted from *. . . and now Miguel* by Joseph Krumgold. Copyright 1953 by Joseph Krumgold. "When first I appear . . .," "A nickel and a dime . . .," and "Why did the lobster . . ." from *The American Riddle Book* by Carl Withers and Dr. Sula Benet. Copyright © 1954 by Carl Withers and Dr. Sula Benet. An Abelard-Schuman Book.

Crown Publishers, Inc. and Clarkson N. Potter, Inc.: "The Walrus and the Carpenter" from *The Annotated Alice* by Lewis Carroll. Introduction and notes by Martin Gardner. Copyright © 1960 by Martin Gardner.

The Dial Press: "I never asked for no allergy" excerpted from the book *Philip Hall Likes Me. I Reckon Maybe.* by Bette Greene. Copyright © 1974 by Bette Greene.

Dodd, Mead & Company: "There Was an Old Lady of Chertsey" and "There Was a Young Girl of Majorca" from *The Complete Nonsense Book* by Edward Lear.

Doubleday & Company, Inc.: "Direction" by Alonzo Lopez from *The Whispering Wind* edited by Terry Allen. Copyright © 1972 by the Institute of American Indian Arts. "Dinky" from *The Collected Poems of Theodore Roethke* by Theodore Roethke. Copyright © 1953 by Theodore Roethke. Text and Melody from "John Henry" by Bascom Lamar Lunsford.

E. P. Dutton: "Bando" (retitled) from *My Side of the Mountain* by Jean George. Copyright © 1959 by Jean George. "Wind is a ghost" from *Whirlwind Is a Ghost Dancing* by Natalia Belting. Text copyright © 1974 by Natalia Belting.

Environmental Action: "This Earth Is Sacred" (titled "All Things Are Connected") by Chief Sealth from *Environmental Action*, November 11, 1972, page 7.

Farrar, Straus and Giroux, Inc.: "The Megrimum" (retitled) from *Kneeknock Rise* by Natalie Babbitt. Copyright © 1970 by Natalie Babbitt. "A Very Talented Cricket" (retitled) from *The Cricket in Times Square* by George Selden. Illustrated by Garth Williams. Copyright © 1960 by George Selden Thompson and Garth Williams.

Four Winds Press, A Division of Scholastic Magazines, Inc.: Eight riddles from *The Nonsense Book* by Duncan Emrich. Text copyright © 1970 by Duncan Emrich.

Grosset & Dunlap, Inc.: "Riddle" from *The Sparrow Bush* by Elizabeth Coatsworth. Copyright © 1966 by Grosset & Dunlap, Inc.

Harcourt Brace Jovanovich, Inc.: Slight adaptation of "Laughing Gas" from *Mary Poppins*, copyright 1934, 1962 by P. L. Travers. "I called to the wind" by Kyorai from *More Cricket Songs: Japanese Haiku*, translated and copyright © 1971 by Harry Behn. "The Tournament" (retitled) abridged and adapted from *Half Magic* by Edward Eager, copyright 1954 by Harcourt Brace Jovanovich, Inc.

Harcourt Brace Jovanovich, Inc., M. T. Parsons and The Hogarth Press: Slight abridgment and adaptation of "Two of Everything" by Li Po from *The Treasure of Li-Po* by Alice Ritchie, copyright 1949 by Harcourt Brace Jovanovich, Inc.; renewed 1977 by M. T. Ritchie.

Harper & Row, Publishers, Inc.: From "Stories from Kansas" (retitled "Which") in *Allegiances* by William Stafford. Copyright © 1968 by William Stafford. "Running away . . ." from *Near the Window Tree: Poems and Notes* by Karla Kuskin. Copyright © 1975 by Karla Kuskin.

Heirs of Knud Rasmussen: "And I think over again . . ." (retitled "Song") from *Intellectual Culture of the Copper Eskimos* translated by Knud Rasmussen.

Holt, Rinehart and Winston, Publishers: "The Secret Sits" from *The Poetry of Robert Frost* edited by Edward Connery Lathem. Copyright 1942 by Robert Frost. Copyright © 1969 by Holt, Rinehart and Winston. Copyright © 1970 by Lesley Frost Ballantine.

Houghton Mifflin Company: "Dangerous Voyage" (retitled) from *Island of the Blue Dolphins* by Scott O'Dell. Copyright © 1960 by Scott O'Dell.

Alfred A. Knopf, Inc.: "Sea Calm" from Selected Poems of Langston Hughes by Langston Hughes. Copyright 1926 by Alfred A. Knopf, Inc.; renewed 1954 by Langston Hughes. "Lincoln Monument: Washington" from The Dream Keeper and Other Poems by Langston Hughes. Copyright 1932 by Alfred A. Knopf, Inc.; renewed 1960 by Langston Hughes.

J. B. Lippincott Company: "A tooter who tooted a flute," "Betty Botter," and "A tree toad loved a she-toad" from A Twister of Twists, A Tangler of Tongues by Alvin Schwartz. Copyright © 1972 by Alvin Schwartz.

Little, Brown and Co. in Association with The Atlantic Monthly Press: "Saved by a Whisker" from By The Great Horn Spoon! by Albert S. Fleischman. Copyright © 1963 by Albert S. Fleischman.

Lothrop, Lee & Shepard Co. (A division of William Morrow & Company): Adaptation of "Something for Davy" (retitled) from Thank You, Jackie Robinson by Barbara Cohen. Copyright © 1974 by Barbara Cohen.

Macmillan Publishing Co., Inc. and Collins Publishers: "Lucy's Adventure" (retitled) from The Lion, The Witch and The Wardrobe by C. S. Lewis. Copyright 1950 by Macmillan Publishing Co., Inc. Copyright renewed © 1978 by Arthur Owen Barfield.

McGraw-Hill Book Company: "Old Ben" from Dawn of Remembered Spring by Jesse Stuart. Copyright © 1972 by Jesse Stuart.

David McKay Co., Inc. and Mrs. Helen Thurber: From Plays and How To Put Them On by Moyne Rice Smith, © 1961 by Moyne Rice Smith. Published by Henry Z. Walck, Inc. Based on the book The Great Quillow by James Thurber, published by Harcourt Brace Jovanovich, Inc. Copyright © 1944 by James Thurber. Copyright © 1972 by Helen W. Thurber.

David McKay Co., Inc. and Ian Serraillier: Slight abridgment of "A Hero's Promise" (retitled) from The Way of Danger by Ian Serraillier. Published by Henry Z. Walck, Inc. © 1962 by Ian Serraillier, and © 1965 Heinemann Educational Books, London.

William Morrow & Co.: "I brought to the New World the gift of devotion" from North Star Shining by Hildegard Hoyt Swift. Copyright 1947 by Hildegarde Hoyt Swift and Lynd Ward.

Rand McNally & Co.: Two riddles from Would You Put Money In a Sand Bank? by Harold Longman. Copyright 1968 by Harold Longman.

Rothco Cartoons, Inc.: "There Was a Young Lady of Bright" by A. H. Reginald Buller from Punch Magazine. © Punch/Rothco.

Charles Scribner's Sons: "Emergency in Space" (retitled) from Farmer in the Sky by Robert A. Heinlein. Copyright 1950 Robert A. Heinlein.

Sterling Publishing Company, Inc.: "Apple Peeling," "Hula Hooping," "String Ball, Largest," and "Pulling with Teeth" from the Guinness Book of World Records. © 1979 by Sterling Publishing Company, New York.

Art Acknowledgments

Chuck Bowden: 31, 207, 255, 293, 341, 403 (adapted from photographs from the following sources: 31, courtesy Atheneum; 293, courtesy Farrar, Straus & Giroux; 341, courtesy Houghton Mifflin; 403, courtesy Little, Brown); Sharon Harker, 64–65 (top), 67, 74–77 (top), 147, 208–211 (top), 213, 295, 359, 378–385 (top), 412; Jerry Smath; 64–65 (bottom), 74–77 (bottom), 208–211 (bottom), 378–385 (bottom).

Cover: Richard Brown

Unit Openers: Jane Teiko Oka

Contents

3 Never Give Up *149*

5 To Live with Nature *297*

1 It Must Be a Trick

A Tricky Twisty Trio

Traditional tongue twisters collected by Alvin Schwartz

Objectives ● To recognize alliteration as a source of verbal humor. ● To compose alliterative sentences and poems.

Betty Botter
　　bought some butter,
But, she said,
　　the butter's bitter.
If I put it
　　in my batter,
It will make
　　my batter bitter.
But a bit
　　of better butter—
That would make
　　my batter better.
So she bought
　　a bit of butter,
Better than
　　her bitter butter.
And she put it
　　in her batter,
And the batter
　　was not bitter.
So 'twas better
　　Betty Botter
Bought a bit
　　of better butter.

Introducing the Poems *Say five times quickly,* The sixth sheik's sheep's sick. *This sentence is called a tongue twister because closely related sounds come one after another, making it difficult to say the sentence. Now we're going to read three tongue-twisting poems.*

Words to Know

vetoed: rejected with authority. (page 15)
tutor: Refer students to the glossary.

Discussion Questions *Which poem do you think was the most difficult to say? Which was the funniest? Alliteration is the repetition of a beginning letter sound in a group of words. Find the alliteration in the poems we read.* (The *b* sounds in "Betty Botter"; the *t* sounds in the last two poems.) *Which words in the last two poems sound the same?* (Toad/toed; tutor/tooter.)

A tree toad loved a she-toad
　　That lived up in a tree.
She was a three-toed tree toad,
　　But a two-toed toad was he.
The two-toed toad tried to win
　　The she-toad's friendly nod,
For the two-toed toad loved the ground
　　On which the three-toed toad trod.
But no matter how the two-toed tree toad tried,
　　He could not please her whim.
In her tree-toad bower,
　　With her three-toed power,
The she-toad vetoed him.

Enriching Activity *Writing.* Write tongue-twister sentences.

A tooter who tooted a flute
　　Tried to tutor two tutors to toot.
Said the two to the tutor,
　　"Is it harder to toot or
To tutor two tutors to toot?"

Illustrated by Marie-Louise Gay

Objectives ● To note the use of detail in portraying a character. ● To speculate about a character's motives. ● To record details in a diary entry. ● To consider how a new friendship develops and changes.

Synopsis of the Story Elizabeth's first glimpse of Jennifer is of two bony feet dangling from a tree branch, and Jennifer's first words are a calm announcement that she is a witch. As Elizabeth gets to know Jennifer, she notices that her new friend does have some uncanny habits and abilities. On Halloween night, Jennifer gives Elizabeth a demonstration of her skills when her trick-or-treat technique produces a wagonload of loot. Elizabeth also ends up with a sackful of treats and much admiration for Jennifer.

Jennifer   **Reading Level** Easy

From a novel by E.L. Konigsburg

Illustrated by Dora Leder

Elizabeth felt she was the loneliest child in the "whole U.S. of A."—until she met Jennifer. Jennifer was unlike anyone Elizabeth had ever known. She never joked or laughed. She didn't talk about the usual things, like sports, parties, and school. But Jennifer did tell Elizabeth a very important secret—that she was a witch. And very soon Elizabeth began to believe it was true.

16

Background The novel *Jennifer, Hecate, MacBeth, William McKinley, and Me, Elizabeth* was a Newbery Honor Book in 1968. It also was in "Fanfare," the *Horn Book's* honor list in 1968 and was on the American Library Association Notable Children's Books list in 1967.

Introducing the Story *What do you know about witches?* (Possible answers: witches have magic powers; they wear black robes and hats.) *In the story you are about to read, a lonely girl named Elizabeth meets a new friend who is most unusual and claims to be a witch. See if you believe that Elizabeth's new friend Jennifer is what she says she is.*

I first met Jennifer on my way to school. It was Halloween, and she was sitting in a tree. I was going back to school from lunch. This particular lunch hour was only a little different from usual because of Halloween. We were told to dress in costume for the school Halloween parade. I was dressed as a Pilgrim.

I always walked the back road to school, and I always walked alone. We had moved to the apartment house in town in September just before school started, and I walked alone because I didn't have anyone to walk with. I walked the back way because it passed through a little woods that I liked. Jennifer was sitting in one of the trees in this woods.

I had my head way back and was watching the leaves when I first saw Jennifer up in the tree. She was dressed as a Pilgrim, too. I saw her feet first. She was sitting on one of the lower branches of the tree swinging her feet. That's how I happened to see her feet first. They were just about the boniest feet I had ever seen. Swinging right in front of my eyes as if I were sitting in the first row at Cinerama. They wore real Pilgrim shoes made of buckles and cracked old leather. The heel part flapped up and down because the shoes were so

big that only the toe part could stay attached. Those shoes looked as if they were going to fall off any minute.

I grabbed the heel of the shoe and shoved it back onto the heel of that bony foot. Then I wiped my hands on my Pilgrim apron and looked up at Jennifer. I didn't know yet that she was Jennifer. She was not smiling, and I was embarrassed.

I said in a loud voice, which I hoped would sound stout red but which came out sounding thin blue, "You're going to lose that shoe."

The first thing Jennifer ever said to me was, "Witches never lose anything."

"But you're not a witch," I said. "You're a Pilgrim, and look, so am I."

"I won't argue with you," she said. "Witches convince; they never argue. But I'll tell you this much. Real witches are Pilgrims, and just because I don't have on a silly black costume and carry a silly broom and wear a silly black hat, doesn't mean that I'm not a witch. I'm a witch all the time and not just on Halloween."

I didn't know what to say, so I said what my mother always says when she can't answer one of my questions. I said, "You better hurry up now, or you'll be late for school."

"Witches are never late," she said.

"But witches have to go to school." I wished I had said something clever.

"I just go to school because I'm putting the teacher under a spell," she said.

"Which teacher?" I asked. "Get it? *Witch* teacher?" I laughed. I was pleased that now I had said something clever.

Jennifer neither laughed nor answered. But I was sure she'd got it. She looked at me hard and said, "Give me those three chocolate chip cookies, and I'll come down and tell you my name, and I'll walk the rest of the way to school with you."

I wasn't particularly hungry for the cookies, but I was hungry for company, so I said, "Okay," and reached out my hand holding the cookies. I wondered how she could tell that they were chocolate chips. They were in a bag.

After Jennifer touched the ground, I saw that she was taller than I. Everybody was. I was the shortest kid in my class. I was always the shortest kid in my class. She was thin. Skinny is what she really was. She came toward my hand and looked hard at the bag of cookies.

"Are you sure you didn't bite any of them?" she demanded.

"Sure I'm sure," I said. I was getting mad, but a bargain's a bargain.

"Well," she said, taking one cookie out of the bag, "My name is Jennifer. Now let's get going." As she said "going," she grabbed the bag with the other two cookies and started to walk.

"Wait up," I yelled. "A bargain's a bargain. Don't you want to know my name?"

"I told you witches are never late, but I can't be responsible for you yet . . . Elizabeth."

She knew my name already! She walked so fast that I was almost convinced that she was a witch; she was practically flying. We got to school just as the tardy bell began to ring. Jennifer's room was a fifth grade just off the corridor near the entrance, and she slipped into her classroom while the bell was still buzzing. My room was four doors further down the hall, and I got to my room *after* the bell had stopped.

After the class finishes the story, ask the students how they think Jennifer would have acted if she had been late for class.

She had said that witches are never late. Being late felt as uncomfortable as my tight Pilgrim dress. No Pilgrim had ever suffered as much as I did. Walking to my seat while everyone stared at me was awful. My desk was in the back of the room; it was a long, long walk. The whole class had time to see that I was a blushing Pilgrim. I knew that I was ready to cry. The whole class didn't have to know that too, so I didn't raise my eyes until I was seated and felt sure that they wouldn't leak. When I looked up, I saw that there were six Pilgrims: three other Pilgrim girls and two Pilgrim boys. That's a lot of Pilgrims for a class of twenty. But none of them could be witches, I thought. After checking over their costumes and shoes, I decided that at least three of them had cousins who had been Pilgrims the year before.

Our lesson that afternoon was short, and I didn't perform too well. I had to tug on my dress a lot and scratch under my Pilgrim hat a lot. I would have scratched other places where the costume itched, but they weren't polite.

At last we were all lined up in the hall. Each class was to march to the auditorium and be seated. Then one class at a time would walk across the stage before the judges. The rest of the classes would be the audience. The classes at the end of the hall marched to the auditorium first.

There were classes on both sides of the hall near my room, and the space for the marchers was narrow. Some of the children had large cardboard cartons over them and were supposed to be packages of cereal or sports cars. These costumes had trouble getting through. Then there was Jennifer. She was last in line. She looked neither to the right nor to the left but slightly up toward the ceiling. I kept my eye on her hoping she'd say "Hi" so that I wouldn't feel so alone standing there. She didn't. But as Jennifer's class passed, Jennifer clop-clopped along in the line with her eyes still up toward the ceiling and passed me a note almost without my knowing. She did it so fast that I wasn't even sure she did it until I felt the note in my hand and crunched it beneath my apron to hide it. Jennifer never took her eyes off the ceiling or broke out of line for even half a step.

Finally, our class got to the auditorium. After I sat down, I opened the note, holding both my hands under my Pilgrim apron. I slowly slipped my hands out and glanced at the note. I was amazed at what I saw. Jennifer's note looked like this:

Meet for Trick or Treat
at
Half after six P.M. o'clock
of this evening.
By the same tree.
Bring two (2) bags.
I hope were good cookies

Point out that Jennifer has used the old-fashioned way of making an *s*. It looks like an *f*.

During the time of the Pilgrims, it was customary to write with a *quill*, a pen made from a large feather.

I studied the note a long time. I thought about the note as I watched the Halloween parade; I wondered if Jennifer used a <u>quill</u> pen. You can guess that I didn't win any prizes for my costume. Neither did Jennifer (even though I thought she should have). We all marched across the stage wearing our masks and stopped for a curtsy or bow (depending on whether you were a girl or a boy) in front of the judges who were sitting at a table in the middle of the stage. Some of the girls who were disguised as boys forgot themselves and curtsied. Then we marched off. Our class was still seated when Jennifer clop-clopped across the stage in those crazy Pilgrim slippers.

She didn't wear a mask at all. She wore a big
brown paper bag over her head and *there were
no holes cut out for her eyes.* Yet, she walked
up the stairs, across the stage, stopped and curtsied, and walked off without tripping or falling or
walking out of those gigantic shoes.

Our family rushed through supper that night.
But the trick or treaters started coming even before we finished. Most of the early ones were
bitsy kids who had to bring their mothers to reach
the door bells for them.

I didn't tell my parents about Jennifer. I mentioned to my mother that I was meeting a friend
at 6:30, and we were going to trick or treat

together. Mom just asked, "Someone from school?" and I just said, "Yes."

The days start getting short, and the evenings start getting cool in late October. So I had to wear my old ski jacket over my costume. I looked like a Pilgrim who had made a bad trade with the Indians. Jennifer was waiting. She was leaning against the tree. She had put on stockings. They were long, black, cotton stockings, and she wore a huge black shawl. She smelled a little bit like moth balls, but I happen to especially like that smell in autumn.

"Hi," I said.

"I'll take the bigger bag," she replied.

She didn't say "please."

I held out the bags. She took the bigger one. She didn't say "thank you." Her manners were unusual. I guessed that witches never said "please" and never said "thank you." All my life my mother had taught me a politeness vocabulary. I didn't mind. I thought that "please" and "thank you" made conversation prettier, just as bows and lace make dresses prettier. I was full of admiration for how easily Jennifer managed without bows or lace or "please" or "thank you."

She opened her bag, stuck her head way down inside, and said:

"Bag, sack, parcel post,
Fill thyself
With goodies most."

She lifted her head out of the bag and tightened her shawl. "We can go now," she said.

"Don't you mean 'Bag, sack, parcel, *poke?*'" I asked. "Parcel *post* is the mail; *poke* is a name for a bag."

Jennifer was walking with her head up, eyes up. She shrugged her shoulders and said, "Poetic license. *Poke* doesn't rhyme."

I shrugged my shoulders and started walking with her. Jennifer disappeared behind a tree. No master spirit had taken her away. She reappeared in a minute, pulling a wagon. It was the usual kind of child's wagon, but to make the sides taller, she had stretched a piece of chicken wire all along the inner rim. Jennifer pulled the wagon, carried her bag, clutched her shawl, and clop-clopped toward the first house. I walked.

I had been trick or treating for a number of years. I began as a bitsy kid, and my mother rang the door bells for me, as other mothers were ringing them for those other bitsy kids that night. I had been a nurse, a mouse (I had worn my sleepers with the feet in), and other things. I had been a Pilgrim before, too. I mentioned that I had been a Pilgrim the year before. All I mean to say is that I'd been trick or treating for years and years and years, and I'd seen lots of trick or treaters come to our house, but I'd never, never, never seen a performance like Jennifer's.

This is the way Jennifer operated: 1. She left the wagon outside the door of the house and out of sight of her victim. 2. She rang the bell. 3. Instead of smiling and saying "trick or treat," she said nothing when the people came to the door.

4. She half fell against the door post and said, "I would like just a drink of water." 5. She breathed hard. 6. The lady or man who answered would say, "Of course," and would bring her a drink of water. 7. As she reached out to get the water, she dropped her big, empty bag. 8. The lady or man noticed how empty it was and said, "Don't you want just a little something?" 9. The lady or man poured stuff into Jennifer's bag. 10. The lady or man put a little something in my bag, too. 11. Jennifer and I left the house. 12. Jennifer dumped the treats into the wagon. 13. Jennifer clop-clopped to the next house with the bag empty again. 14. I walked.

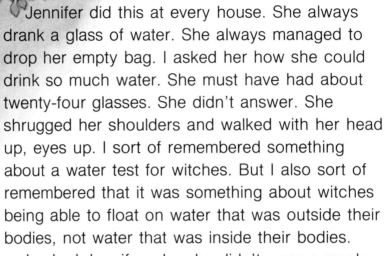

Jennifer did this at every house. She always drank a glass of water. She always managed to drop her empty bag. I asked her how she could drink so much water. She must have had about twenty-four glasses. She didn't answer. She shrugged her shoulders and walked with her head up, eyes up. I sort of remembered something about a water test for witches. But I also sort of remembered that it was something about witches being able to float on water that was outside their bodies, not water that was inside their bodies.

I asked Jennifer why she didn't wear a mask. She answered that one disguise was enough. She told me that all year long she was a witch, disguised as a perfectly normal girl; on Halloween she became undisguised. She may be a witch, I thought, and, of course, she was a girl. But perfect never! And normal never!

I can say that Jennifer collected more treats on that Halloween than I had in all my years put together including the time I was a mouse in my sleepers with the feet in. Because I was with Jennifer each time she went into her act, I managed to collect more treats on that Halloween than I ever had before but not nearly as many as Jennifer. My bag was heavy, though.

Jennifer and I parted about a block from my apartment house. My bag was so heavy that I could hardly hold it with one hand as I pushed the button for the elevator. I put the bag on the floor while I waited. When the elevator arrived, I leaned over to pick up my bundle and heard my Pilgrim dress go *r-r-r-r-r-i-p.* I arrived at our apartment, tired and torn, but happy. Happy because I had had a successful Halloween and happy because my costume had ripped. I wouldn't have to be an itchy Pilgrim another Halloween.

What does Elizabeth think of Jennifer when they first meet? (Possible answer: she finds her unusual, intriguing.) *How does she feel about Jennifer at the end of the story?* (Possible answers: she likes and admires her; she thinks Jennifer is unlike anyone she has ever known.)

Enriching Activities **1.** *Oral expression.* Have each student make up a different spell for Jennifer to say into her trick-or-treat bag or another plan for Jennifer to use when trick-or-treating. Have the students present them to the class. **2.** *Collage.* Have the students work in small groups to create collages of items and symbols associated with Halloween.

Questions

1. Literal/recall Possible answers: Jennifer does not smile (page 18); she does not say "please" or "thank you" (page 25); she is tall and thin (page 20).

2. Literal/recall Possible answers: she knows Elizabeth's name (page 21); she knows three cookies are in the bag (page 19); she recites a poem as if it were a spell (page 25).

3. Interpretive/ inference Possible answer: Jennifer may hope that Elizabeth will be interested enough to become her friend.

4. Vocabulary b. (page 26)

5. Literal/recall and **Interpretive/inference** Possible answers: her old-fashioned writing (page 23); her trick-or-treat methods (pages 26–28).

1. Elizabeth tells you that Jennifer has bony feet. What is another detail she tells about Jennifer?

2. Describe one thing Jennifer does to help convince Elizabeth that she (Jennifer) is a witch.

3. Why does Jennifer want to convince Elizabeth that she (Jennifer) is a witch?

4. When Jennifer says that she uses *poetic license,* what does she mean?
   a. Some poets have permits to write poetry.
   b. Some poets use words in unusual ways to suit their particular needs.
   c. A witch's poems are magic.

5. Describe one thing that Elizabeth admires about Jennifer.

Critical/relating to experience *Diary entries.*

Activity

When Elizabeth first meets Jennifer, she describes the meeting in great detail. Think back to a first meeting you have had with someone who is now a friend. Write a diary entry about that meeting. Give details about the place you met, what you were doing and feeling at that time, and what happened. If you prefer, the meeting you describe can be an imaginary one.

About E. L. KONIGSBURG

Where do authors get ideas for their stories? E. L. Konigsburg, like many others, starts with her own life. "My own children are all visible in my books. They pose for me," she says. Her children are her first editors as well. "I read them what I have written and watch their reactions," she says, "and I revise accordingly."

E. L. Konigsburg (the "E" stands for "Elaine") was born in New York City, but she grew up in Pennsylvania and studied to become a chemist at the University of Pittsburgh. After teaching science, she turned to writing.

E. L. Konigsburg began writing every morning after her three children had left for school. She got the idea for the story about Jennifer from something that happened to her daughter, Laurie. The Konigsburgs had just moved to a new town. Laurie was shy and had a difficult time making new friends. Then she met a tall black girl. The friendship was the beginning of the story. The story itself, of course, came from Mrs. Konigsburg's imagination.

E. L. Konigsburg draws her own pictures for her books. She makes the drawings from photographs of her children.

More Books by E. L. Konigsburg

From the Mixed-Up Files of Mrs. Basil E. Frankweiler (Atheneum, 1967)
Altogether, One at a Time (Atheneum, 1975)
Throwing Shadows (Atheneum, 1979)

The Walrus and the Carpenter

A poem by Lewis Carroll

Illustrations by Robert Van Nutt

based on the drawings of Sir John Tenniel

Objectives ● To enjoy a nonsense poem that tells a story. ● To interpret a poem through various dramatic forms.
Background Lewis Carroll gave the original illustrator, Sir John Tenniel, the choice of a carpenter, a butterfly, or a baronet as the walrus's companion. Each word fit the rhyme scheme and suited the nonsense of the poem.

1 The sun was shining on the sea,
    Shining with all his might:
He did his very best to make
    The billows smooth and bright—
And this was odd, because it was
    The middle of the night.

2 The moon was shining sulkily,
    Because she thought the sun
Had got no business to be there
    After the day was done—
"It's very rude of him," she said,
    "To come and spoil the fun!"

3 The sea was wet as wet could be,
    The sands were dry as dry.
You could not see a cloud, because
    No cloud was in the sky:
No birds were flying overhead—
    There were no birds to fly.

Introducing the Poem   More than a hundred years ago, an English mathematician wrote a very funny, unusual book called Alice's Adventures in Wonderland. His real name was Charles Dodgson, but he chose the pen name of Lewis Carroll. People liked Alice so much that he wrote another book, Through the Looking Glass and What Alice Found There. In these books, strange fantasy characters are always telling Alice something that doesn't make sense. Here is a nonsense poem that two funny gentlemen named Tweedledum and Tweedledee recite to her.

4 The Walrus and the Carpenter
     Were walking close at hand:
   They wept like anything to see
     Such quantities of sand:
   "If this were only cleared away,"
     They said, "it would be grand!"

5 "If seven maids with seven mops
     Swept it for half a year,
   Do you suppose," the Walrus said,
     "That they could get it clear?"
   "I doubt it," said the Carpenter,
     And shed a bitter tear.

6 "O Oysters, come and walk with us!"
     The Walrus did beseech.
   "A pleasant walk, a pleasant talk,
     Along the briny beach:
   We cannot do with more than four,
     To give a hand to each."

33

7 The eldest Oyster looked at him,
   But never a word he said:
The eldest Oyster winked his eye,
   And shook his heavy head—
Meaning to say he did not choose
   To leave the oyster-bed.

8 But four young Oysters hurried up,
   All eager for the treat:
Their coats were brushed, their faces washed,
   Their shoes were clean and neat—
And this was odd, because, you know,
   They hadn't any feet.

9 Four other Oysters followed them,
   And yet another four;
And thick and fast they came at last,
   And more, and more, and more—
All hopping through the frothy waves,
   And scrambling to the shore.

Explain that in stanza
11, the *nonsense* con-
sists of unrelated
objects that are put
together. Have the
students note the ob-
jects the Walrus plans
to talk about. Point
out that this stanza
is famous and often
quoted.

10 The Walrus and the Carpenter
    Walked on a mile or so,
And then they rested on a rock
    Conveniently low:
And all the little Oysters stood
    And waited in a row.

11 "The time has come," the Walrus said,
    "To talk of many things:
Of shoes—and ships—and sealing wax—
Of cabbages—and kings—
And why the sea is boiling hot—
    And whether pigs have wings."

Sealing wax is hot wax used to seal letters.

12 "But wait a bit," the Oysters cried,
    "Before we have our chat;
For some of us are out of breath,
    And all of us are fat!"
"No hurry!" said the Carpenter.
    They thanked him much for that.

35

13 "A loaf of bread," the Walrus said,
    "Is what we chiefly need:
Pepper and vinegar besides
    Are very good indeed—
Now, if you're ready, Oysters dear,
    We can begin to feed."

14 "But not on us!" the Oysters cried,
    Turning a little blue.
"After such kindness, that would be
    A dismal thing to do!"
"The night is fine," the Walrus said.
    "Do you admire the view?

15 "It was so kind of you to come!
    And you are very nice!"
The Carpenter said nothing but
    "Cut us another slice.
I wish you were not quite so deaf—
    I've had to ask you twice!"

36

16 "It seems a shame," the Walrus said,
        "To play them such a trick.
    After we've brought them out so far,
        And made them trot so quick!"
    The Carpenter said nothing but
        "The butter's spread too thick!"

17 "I weep for you," the Walrus said:
        "I deeply sympathize."
    With sobs and tears he sorted out
        Those of the largest size,
    Holding his pocket-handkerchief
        Before his streaming eyes.

18 "O Oysters," said the Carpenter,
        "You've had a pleasant run!
    Shall we be trotting home again?"
        But answer came there none—
    And this was scarcely odd, because
        They'd eaten every one.

Objectives ● To recognize the use of repetition, magic, and fantasy in folk tales. ● To retell a story through pantomime.

Synopsis of the Folk Tale While digging in his vegetable patch, Mr. Hak-Tak finds a large brass pot. He and Mrs. Hak-Tak discover that the pot doubles whatever is put into it, and they soon double their posses-sions. Then Mrs. Hak-Tak tumbles into the pot—and two Mrs. Hak-Taks emerge! This presents a problem until Mr. Hak-Tak falls into the pot and doubles himself.

Introducing the Folk Tale *What would it be like if you suddenly had two of everything? The magic pot in this story makes two of everything—and a little bit of double trouble!*

TWO OF EVERYTHING

A Chinese tale told by Li Po
Illustrated by Jane Teiko Oka

Reading Level Average

Mr. and Mrs. Hak-Tak were rather old and rather poor. They had a small house in a village among the mountains and a tiny patch of green land on the mountain side. Here they grew the vegetables which were all they had to live on. When it was a good season and they did not need to eat up everything as soon as it was grown, Mr. Hak-Tak took what vegetables they could spare in a basket to the next village. There, he sold them for as much as he could get and bought some oil for their lamp, and fresh seeds. Every now and then, but not often, he bought a piece of cotton stuff to make new coats and trousers for himself and his wife. You can imagine they did not often get the chance to eat meat.

Now, one day it happened that when Mr. Hak-Tak was digging in his precious patch, he unearthed a big brass pot. He thought it strange that it should have been there for so long without his having come across it before, and he was disappointed to find that it was empty. Still, he thought they would find some use for the pot, so when he was ready to go back to the house in the evening he decided to take it with him.

Discussion Questions *How does this story differ from a realistic story?* (Possible answers: the story uses magic and fantasy; the magical events are repeated.) *How did the pot help the Hak-Taks?* (Possible answer: they could buy things that made their life easier.) *What humorous problem did the pot cause?* (Mr. Hak-Tak found himself with two wives.) *What made this story funny to you?*

(This type of discussion will help the students recognize that people have different senses of humor.)
Enriching Activity *Story Theater.* Have students pantomime the story as several others read it aloud. To emphasize the doublings in the story, the students might perform in silhouette behind a sheet. See page T44 for more about Story Theater.

It was very big and heavy, and in his struggles to get his arms round it and raise it to a good position for carrying, his purse, which he always took with him in his belt, fell to the ground. So, to be quite sure he had the purse safe, he put it inside the pot and staggered home with his load.

As soon as he got into the house Mrs. Hak-Tak hurried from the inner room to meet him.

"My dear husband," she said, "whatever have you got there?"

"For a cooking pot it is too big; for a bath a little too small," said Mr. Hak-Tak. "I found it buried in our vegetable patch and so far it has been useful in carrying my purse home for me."

"Alas," said Mrs. Hak-Tak. "Something smaller would have done as well to hold any money we have or are likely to have," and she stooped over the pot and looked into its dark inside.

As she stooped, her hairpin—for poor Mrs. Hak-Tak had only one hairpin for all her hair and it was made of carved bone—fell into the pot. She put in her hand to get it out again, and then she gave a loud cry which brought her husband running to her side.

"What is it?" he asked. "Is there a viper in the pot?"

"Oh, my dear husband," she cried. "What can be the meaning of this? I put my hand into the pot to fetch out my hairpin and your purse, and look, I have brought out two hairpins and two purses, both exactly alike."

"Open the purse. Open both purses," said Mr. Hak-Tak. "One of them will certainly be empty."

But not a bit of it. The new purse contained exactly the same number of coins as the old one—for that matter, no one could have said which was the new and which the old—and it meant, of course, that the Hak-Taks had exactly twice as much money in the evening as they had had in the morning.

"And two hairpins instead of one!" cried Mrs. Hak-Tak, forgetting in her excitement to do up her hair which was streaming over her shoulders. "There is something quite unusual about this pot."

"Let us put in the sack of lentils and see what happens," said Mr. Hak-Tak, also becoming excited.

They heaved in the bag of lentils and when they pulled it out again—it was so big it almost filled the pot—they saw another bag of exactly the same size waiting to be pulled out in its turn. So now they had two bags of lentils instead of one.

"Put in the blanket," said Mr. Hak-Tak. "We need another blanket for the cold weather." And, sure enough, when the blanket came out, there lay another behind it.

"Put my wadded coat in," said Mr. Hak-Tak, "and then when the cold weather comes there will be one for you as well as for me. Let us put in everything we have in turn. What a pity we have no meat, for it seems that the pot cannot make anything without a pattern."

41

Then Mrs. Hak-Tak, who was a woman of great intelligence, said, "My dear husband, let us put the purse in again and again and again. If we take two purses out each time we put one in, we shall have enough money by tomorrow evening to buy everything we lack."

"I am afraid we may lose it this time," said Mr. Hak-Tak, but in the end he agreed, and they dropped in the purse and pulled out two, then they added the new money to the old and dropped it in again and pulled out the larger amount twice over. After a while the floor was covered with old leather purses and they decided to throw the money in by itself. It worked quite as well and saved trouble. Every time, twice as much money came out as went in, and every time they added the new coins to the old and threw them all in together. It took them some hours to tire of this game, but at last Mrs. Hak-Tak said, "My dear husband, there is no need for us to work so hard. We shall see to it that the pot does not run away, and we can always make more money as we want it. Let us tie up what we have."

It made a huge bundle in the extra blanket and the Hak-Taks lay and looked at it for a long time before they slept, and talked of all the things they would buy and the improvements they would make in the cottage.

The next morning they rose early and Mr. Hak-Tak filled a wallet with money from the bundle and set off for the big village to buy more things in one morning than he had bought in a whole fifty years.

Mrs. Hak-Tak saw him off and then she tidied up the cottage and put the rice on to boil and had another look at the bundle of money, and made herself a whole set of new hairpins from the pot, and about twenty candles instead of the one which was all they had possessed up to now. After that she slept for a while, having been up so late the night before, but just before the time when her husband should be back, she awoke and went over to the pot. She dropped in a cabbage leaf to make sure it was still working properly, and when she took two leaves out she sat down on the floor and put her arms around it.

"I do not know how you came to us, my dear pot," she said, "but you are the best friend we ever had."

Then she knelt up to look inside it, and at that moment her husband came to the door, and, turning quickly to see all the wonderful things he had bought, she lost her balance and fell into the pot.

Mr. Hak-Tak put down his bundles and ran across and caught her by the ankles and pulled her out. But, oh, mercy, no sooner had he set her carefully on the floor than he saw the kicking legs of another Mrs. Hak-Tak in the pot! What was he to do? Well, he could not leave her there, so he caught her ankles and pulled, and another Mrs. Hak-Tak so exactly like the first that no one would have told one from the other, stood beside them.

"Here's an extraordinary thing," said Mr. Hak-Tak, looking helplessly from one to the other.

"I will not have a second Mrs. Hak-Tak in the house!" screamed the first Mrs. Hak-Tak.

All was confusion. The first Mrs. Hak-Tak shouted and wrung her hands and wept, Mr. Hak-Tak was scarcely calmer, and the second Mrs. Hak-Tak sat down on the floor as if she knew no more than they did what was to happen next.

"One wife is all *I* want," said Mr. Hak-Tak, "but how could I have left her in the pot?"

"Put her back in it again!" cried Mrs. Hak-Tak.

"What? And draw out two more?" said her husband. "If two wives are too many for me, what should I do with three? No! No!" He stepped back quickly as if he was stepping away from the three wives and, missing his footing, lo and behold, he fell into the pot!

Both Mrs. Hak-Taks ran and each caught an ankle and pulled him out and set him on the floor, and there, oh, mercy, was another pair of kicking legs in the pot! Again each caught hold of an ankle and pulled, and soon another Mr. Hak-Tak, so exactly like the first that no one could have told one from the other, stood beside them.

Now the first Mr. Hak-Tak liked the idea of his double no more than Mrs. Hak-Tak had liked the idea of hers. He stormed and raged and scolded his wife for pulling him out of the pot, while the second Mr. Hak-Tak sat down on the floor beside the second Mrs. Hak-Tak and looked as if, like her, he did not know what was going to happen next.

Then the first Mrs. Hak-Tak had a very good idea. "Listen, my dear husband," she said. "Now, do stop scolding and listen, for it is really a good thing that

there is a new one of you as well as a new one of me. It means that you and I can go on in our usual way, and these new people, who are ourselves and yet not ourselves, can set up house together next door to us."

And that is what they did. The first Hak-Taks built themselves a fine new house with money from the pot. Then they built one just like it next door for the new couple, and they lived together in the greatest friendliness, because, as Mrs. Hak-Tak said, "The new Mrs. Hak-Tak is really more than a sister to me, and

the new Mr. Hak-Tak is really more than a brother to you."

The neighbors were very much surprised, both at the sudden wealth of the Hak-Taks and at the new couple who resembled them so strongly that they must, they thought, be very close relations of whom they had never heard before. The neighbors said: "It looks as though the Hak-Taks, when they so unexpectedly became rich, decided to have two of everything, even of themselves, in order to enjoy their money more."

47

Objectives ● To recognize the theme of a play. ● To perform a play.

Synopsis of the Play Hunder, a fierce giant, sits on the hill near a village and demands huge amounts of goods from the villagers. Everyone hopes for a scheme to get rid of the giant, but only Quillow, the toymaker, has a plan. He convinces the giant that he has a disease of the mind, and that the only cure is to bathe in the middle of a distant ocean.

Introducing the Play Put four pennies of different years in a paper bag. Have a volunteer choose one and silently note the year. Ask several students to examine the penny carefully, and then put it back in the bag. Without looking, pick the penny from the bag. (It will be warmer than the others.) If you wish, explain the trick to the class. *Tricks are popular in stories, too.* The Great Quillow *is about a clever trick played on a cruel giant. Read the story to find out who the trickster is.*

Discussion Questions
How does the play show that cleverness can overcome great size and strength? (Quillow tricks Hunder into leaving.) *How do the villagers' opinions of Quillow change?* (At first they think he is idle and worthless; at the end he is their hero.)

The Great Quillow

A play by Moyne Rice Smith
based on the story by James Thurber
Illustrated by Sal Murdocca

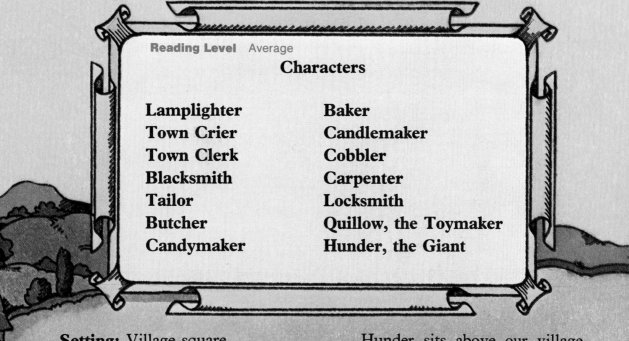

Reading Level Average

Characters

Lamplighter	**Baker**
Town Crier	**Candlemaker**
Town Clerk	**Cobbler**
Blacksmith	**Carpenter**
Tailor	**Locksmith**
Butcher	**Quillow, the Toymaker**
Candymaker	**Hunder, the Giant**

Setting: Village square.
Time: Many years ago.

*The village clock strikes seven.
Lamplighter enters with his long
staff and lights the street lamp.*

Town Crier *(Ringing his bell and
    chanting)*: Town meeting to-
    night. Town meeting tonight.
    Town meeting tonight. . . .

Lamplighter: What good is a
    town meeting when the Giant
Hunder sits above our village
and curses it. What can we do?
He has plundered the villages
of the far countryside. And today the earth shook when he
strode onto our hillside. He
pulled up four trees to make
room to sit down!

Town Crier: The Town Clerk
has gone to hear Hunder's will.
We meet now to hear his demands. *(He continues chanting,
ringing his bell softly.)* Town

meeting tonight. Town meeting tonight. Town meeting tonight. . . .

(The Lamplighter *is joined now by the* Villagers, *who follow the* Town Clerk *onto the stage.)*

Town Clerk *(As he enters, carrying scroll and quill, and takes his place)*: There are ninety-nine other men in the town, but it's the Town Clerk this, and the Town Clerk that, and the Town Clerk everything!

(The Villagers, *who are the* Town Councilors, *mutter and whisper to each other.* Quillow *has followed them in.)*

Town Clerk: Town meeting will come to order! Town meeting will come to order! *(They quiet down.)* I will now call the roll.

Blacksmith: We're all here. You can see that!

Town Clerk *(As each name is called, the* Councilors *answer impatiently.)*: Tailor, Butcher, Candymaker, Blacksmith, Baker, Candlemaker, Lamplighter, Cobbler, Carpenter, Locksmith, Town Crier. *(He looks over his spectacles at* Quillow.) We have a visitor tonight, as usual. *(All turn and look amusedly at* Quillow.) Quillow, the Toymaker. I will make the proper entry in the minutes.

Blacksmith: Never mind the minutes. Read us the demands of Hunder the Giant. *(Cries of* Hear! Hear!*)*

Town Clerk *(Writing with a flourish)*: Quillow, the Toymaker. Now, I will read the minutes of the last meeting.

Candymaker: Let's dispense with the minutes of the last meeting. *(Cries of* Hear! Hear!*)*

Town Clerk: It must be properly moved and duly seconded.

Tailor *(Quickly)*: I do so properly move.

Butcher: And I duly second.

Blacksmith: Now read the demands of Hunder the Giant! *(Cries of* Hear! Hear!*)*

Town Clerk *(Unrolling scroll)*: We come now to the business of the day. I have here the demands of Hunder the Giant. The document is most irregular.

It does not contain a single "greeting" or "whereas" or "be it known by these presents." *(Reads)* "I, Hunder, must have three sheep every morning."

Villagers *(Together)***:** Three sheep!

Butcher *(Aghast)***:** Why that would use up all the sheep in the valley in a week and a fortnight,[1] and there would be no mutton for our own people!

Town Clerk: "I, Hunder, must have a chocolate a day as high and as wide as a spinning wheel."

Candymaker: Why, that would exhaust all the chocolate in my storeroom in three days!

Town Clerk: "I, Hunder, must have a new jerkin[2] made for me in a week and a fortnight."

Tailor *(Gasps)***:** Why, I would have to work night and day to make a jerkin in a week and a fortnight for so large a Giant, and it would use up all the cloth on my shelves and in my basement.

Town Clerk: "I, Hunder, must have a new pair of boots within a week and a fortnight."

Cobbler *(Moans)***:** Why, I would have to work night and day to make a pair of boots for so large a Giant in a week and a fortnight. And it would use up all the leather in my workshop and in my back room.

---

1. **fortnight:** a period of two weeks or fourteen days.
2. **jerkin:** a close-fitting jacket or vest with no sleeves, popular several hundred years ago.

Town Clerk: "I, Hunder, must have an apple pie each morning made of a thousand apples."

Baker: Why, that would use up all the apples and flour and shortening in town in a week and a fortnight. It would take me night and day to make such a pie, so that I could bake no more pies or cakes or cookies, or blueberry muffins or cinnamon buns or cherry boats or strawberry tarts or plum puddings for the people of the town.

Town Clerk: "I, Hunder, must have a house to live in by the time a week and a fortnight have passed."

Carpenter (*Sobs*)**:** Why, I would have to work night and day to build a house for so large a Giant in a week and a fortnight. And all my nephews and uncles and cousins would have to help me, and it would use up all the wood and pegs and hinges and glass in my shop and in the countryside.

Locksmith: I will have to work night and day to make a brass key large enough to fit the key-hole in the front door of the house of so large a Giant. It will use up all the brass in my shop and in the community.

Candlemaker: And I will have to make a candle for his bedside so large it will use up all the wick and tallow in my shop and the world!

Town Clerk: This is the final item. "I, Hunder, must be told a tale each day to keep me amused."

Quillow (*Who has sat all this time with his arms folded and his eyes shut, now opens his eyes and raises his hand*)**:** I will be the teller of tales. I will keep the Giant amused.

Candymaker: Does anyone have any idea of how to destroy the Giant?

(*The* Councilors *think, and then in turn are inspired with a great idea.*)

Lamplighter: I could creep up on him in the dark and set fire to him with my lighter.

Quillow: The fire of your lighter would not harm him any more than a spark struck by a colt-shoe in a meadow.

Blacksmith: Quillow is right. But I could build secretly at night an enormous catapult which would cast a gigantic stone and crush Hunder.

Quillow: He would catch the stone as a child catches a ball, and he would cast it back at the town and squash all our houses.

Tailor: I could put needles in his suit.

Cobbler: I could put nails in his boots.

Candlemaker: I could put gunpowder in his candles.

Candymaker: I could put oil in his chocolates.

Butcher: I could put stones in his mutton.

Baker: I could put tacks in his pies.

Locksmith: I could make the handle of his brass key as sharp as a sword.

Carpenter: I could build the roof of his house insecurely so that it would fall on him.

Quillow: The plans you suggest would merely annoy Hunder as the gadfly annoys the horse and the flea annoys the dog.

Blacksmith: Perhaps the Great Quillow has a plan of his own. *(All laugh.)*

Candymaker: Has the Great Quillow a plan? *(He does not answer.)*

(The Councilors go out slowly and sadly, muttering about their heavy tasks of the night. Quillow sits alone thinking. Suddenly his face lightens. He pantomimes the suggestion of the doll he is going to make. He skips off gleefully as the lights dim to off. The town clock strikes five and the Lamplighter enters and puts out the street light.)

Town Crier *(Enters on tiptoe)*: Sh! Don't wake the Giant.

Lamplighter: Sh! His food may not be ready.

Town Crier *(Softly)***:** Five o'clock, and all's well!

(The Villagers tiptoe on, wearily carrying their foodstuffs. They line up facing the hill with the sleeping Giant.)

Baker: The pie is baked.

Candymaker: The chocolate is made.

Butcher: The sheep are dressed.

Locksmith: I worked all night on the great brass key.

Blacksmith: I helped him with my hammer and anvil.

Candlemaker: I have scarcely begun the enormous candle.

Carpenter: I am weary of sawing and planing.

Tailor: My fingers are already stiff, and I have just started the Giant's jerkin.

Cobbler: My eyes are tired, and I have hardly begun to make his boots.

Town Crier: Where is Quillow? Where is that foolish little fellow?

Lamplighter: He was in his shop at midnight, making toys.

Villagers *(Together)***:** Toys!

Locksmith: He could have helped with the key.

Baker: The pie.

Butcher: The sheep.

Cobbler: The shoes.

(Quillow appears smiling and bowing.)

Blacksmith: Well!

Quillow: Good morning.

Blacksmith: I worked all night with my hammer and anvil helping the locksmith with the great brass key. The Lamplighter tells us YOU spent the night making toys!

Quillow *(Cheerily)*: Making toys, and thinking up a tale to amuse the Giant Hunder.

Blacksmith: And a hard night you must have spent hammering out your tale.

Locksmith: And twisting it.

Carpenter: And leveling it.

Baker: And rolling it out.

Tailor: And stitching it up.

Cobbler: And fitting it together.

Candlemaker: And building it around a central thread.

Butcher: And dressing it up.

Candymaker: And making it not too bitter and not too sweet.

Hunder *(Awakening, his head and shoulders appear above the hillside.)*: HO! HO! *(He claps his hands and the* Villagers *fall backwards. He roars with laughter.)* Bring me my sheep, my pie, my chocolate! *(The* Villagers *lug their foodstuffs across the stage, climb on the bench and heave them up to the* Giant.*)* Tell me your silly names, and what you do. *(Hunder gnaws greedily at his food as the* Villagers *quickly tell their trades, each bowing as he speaks.)*

Hunder: You! You with the white hair, who are you?

Quillow: I am Quillow, the teller of tales.

Hunder: Bow!

Quillow: Wow! *(The others are aghast at his impudence.)*

Hunder *(Scowls with fury, then suddenly laughs)*: You are a fairly droll fellow. Perhaps your tales will amuse me. If they do not, I will put you in the palm of my hand and blow you so far it will take men five days to find you. Now, the rest of you, be off to your work. *(The* Villagers *sneak off in terror, as* Hunder *continues to eat.)* Now, you, tell me a tale.

Quillow *(Sits cross-legged)*: Once upon a time, a Giant came to our town from a thousand leagues away, stepping over the hills and rivers. He was so mighty a Giant that he could

stamp upon the ground with his foot and cause the cows in the fields to turn flip-flops in the air and land on their feet again.

Hunder: Garf! I can stamp upon the ground with my foot and empty a lake of its water.

Quillow: I have no doubt of that, O Hunder. But the Giant who came over the hills and rivers many and many a year ago was a lesser Giant than Hunder. He was weak. He fell ill of a curious malady.[3]

Hunder: Rowf! That Giant was a goose, that Giant was a grasshopper. Hunder is never sick. *(He smites his chest.)*

Quillow: This other Giant had no ailment of the chest or the stomach or the mouth or the ears or the eyes or the arms or the legs.

Hunder: Where else can a Giant have an ailment?

Quillow *(Dreamily)*: In the mind, for the mind is a strange and intricate thing. In lesser men than Hunder it is subject to mysterious maladies.

Hunder: Wumf! Hunder's mind is strong like the rock! *(He smites his forehead.)*

---

3. **malady** (MAL•uh•dee): an illness, usually one lasting a long time.

Quillow: No one to this day knows what brought on this dreadful disease in the mind of the other Giant. He suffered no pain. His symptoms were marvelous and dismaying. First he heard the word. For fifteen minutes one morning, beginning at a quarter of six, he heard the word.

Hunder: Harumph! What was the word the Giant heard for fifteen minutes one day?

Quillow: The word was "woddly." All words were one word to him. All words were "woddly."

Hunder: All words are different to Hunder. And do you call this a tale you have told me? A blithering goose of a Giant hears a word and you call that a tale to amuse Hunder? I hear all words. This is a good chocolate; otherwise I should put you in the palm of my hand and blow you over the housetops.

Quillow (*As the town clock strikes six*): I shall bring you a better tale tomorrow. No one knows to this day what caused the weird illness in the mind of the other Giant. *(Hunder growls, yawns, and sinks his great head onto his arms and goes to sleep.* Quillow *smiles.)*

Quillow (*Calling softly*): Town Crier! Town Crier! (*The* Town Crier *tiptoes on.*) Call the people. Tell them Quillow has a plan to destroy the Giant Hunder. Call them quietly.

Town Crier (*Chanting softly*): Town meeting in the village square. Town meeting in . . .

(As the lights dim into dusk, the Villagers *enter quietly and form a group around* Quillow.*)*

Blacksmith: What is this clown's whim that brings us here like sheep?

(Quillow whispers to the group. They nod and whisper to each other conspiratorially.)

Lamplighter: It will never work.
Candymaker: It is worth trying.
Town Crier: I have a better plan. Let all the women and all the children stand in the streets and gaze sorrowfully at the Giant, and perhaps he will go away.

Candymaker: Let us try Quillow's plan. He has a magic, the little man.

(The lights dim to off. The Villagers *quietly move to either side of the stage and sit. As the lights rise for morning, the* Villagers *are discovered in their places, with* Quillow *sitting cross-legged on the bench below the hillside.)*

Hunder *(Awakening with great noises)*: Tell me a tale, smallest of men, and see to it that I do not nod, or I shall put you in the palm of my hand and blow you through yonder cloud.

Quillow: Once upon a time, there was a King named Anderblusdaferafan, and he had three sons named Ufabrodoborobe, Quamdelrodolanderay and Tristolcomofarasee.

Hunder: Why did this King and his sons have such long and difficult names?

Quillow: Ah, it was because of the King's mother, whose name was Isoldasadelofandaloo. One day as the King and his sons were riding through the magical forest, they came upon a woddly. Woddly woddly woddly woddly. Woddly, woddly, woddly. . . .

WODDLY, WODDLY, WODDLY...

Hunder *(Bellows)*: Say it with words! You say naught but woddly!!

Quillow: Woddly woddly woddly woddly. . . .

Hunder *(Roars)*: Can this be the malady come upon me? Or do you seek to frighten Hunder?

Quillow: Woddly woddly woddly. Woddly woddly woddly.

Hunder *(In terror, shouts at the* Villagers*)*: You, Blacksmith, tell me your name? *(To another)* What is the time of day? . . . Where are you going? . . . How are you feeling? . . . All talk! All talk! Say words!

(The Villagers *carry on conversations with each other using only the word* Woddly*.)*

Hunder *(Silencing them with his roaring)*: It is the malady! I have heard the word! It is the malady! What am I to do to cure the malady? *(The town clock strikes six.)*

Quillow: I was telling you how the King and his three sons rode through the magical forest. . . .

Hunder: I heard the word. All men said the word.

Quillow: What word?

Hunder: Woddly.

Quillow: That is but the first symptom, and it has passed. Look at the chimneys of the town. Are they not red?

Hunder: Yes, the chimneys are red. Why do you ask if the chimneys are red?

Quillow: So long as the chimneys are red, you have no need to worry, for when the second symptom is upon you, the chimneys of the town turn black.

Hunder: I see only red chimneys, but what could have caused Hunder to hear the word?

Quillow *(As the lights dim)*: Rest well. I will tell you another tale tomorrow. *(As Hunder goes to sleep,* Quillow *signals to the Villagers. They quietly move to the chimneys which they pretend to paint. They remove the red cutouts and when they have finished and have returned to their places, the lights come up again for morning.)*

Hunder *(Stirs, rubs eyes, yawns,*

stretches, and then stares): The chimneys! The chimneys are black! The malady is upon me again. Teller of tales, tell me what I must do. The chimneys are black! Look, teller of tales, name me fairly the color of yonder chimneys.

Quillow: The chimneys are red, O Hunder. The chimneys are red. See how they outdo the red rays of the sun.

Hunder: The rays of the sun are red, but the chimneys of the town are black.

Quillow: You tremble, and your tongue hangs out, and these are indeed the signs of the second symptom. But still there is no real danger, for you do not see the blue men. Or do you see the blue men, O Hunder?

Hunder: I see the men of the town staring at me. But their faces are white and they wear clothes of many colors. Why do you ask me if I see blue men?

Quillow: When you see the blue men, it is the third and last symptom of the malady. If that should happen, you must rush to the sea and bathe in the waters or your strength will become the strength of a kitten. Perhaps if you fast for a day and a night, the peril will pass.

Hunder: I will do as you say, teller of tales, for you are wise beyond the manner of men. Bring me no food today, tell me no tale. (*He moans and covers his eyes and sleeps.*)

(*The light dims and the* Villagers *softly steal behind the screens so that when the morning light rises there is no one visible except* Quillow, *the sleeping* Giant, *and the* Town Crier.)

Quillow (*As the town clock strikes five*): Cry the hour. Cry all's well.

Town Crier: Five o'clock! Five o'clock and all's well!

Hunder (*Awakens and looks cautiously at the village*): The chimneys are still black, but I see no blue men. (*He grins, smites his chest and roars.*) HO, Councilors! Bring me my sheep and my pie and my chocolate, for I have a vast hunger. Behold I am still a whole man! I have heard the word and I have seen the chimneys, but I have not beheld the blue men.

Quillow: That is well, for he who beholds the blue men must bathe in the yellow waters in the middle of the sea, or else he will dwindle first to the height of the pussy willow, then to the height of the daffodil, then to the height of the violet, until finally he becomes a small voice in the grass, lost in the thundering of the crickets.

Hunder: But I shall remain stronger than the rock and taller than the oak.

Quillow: If you are stronger than the rock and taller than the oak, then stamp on the ground and make yonder cow in the field turn a flip-flop.

Hunder (*Gleefully*): Behold, I will make the cow turn twice in the air. (*He stamps heavily.*)
(*The blue men slide over the village walls and dance up and down in the air.*)

Hunder (*Cries in anguish*): The blue men! The blue men have come! The world is filled with little blue men!

Quillow: I see no blue men, but you have begun to shrink like the brook in dry weather, and that is the sign of the third symptom.

Hunder *(Shaking with terror)*: The sea! The sea! Point me to the sea!

Quillow: It is many leagues to the east. Run quickly toward the rising sun and bathe in the yellow waters in the middle of the sea.

(Bellowing with anguish, Hunder disappears behind his hillside. As his roaring diminishes, the Villagers *enter.)*

Villagers *(Lifting* Quillow *to their shoulders)*: The Great Quillow!

63

What's So Punny?

RIDDLE ME,
RIDDLE ME,
WHAT IS THAT,
OVER THE HEAD
AND UNDER
THE HAT?

·HAIR.

When first I appear I seem mysterious,
But when I'm explained I'm nothing serious.
—A riddle.

Riddles are among the world's favorite guessing games. For centuries, people everywhere have had fun trying to catch each other with riddles such as the one at the left.

Of all the different kinds of riddles people ask, the trickiest to answer is the *trick question:*

Why is your nose in the middle of your face?
Because it's a scenter.

In many trick questions, like the one above, the answers contain what we call *puns*. A pun is the humorous use of two words that sound alike but have different meanings. In the answer to the riddle about your nose, the word *scenter* sounds like *center*, even though the spellings and meanings of the two words are different. When you read the answer aloud, it means both "nose" (scenter) and "middle" (center).

Here are two more trick questions:

A nickel and a dime were crossing a bridge and the nickel fell off. Why didn't the dime fall too?
It had more sense (cents) than the nickel.

Why did the lobster blush?
Because it saw the salad dressing.

In the riddle about the nickel and the dime, the pun again is made on two words—*cents* and *sense*—that sound alike but have different meanings and spellings. In the riddle about the lobster, the pun is made on two meanings of a word—*dressing*—whose spelling doesn't change.

In each of the following trick questions, the underlined word gives a sensible answer but spoils the pun. Change the word to make a pun. The picture next to each trick question offers a clue to the answer. (Answers are given at the bottom of the page.)

1. What did the kindling wood say to the fireplace?
Good-bye! I've met my <u>fire</u>.

2. Why did the rooster refuse to fight?
Because it was <u>afraid</u>.

3. What did the steak say to the plate?
Pleased to <u>see</u> you.

4. What is the tallest building in town?
The library. It has the most <u>floors</u>.

For fun, write down five of your favorite trick questions. Remember that the answers should be puns. Ask your friends these trick questions to see if they can identify and explain the puns in the answers.

(Answers: 1. match; 2. chicken; 3. meat; 4. stories.)

Food for Thought

Trick questions collected by Duncan Emrich

Objectives ● To identify puns. ● To write riddles and jokes using puns.
Introducing the Puns *What puns can you find on this page?* (Hailing buses; farthest from the bark; sand which is there; beet's all.)

Enriching Activity *Writing puns.* Ask the students to write puns for homonyms or homophones. They might use these examples: *swallow; fly; seal; night/knight; tacks/tax; nose/knows; sail/sale; a loan/alone.*

THAT BEET'S ALL!

What is worse than raining cats and dogs?

(Hailing buses and taxis.)

Why is the end of a dog's tail like the heart of a tree?

(Because it is farthest from the bark.)

Why should people never suffer from hunger in the Sahara desert?

(Because of the sand which is there.)

How many hard-boiled eggs could the giant Goliath eat on an empty stomach?

(One. After that his stomach would not be empty.)

Why is the letter K like flour?

(You can't make cake without it.)

Which is correct?
   The yolk of an egg *is* white?
   The yolk of an egg *are* white?

(Neither; the yolk of an egg is yellow.)

If you were invited out to dinner and on sitting down at the table saw nothing but a beet, what would you say?

(That beet's all!)

Illustrated by Alexandra Wallner

BOOKSHELF

The Great Ringtail Garbage Caper by Timothy Foote. Houghton Mifflin, 1980. A group of daring raccoons organize a scheme to hijack a sanitation truck when their food supply is threatened by overly enthusiastic garbage collectors. **Reading Level** Average

Henry Reed, Inc. by Keith Robertson. Viking Press, 1958. An ingenious boy's summer research firm stirs up hilarious situations all over town. This story has three sequels. **Reading Level** Average

How to Eat Fried Worms by Thomas Rockwell. Franklin Watts, 1973. When Billy bets fifty dollars that he can eat fifteen worms, his family and friends help him invent different ways to cook them. **Reading Level** Easy

The Mouse and the Motorcycle by Beverly Cleary. William Morrow, 1965. After a young mouse named Ralph learns to ride a toy motorcycle, he and the boy who taught him share a series of exciting adventures. Ralph's adventures are continued in **Runaway Ralph.** **Reading Level** Easy

The Amazing Bone by William Steig. Farrar, Straus and Giroux, 1976. Pearl, a pig, meets a talking bone that she invites home to meet her parents. But their journey together is interrupted by unexpected events. **Reading Level** Average

The Mariah Delaney Lending Library Disaster by Sheila Greenwald. Houghton Mifflin, 1977. Mariah Delaney's parents can't understand her delight in thinking of money-making schemes. Mariah's latest venture would shock them—a lending library of books from the Delaneys' collection. **Reading Level** Average

2 Truly Amazing Talents

My Uncle Dan

A poem by Ted Hughes

Objectives ● To enjoy humorous character portraits in two poems. ● To create humorous characters, incidents, and inventions.

Introducing the Poems *The next two poems describe two unusual relatives. See if they are like any relatives you have ever known or heard about.*

My Uncle Dan's an inventor. You may think that's very fine.
You may wish he were your uncle instead of being mine—
If he wanted he could make a watch that bounces when it drops,
He could make a helicopter out of string and bottle tops
Or any really useful thing you can't get in the shops.
        But Uncle Dan has other ideas:
        The bottomless glass for ginger beers,
        The toothless saw that's safe for the tree,
        A special word for a spelling bee
        (Like Lionocerangoutangadder),
        Or the roll-uppable rubber ladder,
        The mystery pie that bites when it's bit—
        My Uncle Dan invented it.
My Uncle Dan sits in his den inventing night and day.
His eyes peer from his hair and beard like mice from a load of hay.
And does he make the shoes that will go for walks without your feet?
A shrinker to shrink instantly the elephants you meet?
A carver that just from the air carves steaks cooked and ready to eat?
        No, no, he has other intentions—
        Only perfectly useless inventions:
        Glassless windows (they never break),
        A medicine to cure the earthquake,
        The unspillable screwed-down cup,
        The stairs that go neither down nor up
        The door you simply paint on a wall—
        Uncle Dan invented them all.

Discussion Questions *Which of Uncle Dan's inventions would you most like to own? Why? Do you think Uncle Dan will ever become rich or famous? Why or why not?* (Possible answer: no, because his inventions are impractical or useless.)

Enriching Activities **1.** *Creative thinking/ inventions.* Have the students think up other inventions that Uncle Dan might try to create. Some students may want to construct three-dimensional models and explain them to the class. **2.** *Writing.* Have the students create original characters and write a paragraph explaining what makes them unusual or unique.

LIONOCERANGOUTANGADDER

Illustrated by Mila Lazarevich

71

My Aunt Dora

A poem by Ted Hughes

You've heard how a green thumb
Makes flowers come
Quite without toil
Out of any old soil.

Well, my aunt's thumbs were green.
At a touch, she had blooms
Of prize chrysanthemums—
The grandest ever seen.

People from miles around
Came to see those flowers
And were truly astounded
By her unusual powers.

One day a little weed
Pushed up to drink and feed
Among the pampered flowers
At her water-can showers.

Day by day it grew
With ragged leaves and bristles
Till it was tall as me or you—
It was a king of thistles.

72

"Prizes for flowers are easy,"
My aunt said in her pride.
"But was there ever such a weed
The whole world wide?"

She watered it, she tended it,
It grew alarmingly.
As if I had offended it,
It bristled over me.

"Oh, Aunt!" I cried. "Beware of that!
I saw it eat a bird."
She went on polishing its points
As if she hadn't heard.

"Oh, Aunt!" I cried. "It has a flower
Like a lion's beard—"
Too late! It was devouring her
Just as I had feared!

Her feet were waving in the air—
But I shall not proceed.
Here ends the story of my aunt
And her ungrateful weed.

Illustrated by Mila Lazarevich

Writing Quatrains by Myra Cohn Livingston

Think of some of the old songs, verses, and rhymes that you remember best. Why do you remember them so well? There may be several reasons—perhaps they are fun and easy to say, and maybe they are written in a four-line pattern called a *quatrain.* You may wish to know that the word quatrain comes from the Latin word *quattor* (KWAH•tor) meaning "four." *Cuatro* (KWAH•troh) in Spanish also means four.

The quatrain is often a complete verse by itself, like the rhyming quatrain below.

As I was standing in the street,	A
As quiet as could be,	B
A great big ugly man came up	C
And tied his horse to me.	B

There is a rhyming pattern in this quatrain. To find it, look at the last word in each line and at the letter beside it. We use letters to label the sounds of these end-words so that we can describe and talk about the rhyming pattern. In line 1 the word *street* has a sound you can call A. In line 2 the word *be* has a different sound than *street* so it is labeled B. Line 3 ends with *up*, a still different sound, so it is called C. But the *me* in line 4 rhymes with *be* in line 2, so it is called B also. The pattern for this rhyming quatrain is A—B—C—B.

Objectives ● To identify quatrains and their rhyming patterns. ● To write a quatrain.
Introducing the Lesson *You have read many different kinds of poems. Some poems rhyme; some do not. Some are limericks and some are haiku. Today we will study the quatrain (kwo′·trān).*

Write on the board the quatrain "As I was standing in the street . . ." (page 74) and underline the end words. Explain that the end words form the rhyming pattern A–B–C–B. Read the verse aloud to be sure the students hear the rhyme scheme.

Although A–B–C–B is the rhyming pattern poets use most often in writing a quatrain, there are many others. Notice the pattern that X. J. Kennedy uses in this first verse from his poem, "Hickenthrift and Hickenloop."

Hickenthrift and Hickenloop	A
Stood fourteen mountains high.	B
They'd wade the wind, they'd have to stoop	A
To let the full moon by.	B

In lines 1 and 3, the last words rhyme (*Hickenloop* and *stoop*), so they are both called A, just as *high* in line 2 and *by* in line 4 rhyme and are called B. This pattern is called A–B–A–B and is a little harder to write than the A–B–C–B pattern.

There are a number of rhyming patterns you can use in a quatrain. The following three quatrains use patterns that are different from the two patterns you've learned about. Can you tell the rhyme pattern for each one? (The answers are upside down on the next page.)

1. I went to the animal fair.
   The birds and the beasts were there.
   The big baboon, by the light of the moon,
   Was combing his auburn hair.

Have the students clap out the rhythm in some of the quatrains. Note that the rhythm, as well as the rhyme, follows a consistent pattern.

75

Write these quatrains on the board. Have the students underline the rhyming words and identify the rhyme pattern.

2. I had a little pig, his name was Ben,
   He learned how to count from one to ten.
   I dressed him up to look like a clerk
   With a collar and a suit and sent him to work.

3. O what's the weather in a Beard?
   It's windy there, and rather weird,
   And when you think the sky has cleared
   —Why, there is Dirty Dinky.

The third quatrain above, which has a more unusual pattern, is from Theodore Roethke's poem "Dinky" on

(Answers: 1. A–A–B–A; 2. A–A–B–B; 3. A–A–A–B.)

76

page 216. In each quatrain in that poem, the first three
lines (A) all rhyme, and the last line (B) is repeated
throughout the poem.

It is possible also to write a quatrain with no rhyming words, like this part of the poem "Which" by
William Stafford.

> Which of the horses
> we passed yesterday whinnied
> all night in my dreams?
> I want that one.

Quatrains offer many possibilities for your own
writing. Quatrains can be funny or serious. If you like
to write riddles, the quatrain is a good pattern to use
for these. If you want to write poetry, just one quatrain
can make a whole poem, or you can put together two,
three, or many quatrains into a much longer poem.
You can even use quatrains to tell a story, as Ted
Hughes does in his poem "My Aunt Dora" on page 72.
Because they can be used alone or in many combina-
tions, quatrains are the "building blocks" of poetry.

When you *do* write your own quatrain, keep in mind
that, whether or not you use rhyme, you will always
need *rhythm*. To keep a good rhythm, try to use about
the same number of syllables in all of the lines and say
your verse aloud. You'll be able to hear if a line seems
too short or too long for all the others.

77

Objectives ● To recognize fantasy devices. ● To examine the elements of humor in a fantasy. ● To dramatize a humorous fantasy.

Synopsis of the Story When Jane and Michael Banks go with Mary Poppins to visit her uncle, Mr. Wigg, they discover him on the ceiling. Mr. Wigg explains that he is floating because he is filled with Laughing Gas. (Continued on next page.)

Laughing Gas

From the novel *Mary Poppins* by P.L. Travers

Illustrated by Bert Dodson

Reading Level Challenging

Soon Jane and Michael are laughing and floating, too. Mary Poppins disapproves of their behavior, but joins them in mid-air. Then Mr. Wigg's landlady, Miss Persimmon, enters the room, and, thanks to Mary Poppins, finds herself waddling through the air. When Mary Poppins announces that it is time to go, the sad thought makes Mr. Wigg, Jane, and Michael return to earth.

Introducing the Story *Who has heard of Mary Poppins? How would you describe her?* (Possible answer: she is a governess who seems strict and solemn, but has magical powers.) *What words can you think of that describe different kinds of laughter?* (Possible answers: howl; titter; giggle; chuckle; belly laugh; roar.) Have volunteers demonstrate each. *In the story we are about to read, laughter has a very strange effect on some of the characters.*

Word to Know
   mirth (page 89): Refer the students to the glossary.

Jane and Michael Banks were glad that the woman who had been taking care of them had gone, for they had never liked her. Anything, they thought, would be better than Katie Nanna—if not much *better.*

But they weren't expecting a nanny¹ quite like Mary Poppins, who blew into their house, slid up *the bannister to the second floor, and unpacked a roomful of items from an empty suitcase! True, she seemed to be a rather severe nanny, with her sharp words, frowns, and lack of patience. But Michael and Jane quickly came to be very fond of Mary Poppins and her magical ability to bring impossible events into their lives.*

Mary Poppins, Jane, and Michael turned the corner and pulled the bell of Number Three, Robertson Road. Jane and Michael could hear it faintly echoing from a long way away and they knew that in one minute, or two at the most, they would be having tea with Mary Poppins's uncle, Mr. Wigg, for the first time ever.

"If he's in, of course," Jane said to Michael in a whisper.

---

1. nanny: in England, a child's nurse.

At that moment the door flew open and a thin, watery-looking lady appeared.

"Is he in?" said Michael quickly.

"I'll thank you," said Mary Poppins, giving him a terrible glance, "to let *me* do the talking."

"How do you do, Mrs. Wigg," said Jane politely.

"Mrs. Wigg!" said the thin lady, in a voice even thinner than herself. "How dare you call me Mrs. Wigg? No, thank you! I'm plain Miss Persimmon *and* proud of it. Mrs. Wigg indeed!" She seemed to be quite upset, and they thought Mr. Wigg must be a very odd person if Miss Persimmon was so glad not to be Mrs. Wigg.

"Straight up and first door on the landing," said Miss Persimmon, and she went hurrying away down the passage saying: "Mrs. Wigg indeed!" to herself in a high, thin, outraged voice.

Jane and Michael followed Mary Poppins upstairs. Mary Poppins knocked at the door.

"Come in! Come in! And welcome!" called a loud, cheery voice from inside. Jane's heart was pitter-pattering with excitement.

"He *is* in!" she signalled to Michael with a look.

Mary Poppins opened the door and pushed them in front of her. A large cheerful room lay before them. At one end of it a fire was burning brightly and in the center stood an enormous table laid for tea—four cups and saucers, piles of bread and butter, crumpets, coconut cakes, and a large plum cake with pink icing.

"Well, this is indeed a Pleasure," a huge voice greeted them, and Jane and Michael looked round for

In the United States, *crumpets* (line 4 from the foot of the page) are called *English muffins*.

Explain that *Pleasure* begins with a capital letter because some British writers continue to follow the style of capitalization used in the seventeenth century.

its owner. He was nowhere to be seen. The room
appeared to be quite empty. Then they heard Mary
Poppins saying crossly:

"Oh, Uncle Albert—not *again?* It's not your birthday, is it?"

And as she spoke she looked up at the ceiling.
Jane and Michael looked up too and to their surprise
saw a round, fat, bald man who was hanging in the
air without holding on to anything. Indeed, he appeared to be *sitting* on the air, for his legs were
crossed and he had just put down the newspaper
which he had been reading when they came in.

"My dear," said Mr. Wigg, smiling down at the children, and looking apologetically at Mary Poppins, "I'm very sorry, but I'm afraid it *is* my birthday."

"Tch, tch, tch!" said Mary Poppins.

"I only remembered last night and there was no time then to send you a postcard asking you to come another day. Very distressing, isn't it?" he said, looking down at Jane and Michael.

"I can see you're rather surprised," said Mr. Wigg. And, indeed, their mouths were so wide open with astonishment that Mr. Wigg, if he had been a little smaller, might almost have fallen into one of them.

"I'd better explain, I think," Mr. Wigg went on calmly. "You see, it's this way. I'm a cheerful sort of man and very <u>disposed</u> to laughter. You wouldn't believe, either of you, the number of things that strike me as being funny. I can laugh at pretty nearly everything, I can."

Disposed means inclined toward.

And with that Mr. Wigg began to bob up and down, shaking with laughter at the thought of his own cheerfulness.

"Uncle Albert!" said Mary Poppins, and Mr. Wigg stopped laughing with a jerk.

"Oh, beg pardon, my dear. Where was I? Oh, yes. Well, the funny thing about me is—all right, Mary, I won't laugh if I can help it!—that whenever my birthday falls on a Friday, well, it's all up with me. Absolutely U.P.," said Mr. Wigg.

"But why——?" began Jane.

"But how——?" began Michael.

"Well, you see, if I laugh on that particular day I become so filled with Laughing Gas that I simply can't keep on the ground. Even if I smile it happens. The first funny thought, and I'm up like a balloon. And until I can think of something serious I can't get down again." Mr. Wigg began to chuckle at that, but he caught sight of Mary Poppins's face and stopped the chuckle, and continued:

"It's awkward, of course, but not unpleasant. Never happens to either of you, I suppose?"

Jane and Michael shook their heads.

"No, I thought not. It seems to be my own special habit. Once, after I'd been to the Circus the night before, I laughed so much that—would you believe it?—I was up here for a whole twelve hours, and couldn't get down till the last stroke of midnight. Then, of course, I came down with a flop because it was Saturday and not my birthday any more. It's rather odd, isn't it? Not to say funny?

"And now here it is Friday again and my birthday, and you two and Mary P. to visit me. Oh, don't make me laugh, I beg of you——" But although Jane and Michael had done nothing very amusing, except to stare at him in astonishment, Mr. Wigg began to laugh again loudly, and as he laughed he went bouncing and bobbing about in the air, with the newspaper rattling in his hand and his spectacles half on and half off his nose.

Floundering means stumbling about.

A *gas bracket* is a wall lamp that brings gas into the room to be burned for light.

He looked so comic, floundering in the air like a great human bubble, clutching at the ceiling sometimes and sometimes at the gas bracket as he passed it, that Jane and Michael, though they were trying

84

hard to be polite, just couldn't help doing what they did. They laughed. *And* they laughed. They shut their mouths tight to prevent the laughter escaping, but that didn't do any good. And presently they were rolling over and over on the floor, squealing and shrieking with laughter.

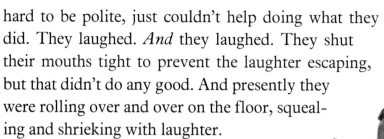

"Really!" said Mary Poppins.
"Really, *such* behavior!"

"I can't help it, I can't help it!" shrieked Michael as he rolled into the fender. "It's so terribly funny. Oh, Jane, *isn't* it funny?"

Jane did not reply, for a curious thing was happening to her. As she laughed she felt herself growing lighter and lighter, just as though she were being pumped full of air. It was a curious and delicious feeling and it made her want to laugh all the more. And then suddenly, with a bouncing bound, she felt herself jumping through the air. Michael, to his astonishment, saw her go soaring up through the room. With a little bump her head touched the ceiling and then she went bouncing along it till she reached Mr. Wigg.

"*Well!*" said Mr. Wigg, looking very surprised indeed. "Don't tell me it's *your* birthday, too?" Jane shook her head.

"It's not? Then this Laughing Gas must be catching! Hi—whoa there, look out for the mantelpiece!" This was to Michael, who had suddenly risen from the floor and was swooping through the air, roaring with laughter, and just grazing the china ornaments on the mantelpiece as he passed. He landed with a bounce right on Mr. Wigg's knee.

"How do you do," said Mr. Wigg, heartily shaking Michael by the hand. "I call this really friendly of you—bless my soul, I do! To come up to me since I couldn't come down to you—eh?" And then he and Michael looked at each other and flung back their heads and simply howled with laughter.

"I say," said Mr. Wigg to Jane, as he wiped his eyes. "You'll be thinking I have the worst manners

in the world. You're standing and you ought to be sitting—a nice young lady like you. I'm afraid I can't offer you a chair up here, but I think you'll find the air quite comfortable to sit on. I do."

Jane tried it and found she could sit down quite comfortably on the air. She took off her hat and laid it down beside her and it hung there in space without any support at all.

"That's right," said Mr. Wigg. Then he turned and looked down at Mary Poppins.

"Well, Mary, we're fixed. And now I can inquire about *you*, my dear. I must say, I am very glad to welcome you and my two young friends here today— why, Mary, you're frowning. I'm afraid you don't approve of—er—all this."

He waved his hand at Jane and Michael, and said hurriedly:

"I apologize, Mary, my dear. But you know how it is with me. Still, I must say I never thought my two young friends here would catch it, really I didn't, Mary! I suppose I should have asked them for another day or tried to think of something sad or something—"

"Well, I must say," said Mary Poppins primly, "that I have never in my life seen such a sight. And at your age, Uncle—"

"Mary Poppins, Mary Poppins, do come up!" interrupted Michael. "Think of something funny and you'll find it's quite easy."

"Ah, now do, Mary!" said Mr. Wigg persuasively.

"We're lonely up here without you!" said Jane, and held out her arms towards Mary Poppins. "*Do* think of something funny!"

"Ah, *she* doesn't need to," said Mr. Wigg sighing. "She can come up if she wants to, even without laughing—and she knows it." And he looked mysteriously and secretly at Mary Poppins as she stood down there on the hearthrug.

"Well," said Mary Poppins, "it's all very silly and undignified, but, since you're all up there and don't seem able to get down, I suppose I'd better come up, too."

With that, to the surprise of Jane and Michael, she put her hands down at her sides and without a laugh, without even the faintest glimmer of a smile, she shot up through the air and sat down beside Jane.

"How many times, I should like to know," she said snappily, "have I told you to take off your coat when you come into a hot room?" And she unbuttoned Jane's coat and laid it neatly on the air beside the hat.

"That's right, Mary, that's right," said Mr. Wigg contentedly, as he leaned down and put his spectacles on the mantelpiece. "Now we're all comfortable—"

"There's comfort *and* comfort," sniffed Mary Poppins.

"And we can have tea," Mr. Wigg went on, apparently not noticing her remark. And then a startled look came over his face.

"My goodness!" he said. "How dreadful! I've just realized—that table's down there and we're up here. What *are* we going to do? We're here and it's there. It's an awful tragedy—awful! But oh, it's terribly comic!" And he hid his face in his handkerchief and laughed loudly into it. Jane and Michael, though they did not want to miss the crumpets and the cakes, couldn't help laughing too, because Mr. Wigg's <u>mirth</u> was so infectious.

Mr. Wigg dried his eyes.

"There's only one thing for it," he said. "We must think of something serious. Something sad, very sad. And then we shall be able to get down. Now— one, two, three! Something *very* sad, mind you!"

They thought and thought, with their chins on their hands.

Michael thought of school, and that one day he would have to go there. But even that seemed funny today and he had to laugh.

Jane thought: "I shall be grown up in another fourteen years!" But that didn't sound sad at all, but quite nice and rather funny. She could not help smiling at the thought of herself grown up, with long skirts and a handbag.

"There was my poor old Aunt Emily," thought Mr. Wigg out loud. "She was run over by an omnibus. Sad. Very sad. Unbearably sad. Poor Aunt Emily. But they saved her umbrella. That was funny, wasn't it?" And before he knew where he was, he was heaving and trembling and bursting with laughter at the thought of Aunt Emily's umbrella.

"It's no good," he said, blowing his nose. "I give it up. And my young friends here seem to be no better at sadness than I am. Mary, can't *you* do something? We want our tea."

To this day Jane and Michael cannot be sure of what happened then. All they know for certain is that, as soon as Mr. Wigg had appealed to Mary Poppins, the table below began to wriggle on its legs. Presently it was swaying dangerously, and then with a rattle of china and with cakes lurching off their plates on to the cloth, the table came soaring through the room, gave one graceful turn, and landed beside them so that Mr. Wigg was at its head.

"Good girl!" said Mr. Wigg, smiling proudly upon her. "I knew you'd fix something. Now, will you take the foot of the table and pour out, Mary? And the guests on either side of me. That's the idea," he said, as Michael ran bobbing through the air and sat down on Mr. Wigg's right. Jane was at his left hand. There they were, all together, up in the air and

the table between them. Not a single piece of bread-and-butter or a lump of sugar had been left behind.

Mr. Wigg smiled contentedly.

"It is usual, I think, to begin with bread-and-butter," he said to Jane and Michael, "but as it's my birthday we will begin the wrong way—which I always think is the *right* way—with the Cake!"

And he cut a large slice for everybody.

"More tea?" he said to Jane. But before she had time to reply there was a quick, sharp knock at the door.

"Come in!" called Mr. Wigg.

The door opened, and there stood Miss Persimmon with a jug of hot water on a tray.

"I thought, Mr. Wigg," she began, looking searchingly round the room, "you'd be wanting some more hot— Well, I never! I simply *never!*" she said, as she caught sight of them all seated on the air round the table. "Such goings on I never did see. In all my born days I never saw such. I'm sure, Mr. Wigg, I always knew *you* were a bit odd. But I've closed my eyes to it—being as how you paid your rent regular. But such behavior as this—having tea in the air with your guests—Mr. Wigg, sir, I'm astonished at you! It's that undignified, and for a gentleman of your age—I never did—"

"But perhaps you will, Miss Persimmon!" said Michael.

"Will what?" said Miss Persimmon haughtily.

"Catch the Laughing Gas, as we did," said Michael.

Miss Persimmon flung back her head scornfully.

"I hope, young man," she retorted, "I have more respect for myself than to go bouncing about in the air like a rubber ball on the end of a bat. I'll stay on my own feet, thank you, or my name's not Amy Persimmon, and—oh dear, oh *dear*, my goodness, oh *DEAR*—what *is* the matter? I can't walk, I'm going, I—oh, help, *HELP!*"

For Miss Persimmon, quite against her will, was off the ground and was stumbling through the air, rolling from side to side like a very thin barrel, balancing the tray in her hand. She was almost weeping with distress as she arrived at the table and put down her jug of hot water.

"Thank you," said Mary Poppins in a calm, very polite voice.

Then Miss Persimmon turned and went wafting down again, murmuring as she went: "So undignified—and me a well-behaved, steady-going woman. I must see a doctor—"

When she touched the floor she ran hurriedly out of the room, wringing her hands, and not giving a single glance backwards.

"So undignified!" they heard her moaning as she shut the door behind her.

"Her name can't be Amy Persimmon, because she *didn't* stay on her own feet!" whispered Jane to Michael.

But Mr. Wigg was looking at Mary Poppins—a curious look, half-amused, half-accusing.

"Mary, Mary, you shouldn't—bless my soul, you shouldn't, Mary. The poor old body will never get over it. But, oh, my Goodness, didn't she look funny waddling through the air—my Gracious Goodness, but didn't she?"

And he and Jane and Michael were off again, rolling about the air, clutching their sides and gasping with laughter at the thought of how funny Miss Persimmon had looked.

"Oh dear!" said Michael. "Don't make me laugh any more. I can't stand it! I shall break!"

"Oh, oh, oh!" cried Jane, as she gasped for breath, with her hand over her heart. "Oh, my Gracious, Glorious, Galumphing Goodness!" roared Mr. Wigg, dabbing his eyes with the tail of his coat because he couldn't find his handkerchief.

Galumphing, a word invented by Lewis Carroll, means *marching triumphantly.* Here Mr. Wigg uses the word to express his mirth.

"IT IS TIME TO GO HOME." Mary Poppins's voice sounded above the roars of laughter like a trumpet.

And suddenly, with a rush, Jane and Michael and Mr. Wigg came down. They landed on the floor with a huge bump, all together. The thought that they would have to go home was the first sad thought of the afternoon, and the moment it was in their minds the Laughing Gas went out of them.

Jane and Michael sighed as they watched Mary Poppins come slowly down the air, carrying Jane's coat and hat.

Mr. Wigg sighed, too. A great, long, heavy sigh.

"Well, isn't that a pity?" he said soberly. "It's very sad that you've got to go home. I never enjoyed an afternoon so much—did you?"

"Never," said Michael sadly, feeling how dull it was to be down on the earth again with no Laughing Gas inside him.

"Never, never," said Jane, as she stood on tiptoe and kissed Mr. Wigg's withered-apple cheeks. "Never, never, never, never. . . !"

Discussion Question *People laugh at things that are unexpected or seem foolish. What are some of the things that make this story funny?* (Possible answers: people drinking tea in mid-air; Mr. Wigg's personality; Mary Poppins's disapproval; Miss Persimmon's reaction to floating.)
Enriching Activities   1. *Improvisation.* Have the students form groups of five, each student taking the part of a story character.

Have each group improvise a section of the story.   **2.** *Point-of-view writing.* Ask the students to imagine that they are Jane or Michael Banks, and that they are in class on a Friday that is their birthday. Have them write paragraphs explaining what might happen if they suddenly found themselves laughing uncontrollably and floating toward the ceiling. Remind them to write in the first person.

Questions

1. How did Jane and Michael get up to the ceiling? How did Mary Poppins get there? How did Miss Persimmon get there?

2. When would Mr. Wigg rise in the air? When do you suppose Mary Poppins could rise in the air? Why do you say so?

3. If Mary Poppins played tricks on people, as she did to Miss Persimmon, why did she act so strict and stern?

4. Match the following to show what a person might say if he or she were apologetic, persuasive, or scornful.

    apologetic   a. "How dare you speak to me!"

    persuasive   b. "I'm sorry."

    scornful   c. "*Please* change your mind."

Activity

Interpretive/extrapolation Creating fantasy devices. Ask the students to share their ideas. They may suggest fantasy devices such as time machines or animals that talk.

The story "Laughing Gas" is a kind of highly imaginative story called a *fantasy*. In the story, the laughing gas which makes people float is used as a *fantasy device*—something the author created to make the story more fanciful. Use your imagination to create a new fantasy device for another funny Mary Poppins adventure. Then write a paragraph describing the device's magical effects.

1. Literal/recall Jane and Michael laughed, and that made them rise to the ceiling (page 86). Mary Poppins used her magical powers (page 88). **Interpretive/inference** Mary Poppins made Miss Persimmon float (page 93).

2. Literal/recall Mr. Wiggs floated in the air when his birthday was on a Friday (page 83). **Interpretive/inference** Mary Poppins could fly whenever she wished to because she had magical powers.

3. Interpretive/ inference Possible answers: she wanted to conceal her magical powers; she thought that her manner kept people in line even though they were having fun.

4. Vocabulary apologetic—b. (page 83); persuasive—c. (page 88); scornful—a. (page 92).

Fast on Their Feet

Three limericks

Objective ● To recognize and to enjoy limericks.
Introducing the Poems Limericks are funny, nonsense poems written in five lines. Many limericks start with the words There was a . . . . Many of them are about people. These limericks will introduce you to three women with unusual and funny talents.

There was a young lady of Bright,
Whose speed was far faster than light.
    She set out one day
    In a relative way,
And returned home the previous night.

—A. H. Reginald Buller

There was an Old Lady of Chertsey,
Who made a remarkable curtsy;
    She twirled round and round,
    Till she sank underground,
Which distressed all the people of Chertsey.

—Edward Lear

96

Words to Know

relative: pertaining to the theory of relativity; she broke the time barrier by moving faster than the speed of light. (page 96)

previous: coming before. (page 96)

Discussion Question *Look at the first two lines of each limerick. What information is given?* (The main character; a place name; the situation.)

Enriching Activities **1.** *Related reading.* The students might enjoy reading selections from *Laughable Limericks* by Sara and John Brewton (T. Y. Crowell, 1965) or *Lollygag of Limericks* by Myra Cohn Livingston (Atheneum, 1978). **2.** *Cartoons.* Have the students draw cartoons showing the Young Lady of Bright accomplishing other impossible feats.

Majorca /mə·jôr′·kə/ (line 1) is a large island off the eastern coast of Spain. Note the near- or *slant* rhyme of *Majorca* and *walker.*

A *stile* is a step, or series of steps, on each side of a fence or wall.

There was a Young Girl of Majorca,
Whose Aunt was a very fast walker;
    She walked seventy miles,
    And leaped fifteen stiles,
Which astonished that Girl of Majorca.

—Edward Lear

Illustrated by Marie-Louise Gay

Can You Believe It?

Articles from the *Guinness Book of World Records*

Objectives • To enjoy reading articles about world records. • To write an article about a fictional world record.

Background The *Guinness Book of World Records*, published by the Guinness Brewery Company in Dublin, Ireland, first appeared in 1956. This best-selling reference book reports world records for the biggest, smallest, heaviest, longest, and best in the human and natural worlds. Every record published in the book is carefully checked and documented.

APPLE PEELING

The longest single unbroken apple peel on record is 172 feet 4 inches peeled by Kathy Wafler, 17, of Wolcott, New York, in 11 hours 30 minutes at the Long Ridge Mall, Rochester, N.Y., on October 16, 1976. The apple weighed 20 ounces.

HULA HOOPING

The highest claim for sustaining gyrating hoops is 62 set by Jo Ann Barnes, 15, of Inglewood, California, co-champion of the 1976 U.S. National Contest at Six Flags Over Georgia, near Atlanta, on October 3, 1976. The longest recorded marathon is 54 hours by Kym Coberly of Denton, Texas, October 7–9, 1978.

STRING BALL, LARGEST

The largest balls of string on record are 11 feet in diameter weighing $5\frac{1}{2}$ tons, one of which was amassed by Francis A. Johnson of Darwin, Minnesota, since 1950, and another by Frank Stoeber of Cawker City, Kansas, since at least 1962.

PULLING WITH TEETH

The "strongest teeth in the world" belong to "Hercules" John Massis (b. Wilfried Oscar Morbée, June 4, 1940) of Oostakker, Belgium, who on November 8, 1978, demonstrated the ability to pull 3 railroad cars weighing 140 tons on a level track outside Stockholm, Sweden, with a bit in his teeth. At Evry, France, on March 19, 1977, he raised a

weight of $513\frac{5}{8}$ lbs. to a height of 6 inches from the ground with a bit in his teeth. Massis prevented a helicopter from taking off using only a mouth harness in Los Angeles on April 7, 1979, for the "Guinness Spectacular" ABC–TV show.

Illustrated by Jerry Smath

Objectives • To review the concept of a fantasy device. • To recognize that actions reveal a character's traits. • To create an original story using a fantasy device. • To dramatize a story using Readers Theatre.

Synopsis of the Story The excited Bellini family returns to their newsstand in Times Square to see if Chester, Mario's pet cricket, will sing again. He does, and Mr. Smedley, a music teacher and regular customer, hears him. Astonished, Mr. Smedley writes to the New York *Times* about Chester's talent. When his letter is published, hundreds of New Yorkers crowd around the newsstand to hear Chester. Soon his concerts draw enormous crowds, and business at the newsstand is tremendous. Chester becomes a famous and beloved musician.

A Very Talented Cricket

From the novel *The Cricket in Times Square* by George Selden

Illustrated by Garth Williams

Reading Level Challenging

Background In 1961, the novel *The Cricket in Times Square* was a Newbery Honor Book and was in "Fanfare," the *Horn Book*'s honor list.

Introducing the Story *At night, male crickets rub the scraper part of one wing against the ridge-like part of another wing to make a regular high-pitched chirping sound. What would you do if you heard a cricket chirping a tune? The cricket in this story has an unusual talent. Let's see what happens when people discover what he is able to do.*

Trapped under the roast beef sandwiches in a picnic basket, Chester the country cricket arrives at the Times Square subway station in New York City. Wriggling free, Chester is found by Mario Bellini, a lonely boy who helps his parents run a tiny newsstand. Soon, Chester has a home in a matchbox on the newsstand counter and two new friends—a talkative mouse named Tucker and Tucker's thoughtful friend, Harry the Cat.

Chester, Tucker, and Harry all live happily at the newsstand until one night when their carelessness causes a fire that just about puts the Bellini newsstand out of business. Convinced that the cricket has brought the family bad luck, Mama Bellini says Chester must go. Then Chester begins to chirp a mournful and lovely tune he learned from the radio. Tears come to Mama's eyes—it is her favorite song—and the Bellinis learn of Chester's unique musical talent. So begins the most remarkable week in Chester Cricket's life.

The next morning, which was the last Sunday in August, all three Bellinis came to open the news-stand. They could hardly believe what had happened yesterday and were anxious to see if Chester would continue to sing familiar songs. Mario gave the cricket his usual breakfast of mulberry leaves and water, which Chester took his time eating. He could see that everyone was very nervous and he sort of enjoyed making them wait. When breakfast was over, he had a good stretch and limbered his wings.

Since it was Sunday, Chester thought it would be nice to start with a hymn, so he chose to open his concert with "Rock of Ages." At the sound of the first notes, the faces of Mama and Papa and Mario broke into smiles. They looked at each other and their eyes told how happy they were, but they didn't dare to speak a word.

During the pause after Chester had finished "Rock of Ages," Mr. Smedley came up to the news-stand to buy his monthly copy of *Musical America*. His umbrella, neatly folded, was hanging over his arm as usual.

"Hey, Mr. Smedley—my cricket plays hymns!" Mario blurted out even before the music teacher had a chance to say good morning.

"And opera!" said Papa.

"And Italian songs!" said Mama.

"Well, well, well," said Mr. Smedley, who didn't believe a word, of course. "I see we've all become very fond of our cricket. But aren't we letting our imagination run away with us a bit?"

"Oh, no," said Mario. "Just listen. He'll do it again."

Chester took a sip of water and was ready to play some more. This time, however, instead of "Rock of Ages," he launched into a stirring performance of "Onward Christian Soldiers."

Mr. Smedley's eyes popped. His mouth hung open and the color drained from his face.

"Do you want to sit down, Mr. Smedley?" asked Papa. "You look a little pale."

"I think perhaps I'd better," said Mr. Smedley, wiping his forehead with a silk handkerchief. "It's rather a shock, you know." He came inside the newsstand and sat on the stool so that his face was just a few inches away from the cricket cage. Chester chirped the second verse of "Onward Christian Soldiers," and finished with a soaring "Amen."

"Why the organist played that in church this morning," exclaimed the music teacher breathlessly, "and it didn't sound *half* as good! Of course the cricket isn't as loud as an organ—but what he lacks in volume, he makes up for in sweetness."

"That was nothing," said Papa Bellini proudly. "You should hear him play *Aïda*."

"May I try an experiment?" asked Mr. Smedley.

All the Bellinis said yes at once. The music teacher whistled the scale—do, re, mi, fa, sol, la, te, do. Chester flexed his legs, and as quickly as you could run your fingers up the strings of a harp, he had played the whole scale.

Mr. Smedley took off his glasses. His eyes were moist. "He has absolute pitch," he said in a shaky voice. "I have met only one other person who did. She was a soprano named Arabella Hefflefinger."

Chester started to play again. He went through the two other hymns he'd learned—"The Rosary" and "A Mighty Fortress Is Our God"—and then did the violin concerto. Naturally, he couldn't play it just as it was written without a whole orchestra to back him up, but he was magnificent, all things considered.

Once Mr. Smedley got used to the idea that he was listening to a concert given by a cricket, he enjoyed the performance very much. He had special praise for Chester's "phrasing," by which he meant the neat way the cricket played all the notes of a passage without letting them slide together. And

Someone with *absolute pitch* can reproduce notes in the correct pitch—none are too high or too low.

A *soprano* is a singer with a high-pitched voice.

A *concerto* /kən·cher′·tō/ is a piece of classical music written for an orchestra and solo instruments. Most concertos have three parts, or *movements*.

104

sometimes, when he had been deeply moved by a section, the music teacher would touch his chest over his heart and say, "That cricket has it *here!*"

As Chester chirped his way through the program, a crowd collected around the newsstand. After each new piece, the people applauded and congratulated the Bellinis on their remarkable cricket. Mama and Papa were fit to burst with pride. Mario was very happy too, but of course he had thought all summer that Chester was a very unusual person.

When the playing was over, Mr. Smedley stood up and shook hands with Papa, Mama, and Mario. "I want to thank you for the most delightful hour I have ever spent," he said. "The whole world should know of this cricket." A light suddenly spread over his face. "Why I believe I shall write a letter to the music editor of the New York *Times*," he said. "They'd certainly be interested."

And this is the letter Mr. Smedley wrote:

To the Music Editor of the New York Times *and to the People of New York—*

Rejoice, oh New Yorkers—for a musical miracle has come to pass in our city! This very day, Sunday, August 28th, surely a day which will go down in musical history, it was my pleasure and privilege to be present at the most beautiful recital ever heard in a lifetime devoted to the sublime art. (Music, that is.) Being a musicologist myself, and having graduated—with honors—from a well-known local school of music, I feel I am qualified to judge such matters, and I say, without hesitation, that never have such strains been heard in New York before!

A *musicologist* studies the history and science of music.

Strains are musical sounds.

105

Perchance is an old-fashioned word for *perhaps*.

Operatic music is classical music that features singers. *Symphonic* music is classical music played by an orchestra.

Carnegie Hall is a concert hall in New York City.

Opera lovers go to the *Metropolitan Opera House* (line 18), the *Met,* to hear the finest operatic singers in the world.

Implore (line 20) means *plead*.

"But who was the artist?" the eager music lover will ask. *"Was it perchance some new singer, just lately arrived from a triumphant tour of the capitals of Europe?"*

No, music lovers, it was not!

"Then was it some violinist, who pressed his cheek with love against his darling violin as he played?"

Wrong again, music lovers.

"Could it have been a pianist—with sensitive, long fingers that drew magic sounds from the shining ivory keys?"

Ah—music lovers, you will never guess. It was a cricket! A simple cricket, no longer than half my little finger—which is rather long because I play the piano—but a cricket that is able to chirp operatic, symphonic, and popular music. Am I wrong then in describing such an event as a miracle?

And where is this extraordinary performer? Not in Carnegie Hall, music lovers—nor in the Metropolitan Opera House. You will find him in the newsstand run by the Bellini family in the subway station at Times Square. I urge—I implore!—every man, woman, and child who has music in his soul not to miss one of his illustrious— nay, his glorious—concerts!

enchantedly yours,
Horatio P. Smedley

P.S. I also give piano lessons. For information write to:
H. P. Smedley
1578 West 63rd Street
New York, N. Y.

The music editor of the New York *Times* was quite surprised to get Mr. Smedley's letter, but he believed in the freedom of the press and had it printed on the theatrical and musical page of the paper. The next morning, thousands of people—at home, over the breakfast table, and on buses and trains coming into New York—read about Chester.

The Bellinis got to the newsstand very early. Papa opened the *Times* bundle and thumbed through a copy looking for the letter. When he found it, he read it aloud to Mama and Mario. Then he folded the paper and put it back on the stack to be sold.

"So," said Papa. "We have a <u>celebrity</u> in our midst." A *celebrity* is a famous person.

The celebrity was just at that moment having himself a big yawn in the cricket cage. He had been up most of the night with his manager and Harry Cat, learning new pieces. After eating breakfast and having another stretch, he tested his wings against each other, like a violinist making sure that his violin is in tune. The wings were fine. This time of year they almost itched to chirp. Chester ran over the scales a few times and started to play.

His first selection was something he had heard the night before called "A Little Night Music." It was by a man named <u>Mozart</u>. Chester and Tucker and Harry had all been delighted by "A Little Night Music." They thought it was a very good piece for the cricket to learn because they had heard it first at night, and also because Chester was quite a little person himself. It was lovely music too, with little tunes that sounded like insects hopping around and having a grand time.

Wolfgang Amadeus Mozart (1756–1791) was one of the greatest composers of classical music.

As Chester played, the station began to fill up with the usual commuters. People collected around the newsstand—some drawn by the chirping, and others because they wanted to see the cricket they'd read about. And as always in New York, when a little crowd formed, more people came just to see what the others were looking at. Bees do that, and so do human beings.

Somebody asked who was playing.

"A cricket," a man answered.

"Oh, stop joking!" the first man said and burst out laughing.

In front of him a little lady with a feather in her hat, who was enjoying the music, turned around and whispered "Shhhh!" very angrily.

In another part of the station a man was reading Mr. Smedley's letter, and two other men were also reading it over his shoulders.

"My gosh!" said the one on the right. "A cricket. Who would have believed it?"

"It's a fake," said the man on the left. "Probably a record."

The man in the middle, who owned the paper, snapped it shut. "It *isn't* a fake!" he said. "It's a little living creature—and it sings beautifully! I'm going to give up my season ticket at the Philharmonic."

Everywhere people were talking and arguing and listening to Chester.

Mario made a pile of old magazines and put the cricket cage on top of them so everyone could see better and hear more clearly. When Chester finished one number, a shout of "More! More!" rang through the station. The cricket would catch his breath, have a sip of water, flex his wings, and begin a new selection as fast as he could.

And the crowd grew and grew. Mama Bellini had never seen such a crowd around the newsstand. But she wasn't one to be so <u>dazed</u> by good fortune that she missed out on such a chance. Taking a bundle of *Times* under one arm, she worked her way around, murmuring softly—so as not to disturb the music lovers—"Read about the cricket, read about the cricket. It's in the New York *Times*."

Dazed means *stunned* or *startled and confused.*

109

People snapped up the papers like candy. Mama had to keep going back to the newsstand for new loads. And in less than half an hour the whole stock of the *Times* had been sold.

"Don't sit with your eyes shut," Mama whispered to Papa. (Papa Bellini was one of those people who enjoy listening to music most with their eyes closed.) She put a bunch of *Musical America* into his arms. "Try these. It's a good time now."

Papa sighed, but did as she asked him. And in a little while all the copies of *Musical America* were gone too. It is safe to say that there had never been such an interest in music in the Times Square subway station as there was on that morning.

Over in the drainpipe, Tucker Mouse and Harry Cat were listening too—Harry with his eyes closed like Papa Bellini. There were so many human beings that they couldn't even see the newsstand. But they could hear Chester chirping away on the other side of all the heads and legs and backs. His clear notes filled the station.

"Didn't I tell you?" said Tucker between pieces. "Look at them all. There's a fortune in this. I wish one of us was big enough to pass the hat."

But Harry only smiled. He was happy right where he was, just sitting, enjoying the music.

And the crowd kept on growing. That first day alone, there were seven hundred and eighty-three people late to work because they had stopped to listen to Chester.

During the next few days, other papers besides the *Times* began to run articles on the cricket. Even

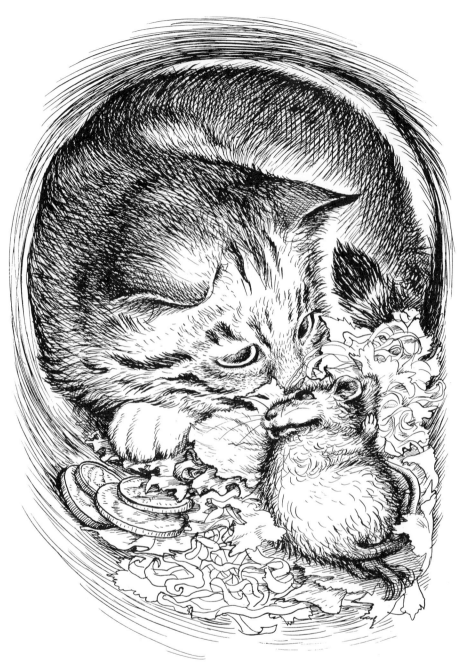

Musical America sent an editor (an assistant editor) down to hear a recital. And Chester was news on the radio and television. All the announcers were talking about the remarkable insect who was delighting <u>throngs</u> in the Times Square subway station.

Throngs are crowds of people.

The Bellinis decided that the best times for Chester to play were early in the morning and late in the afternoon, since that was when the station was the fullest. Concerts began at eight A.M. and four-thirty P.M. and usually lasted an hour and a half—not including encores.

Business boomed at the newsstand. Mama made sure that extra loads of magazines and newspapers were delivered. But even so, by closing time they had sold out completely. Mama Bellini, by the way, turned out to be the best friend a cricket ever had. At noon she would rush home and fix Chester some delicacy for lunch, like a midget fruit salad or an entire vegetable dinner so small you could serve it on a silver dollar. Chester really preferred his mulberry leaves, but he ate everything so as not to hurt her feelings.

Sai Fong, from whom Mario had bought a cage for Chester, had seen Chester's picture in the paper. He kept Mario supplied with leaves. He and another Chinese gentleman dug out two collapsible chairs from his attic and came uptown every day at eight and four-thirty to hear Chester's new programs.

Mr. Smedley was there at least once a day too. He brought a tape recorder and made recordings of all the new pieces Chester learned. And during the intermissions—there was always an intermission of ten minutes halfway through the concert—he delivered short talks on musical appreciation to the audiences.

So by Thursday, Chester Cricket was the most famous musician in New York City.

Discussion Questions *What does Mama Bellini do when Chester draws large crowds to the newsstand?* (She sells newspapers and magazines.) *What does this tell you about her?* (Possible answer: she is clever and cares about making money.) *What does Papa Bellini do?* (He listens to the music with his eyes closed.) *What does this tell you about him?* (Possible answer: he loves beautiful music.) *What does Mr. Smedley do during the concerts, and what does this tell you*

about him? (He gives lectures during intermissions; he loves teaching music.)
Enriching Activity *Readers Theatre.* Choose several students to take the parts of the narrator and the characters in the story. Have them select favorite scenes from the story to tape record or read aloud using the Readers Theatre techniques on page T43. Some students might write and record a commercial for Chester's concerts.

Questions

1. What is the story's main fantasy device—something not likely to be believed if it happened in "real" life?

1. Interpretive/inference A cricket that plays music (page 102).

2. How did Chester refresh himself between songs in a concert? **2. Literal/recall** Chester would have a sip of water and flex his wings (pages 102, 108).

3. Why did Mr. Smedley put a P.S. in his letter?

4. The story contains details that show people being pleasant and kind to others. Write about two such details.

5. Write the meaning of each root word and the words built from each one.

Root word

perform	performer	performance
record	recorder	recording
music	musician	musical

Activity **Critical/relating to experience** *Writing letters.*

Mr. Smedley wrote a letter to the editor of a newspaper to express his excitement about an extraordinary event he had attended. Write a letter to the editor of your local newspaper. Tell about an unusual event that you have attended. Describe what you thought was exciting or interesting about this event, and what made it unusual. The event you describe may be either partly or entirely imaginary.

3. Interpretive/inference He wanted to find more piano students (page 106).

4. Literal/recall Possible answers: Mr. Smedley wrote a letter about Chester (page 105); Mama prepared special food for Chester (page 112).

5. Vocabulary *perform*—to act, play music, or sing for an audience; *performer*—one who performs (page 106); *performance*—the act of performing (page 102); *record*—to register sound on a phonograph disc or magnetic tape; *recorder*—a machine used for recording (page 112); *recording*—a tape or phonograph disc that registers sound (page 112); *music*—a composition produced by combining and regulating sounds of varying pitch (page 106); *musician*—a person who makes music a profession, such as a conductor or performer (page 112); *musical*—skilled in music (page 101).

113

Objectives   ● To extrapolate events resulting from a change in plot.   ● To identify a character's motives.   ● To discuss the concepts of heroism and honor.   ● To recognize and list new vocabulary.

Synopsis of the Story   A wish on a magic coin transports four children to a jousting tournament at Camelot. As they watch Launcelot win match after match, one of the children, Katharine, decides to challenge Sir Launcelot. Through the magic of the coin, Katharine becomes Sir Kath and defeats the famous knight. Merlin confronts Katharine with her undeserved victory and uses the coin to return Camelot to the time before the tournament. The children wish themselves home, never to travel into the past again.

Reading Level   Challenging

The Tournament

From the novel *Half Magic* by Edward Eager

Illustrated by Jerry Smath

The *Round Table* (line 13) was the circular table where King Arthur met with his knights.

The old coin that Jane found looked almost like a nickel, but it bore strange signs and worked a strange magic—it granted half the wishes its owners made. Soon Jane, her brother Mark, and her sisters Katharine and Martha were all wishing on the magic charm.

Katharine remembered to double her wishes when her turn came. "I wish," she said, "that we may go back twice as far as to the days of King Arthur, and see two tournaments, and go on two quests, and do two good deeds." With the charm's "half magic," the four children found themselves in the England of King Arthur's time. The quest that followed led them to Sir Launcelot, the greatest knight of the Round Table, who was locked in a dungeon by his enemy, Morgan le Fay. With the charm's help, Katharine rescued Sir Launcelot. But was he grateful? Not a bit. He preferred to escape without the help of magic. So an angry Katharine undid her good deed and wished herself and the others to a tournament at Camelot. When they arrive, Katharine still has half of two good deeds to do.

114

Background   The novel *Half Magic* was on the American Library Association Notable Children's Books list in 1954.

Introducing the Story   *King Arthur, one of the most famous British kings, may or may not have existed, but there are many stories about this legendary king and his knights. In this story, four children have an adventure with King Arthur's greatest knight, Sir Launcelot.*

Words to Know

tournament: a sport in which knights on horseback tried to unseat one another with lances or swords. (Point out the word in the title)

Camelot (kam′·ə·lot): the town where King Arthur had his court. (page 114)

combat: fighting with weapons. (page 118)

trice: a moment. (page 121)

"I can't get used to this being rushed around," complained Martha, as she found herself somewhere else for the third time in three minutes. "Where are we now, and when is it?"

"Camelot, I should think," said Katharine, "in tournament time! Look!"

Jane and Mark and Martha looked. Camelot and the field of tournament looked exactly as you would expect them to look, from the descriptions in *The Boy's King Arthur* and the wonderful books of Mr. T. H. White. Trumpets were blowing clarion calls, and pennons fluttered on the blue air, and armor flashed in the bright light. Gallant knights and trusty squires and faithful pages and ladies fair were crowding into the stands in hundreds to watch the chivalrous sport.

The four children had front-row grandstand seats, for Katharine had made that a part of her wish. They looked around them, taking in the sights.

King Arthur sat enthroned on a high platform at one end of the field. The children could see him clearly, with his kind, simple, understanding face like the warm sun come to shine on merry England. Queen Guinevere was seated at his right, and Merlin, the magician, thin and wise and gray-bearded, at his left.

And now the trumpets blew an extra long fanfare, and the tournament began.

Sir Launcelot was among the first to ride out on the field. The children recognized him by his armor.

"I told you he'd come out all right," said Katharine, a bit bitterly.

But when Sir Launcelot got going in that tournament, even Katharine had to admire him.

He smote down five knights with his first spear, and four knights with his second spear, and unhorsed three more with his sword, until all the people sitting round on the benches began crying out, "Oh, Gramercy, what marvelous deeds that knight doth do in that field!"

Jane sighed a satisfied sigh. "Kind of glorious, isn't it?" she murmured.

"It's the most wonderful age in human history," said Mark solemnly. "If only it didn't have to end!"

Gramercy is an archaic expression of surprise or thanks.

117

"Why did it?" asked Martha, who hadn't read *The Boy's King Arthur* yet.

"Partly 'cause some of the other knights got tired of being knocked down all the time and having Launcelot always win," Mark told her.

"Yes," said Katharine, in rather a peculiar voice, "it would really be a good deed, in a way, if somebody knocked *him* down for a change, wouldn't it?"

Mark gave her a sharp look, but just then Sir Launcelot started knocking down more knights, and he had to watch the field. When he looked again, Katharine wasn't there.

Mark nudged Jane hard, as a horrible thought came into his mind.   Nudged means *pushed*.

Jane turned and saw the empty spot where Katharine had been, and Mark could tell that she was having the same thought, too.

Just then there was an interruption in the tournament. A strange knight rode out on the field of combat and straight up to King Arthur's platform.

"I crave your Majesty's permission to challenge Sir Launcelot to single combat!" cried the strange knight in a voice loud enough for the children to hear clearly from where they sat.

The hearts of Jane and Mark sank.

Even Martha now guessed the horrid truth. "How dare she?" she whispered.

"I don't know," said Mark. "She's been getting too full of herself ever since we started this wish!"

"Wait till I get her home!" said Jane grimly.

"How call they you, strange sir?" King Arthur was saying, meanwhile, "and whence do you hail?"

"They call me Sir Kath," said the strange knight, "and I hail from Toledo, Ohio."

"I know not this Toledo," said King Arthur, "but fight if you will. Let the combat begin."

The trumpets sounded another clarion call, the strange knight faced Sir Launcelot, and there began the strangest combat, it is safe to say, ever witnessed by the knights of the Round, or any other, Table.

The intrepid Katharine thought herself very clever at this moment. She had wished she were wearing two suits of armor and riding two horses, and she had wished she were two and a half times as tall and strong as Sir Launcelot, and she had wished that she would defeat him twice. And immediately here she was, wearing one suit of armor and riding one horse, and she was one and a quarter times as tall and strong, and she couldn't wait to defeat him once.

But in her cleverness she had forgotten one thing. She had forgotten to wish that she knew the rules of jousting. And here she was, facing the greatest knight in the world, and she didn't know how to start. She knew she'd win in the end, because she'd wished it that way, but what was she to do in the beginning and middle?

Before she could work out another wish to take care of this, Sir Launcelot rode at her, struck her with his <u>lance</u>, and knocked her back onto her horse's tail. Then he rode at her from the opposite direction and knocked her forward onto her horse's neck.

The crowd roared with laughter.

The feelings of Jane, Mark and Martha may well be imagined.

Point out the *lance* (line 27) in the illustration.

As for the feelings of Katharine, they knew no bounds. She still held the magic charm clutched in one hot hand, and she wasn't bothering about correct arithmetic now.

"I wish I could fight ten times as well as you, you bully! Yah!" were the words that the valiant Sir Kath spoke upon the field. It was a cry of pure temper.

And immediately she could fight five times as well as Sir Launcelot, and everyone knows how good *he* was.

A *valiant* person (line 6) is brave and courageous. Point out the irony intended here.

What followed would have to be seen to be believed. Katharine came down like several wolves on the fold. She seemed to spring from all sides at once. Her sword flashed like a living thunderbolt. Her lance whipped about, now here, now there, like a snake gone mad.

"Zounds!" cried the people, and "Lackaday" and "Wurra wurra!"

Jane, Mark and Martha watched with clasped hands.

If Sir Launcelot had not been the greatest knight in the world, he would never have lived to tell the tale. Even as it was, the end was swift. In something less than a trice he was unseated from his horse, fell to the ground with a crash, and did not rise again.

Katharine galloped round and round the field, bowing graciously to the applause of the crowd.

But she soon noticed that the crowd wasn't applauding very loudly. And it was only the traitorous knights like Sir Mordred and Sir Agravaine, the ones who were jealous of Launcelot, who were applauding at all.

The rest of the crowd was strangely silent. For Launcelot, the flower of knighthood, the darling of the people's hearts, the greatest champion of the Round Table, had been defeated!

Queen Guinevere looked furious. King Arthur looked sad. The attendant knights, except for the traitorous ones, looked absolutely wretched. Merlin looked as if he didn't believe it.

Jane and Mark and Martha looked as though they believed it, but didn't want to.

And it was then that the full knowledge of what she had done swept over Katharine.

She had succeeded and she had failed. She had defeated the greatest knight in history. But she had pretended to herself that she was doing it for a good deed. Really it had been just because she was annoyed with Launcelot for not appreciating her help enough, back in Morgan le Fay's castle.

Her cheeks flamed and she felt miserable. It was hot inside her helmet suddenly, and she dragged it off. Then she remembered too late that she'd forgotten something else when she made her wish. She had wished to be in armor, and to be on horseback, and to be tall and strong, and to win. But she had forgotten to say anything about not being Katharine any longer.

Now, as the helmet came away, her long brown hair streamed down onto her shoulders, and her nine-year-old face blinked at the astonished crowd.

Those sitting nearest the ringside saw. Sir Mordred tittered. Sir Agravaine sneered. The mean knights who were jealous of Sir Launcelot began to laugh, and mingled with the laughter were the cruel words, "Beaten by a girl!"   Mingled means mixed.

Sir Launcelot came to and sat up. He heard the laughter. He looked at Katharine. Katharine looked away, but not before he had recognized her. He got to his feet. There was silence all round the field; even the mean knights stopped laughing.

Sir Launcelot came over to Katharine. "Why have you done this to me?" he said.

"I didn't mean to," said Katharine.

With flushed cheeks, but with head held high, Sir
Launcelot strode to King Arthur's platform and knelt
in the dust before it. In a low voice he asked leave to
go on a far quest, a year's journey away at least, that
he might hide his shame till by a hundred deeds of
valor he would win back his lost honor.

Flushed cheeks have turned red.

King Arthur did not trust himself to speak. He
nodded his consent.

In medieval times, *honor* was the glory and respect won by skill in battle.

Queen Guinevere did not even look at Sir Launcelot
as he walked away from the field of tournament.

Merlin spoke a word in King Arthur's ear. King
Arthur nodded. He rose, offered an arm to Guinevere,
and led her from the stand. Merlin spoke another
word, this time to the attendant knights. They began
clearing the people from the field.

Most of the people went quietly, but three
children in the front row of the grandstand put up
quite a fuss, saying that they had to find their sister
Katharine, who'd done something terrible. But a
sister was a sister and they'd stick up for her,
anyway. The knights cleared them away with the rest.

Presently, after what seemed like at least a year,
Katharine found herself alone before Merlin. She was
crying.

Merlin looked at her sternly.

"Fie on your weeping," he said. "I wot well that
ye be a false enchantress, come here in this guise to
defeat our champion and discredit our Table Round!"

"I'm not! I didn't!" said Katharine.

"Ye be, too!" said Merlin, "and you certainly
have! After today our name is mud in Camelot!"

"Oh, oh," wept Katharine.

"Silence, sorceress," said Merlin. He waved his wand at her. "I command that you appear before me in your true form!"

Immediately Katharine wasn't tall or strong or in armor any more, but just Katharine.

Merlin looked surprised.

"These fiends begin early!" he said. "However, doubtless ye be but the instrument of a greater power." He waved his wand again. "I command that your allies, cohorts, aids, accomplices and companions be brought hither to stand at your side!"

Jane and Mark and Martha appeared beside Katharine, looking nearly as unhappy and uncomfortable as she.

Merlin looked really quite startled. Then he shook his head sadly.

"So young," he said, "and yet so wicked!"

"We're not!" said Martha, making a rude face.

The behavior of the others was more seemly.

"You see, sir," began Mark.

"We didn't mean to," began Jane.

"Let me," said Katharine. "I started it."

And in a rush of words and tears she told Merlin everything, beginning with the charm, and her wish to travel back in time, and going on to what she had hoped to do, and what she'd done and where she'd gone wrong.

"I wanted to do a good deed," she said, "and I *did* one when I rescued Launcelot from that old dungeon. But then he wasn't properly grateful at all and made me undo it so he could rescue himself, all for the sake of his old honor! And that made me cross! And just now I pretended I was defeating him so the other knights wouldn't be so jealous of him, but really I was just trying to get back at him for being so stuck-up! And I always wanted to fight in a real tournament, anyway!"

Doubtless is another word for *without doubt,* or *certainly.*

Here an *instrument* (line 2) means something used to accomplish some purpose.

Hither (line 5) means *here.*

"Well, now you have," said Merlin, "and what good did you do by it? Just made everybody thoroughly unhappy!"

"I know," said Katharine.

"That's what comes of meddling," said Merlin. "There is a pattern to history, and when you try to change that pattern, no good may follow."

Katharine hung her head.

"However," went on Merlin, and to the surprise of the four children, he was smiling now, "all is not lost. I have a few magic tricks of my own, you know. Let me see, how shall I handle this? I *could* turn time back, I suppose, and make it as though this day had never happened, but it would take a lot out of me."

"Really?" said Katharine in surprise. "It would be a mere nothing to *us!*"

Merlin looked at her a bit grimly.

"Oh, it would, would it?" he said.

"Oh, yes," went on Katharine happily. "I could wish Launcelot were twice as near as here again, and then I could wish that he'd defeat me twice, and then I could wish that the people would honor him twice as much as they ever did, and then I could wish . . ."

"Hold!" cried Merlin, in alarm. "A truce to your wishes, before you get us in worse trouble! I think I had best see this wonderful charm of yours." He made a <u>pass</u> at Katharine with his wand. "If there be any magic among you, let it appear now or forever hold its peace."

Merlin made a *pass*, or wave, of his wand.

126

Katharine's hot hand, which for so long had clutched the charm, opened in spite of itself, and the charm lay in plain sight on her palm.

Merlin looked at it. His eyes widened. He swept his tall hat from his head and bowed low before the charm, three times. Then he turned to the children.

"This is a very old and powerful magic," he said. "Older and more powerful than my own. It is, in fact, too powerful and too dangerous for four children, no matter how well they may intend, to have in their keeping. I am afraid I must ask you to surrender it."

He made another pass with his wand. The charm leaped gracefully from Katharine's hand to his own.

Mark spoke.

"But it came to us in our own time," he said, "and that's a part of history, too, just as much as this is. Maybe we were *meant* to find it. Maybe there's some good thing we're supposed to do with it. There is a pattern to history, and when you try to change that pattern, no good may follow."

Merlin looked at him.

"You are a wise child," he said.

"Just average," said Mark modestly.

"Dear me," said Merlin. "If that be so, if all children be as sensible as you in this far future time you dwell in . . ." He broke off. "What century did you say you come from?"

"We didn't," said Mark, "but it's the twentieth."

"The twentieth century," mused Merlin. "What a happy age it must be—truly the Golden Age that we are told is to come."

He stood thinking a moment. Then he smiled.

"Very well. Go back to your twentieth century," he said, "and take your magic with you, and do your best with it. But first, I have something to say."

He held the charm at arm's length, rather as though he feared it might bite him, and addressed it with great respect.

"I wish," he said, "that in six minutes it may be as though these children had never appeared here. Except that they—and I—will remember. And I further wish that our tournament may begin all over again and proceed as originally planned by history. Only twice as much so," he added, to be on the safe side.

"Now may I have it back, please?" Katharine asked, when he had done.

"In a minute,'" said Merlin. "By the way, have you been making a lot of wishes lately? It feels rather worn out to me. It won't last forever, you know."

"Oh dear, we were afraid of that," said Jane. "How many more do we get?"

"That would be telling," said Merlin. "But you'd best not waste too many. It might be later than you think."

"Oh!" cried Martha. "Maybe we'll never get home!"

"Don't worry," said Merlin, smiling at her. "There are still a few wishes left for you. And one more for me." Again he held the charm out before him.

"And I thirdly wish," he said, "for the future protection of the world from the terrible good intentions of these children and for their protection against their own folly. May this charm, for twice the length of time that it shall be in their hands, grant no further wishes carrying said children out of their own century and country, but may they find whatsoever boon the magic may have in store for them in their own time and place." He put the charm into Katharine's hands. "And now you'd best be going. Because in less than a minute by my wish, it will be as though you'd never appeared here. And if you aren't home when that happens, goodness knows where you *will* be!"

"But what about the good deed I wished?" said Katharine. "None of the ones I tried worked out!"

An *ideal* (line 7) is a goal, an idea of what would be perfect.

"My child," said Merlin, and his smile was very kind now, "you have done your good deed. You have brought me word that for as far into time as the twentieth century, the memory of Arthur and of the Round Table, which I helped him to create, will be living yet. And that in that far age people will still care for the ideal I began, enough to come back through time and space to try to be of service to it. You have brought me that word, and now I can finish my work in peace and know that I have done well. And if that's not a good deed, I should like to know what is. Now good-bye. Wish quickly. You have exactly seventeen seconds."

Katharine wished.

And because their mother had been worried yesterday by their being so long away, Katharine put in that when they got home, they should only have been gone two minutes, by real time.

This was really quite thoughtful of Katharine. Perhaps she, too, like Mark the day before, had learned something during her day of adventure.

The next thing the four children knew, they were sitting together in Katharine and Martha's room, and it was still that morning, and they had only been away from home a minute. Yet that minute was packed with memories.

"Did we dream it?" Katharine asked.

"I don't think so, or we wouldn't all remember it," said Mark.

"And we all do, don't we?" said Jane.

And they all did.

130

Discussion Questions *After she had won the joust, why was Katharine unhappy?* (She had wanted to do a good deed but was unsuccessful; she realized that everyone except the jealous knights admired Launcelot.) *The people of Camelot and Launcelot were unable to accept his loss of the match. Launcelot believed that he had also lost his honor, his dignity, and his reputation. Do people today still expect their heroes to be perfect? Why or why not?*

Enriching Activity *Vocabulary.* Ask the students to guess the meanings of the archaic words in the story (*fie, wot,* and so on) and to verify them in a dictionary. Then have them begin a list of new words encountered in their reading. Point out that the glossary of their textbook (page 413) includes many of these. Encourage them to consult dictionaries and to write sentences using the words. From time to time, remind the students to continue their lists.

Questions

1. What good deed did Katharine *intend* to do? According to Merlin, what good deed did she *actually* do?

2. How might Launcelot's defeat have changed the history of Camelot?

3. Merlin, and later Mark, said, "There is a pattern to history, and when you try to change that pattern no good may follow." Who meant "We are part of the pattern"? Who meant "You are *not* part of the pattern"?

4. Choose the word that means the same as each underlined word from the story.

   fearless   resounding   courage

   a. "Trumpets were blowing <u>clarion</u> calls."
   b. Launcelot planned "a hundred deeds of <u>valor</u>."
   c. "The <u>intrepid</u> Katharine" thought herself clever.

1. Literal/recall
She wanted to defeat Launcelot so the other knights would no longer be jealous of him (page 125); Katharine brought Merlin the good news that the Round Table was remembered in the future (page 130).

2. Interpretive/ extrapolation
Possible answer: if Launcelot had been discredited, he might not be remembered today.

3. Interpretive/ inference Mark meant "We are . . . ." (page 128) Merlin meant "You are *not* . . . ." (page 126)

4. Vocabulary
a. resounding (page 116); b. courage (page 123); c. fearless (page 119).

Activity

The half-magic coin has fallen into your hands, but it no longer grants wishes for trips into the past. You might wish for a trip into the future. Describe the time and place you visit, one exciting thing that happens there, and the special talents you wish for.

Interpretive/ extrapolation
Writing. Remind the students to double their wishes.

Objectives • To recognize the elements of myth. • To note how a main character solves a problem. • To write a story about a legendary hero in a modern setting.

Synopsis of the Legend Theseus, the prince of Athens, joins fourteen young Athenians who are to be sacrificed to the Minotaur of Crete. They sail toward Crete and meet Minos, the king of the island and caretaker of the Minotaur. In the palace on Crete, Theseus meets Ariadne, King Minos's daughter, and falls in love with her. Ariadne tells him how to kill the Minotaur and find his way out of the Labyrinth. The Athenians then escape from Crete, and Ariadne and Theseus are wed as they sail to Athens.

Reading Level Challenging

A HERO'S PROMISE

A Greek legend retold by Ian Serraillier

Illustrated by Kinuko Craft

Stories about Theseus,[1] one of the greatest heroes of ancient Greece, have been told for centuries. The story of his struggle with the Minotaur[2] is but one of many tales about Theseus' strength and bravery.

---

1. **Theseus** (THEE·see·uhs).
2. **Minotaur** (MIN·uh·tawr).

132

Background   Theseus, the favorite hero of the ancient Athenians, had mortal parents but was related through his mother's family to the sea god Poseidon. The slaying of the Minotaur is one of the myths about Theseus's adventures as a young man.

Introducing the Legend   *The ancient Greeks developed many legends about gods, goddesses, and ordinary people. This story tells some of the heroic exploits of young Theseus, a favorite of the sea god Poseidon. As you read, note which acts are the work of the gods, and which are the result of courage and loyalty.*

Theseus was a long-lost son of King Aegeus[3] of the ancient Greek city of Athens. Many years before this story begins, King Aegeus had caused the death of Androgeus,[4] the son of King Minos[5] of Crete.[6] As punishment, Minos demanded a human sacrifice from the people of Athens. Every year for ten years the people of Athens had sent seven boys and seven girls to the island of Crete, where King Minos forced them to enter the Labyrinth.[7] The huge maze was the home of the terrible Minotaur, half man and half beast, who ate only human flesh. No one who entered the Labyrinth had ever escaped.

When Theseus came at last to his father's city, he was horrified to learn of this cruel punishment. Theseus felt that his father Aegeus and the people of Athens had paid far too much for one misdeed. He made a promise to the fourteen doomed young people: "Do not despair. I will go with you and kill the Minotaur. None of you will die."

---

3. **Aegeus** (EE·jee·uhs).
4. **Androgeus** (An·DRAH·jee·uhs).
5. **Minos** (MY·nuhs).
6. **Crete** (KREET).
7. **Labyrinth** (LAB·uh·rinth).

A *black sail* on the Athenian ships symbolized the deaths of the fourteen youths.

Unfurled (line 11) means *opened* or *unrolled.*

Amidships (line 13) means *in the middle of the ship.*

Vain means *conceited.*

In the harbor the ship was already waiting. The helmsman was standing by the steering oar. The pilot at the prow and the thirty oarsmen on their benches were impatient to be off. As the victims embarked, their families and friends followed them up the gangplank, pressing on them food for the voyage, embracing them, clinging to them. And when the ship drew slowly away, they stretched out their hands to them over the water.

Outside the harbor the sailors hauled the black sail up to the masthead and unfurled it. The north wind filled it, and the ship sped away over the waves. But the victims, huddled together amidships, were cold and lonely as the sea, and the crying gulls above their heads echoed their misery.

They sailed past the islands of Aegina[8] and Milos,[9] and on the third day out they sighted far off the cliffs of Crete. A ship came out to meet them.

"She has a golden sail painted with royal dolphins," said the pilot. "King Minos himself must be on board."

The sails of both ships were lowered and the oarsmen took over. The Cretan ship drew alongside. King Minos was standing at the prow, splendid in a golden embroidered cloak that streamed behind him in the breeze. He was a great warlord and a lover of beautiful things, but he was also vain.

When the two ships were close enough for the oarsmen to touch hands, he leaped aboard the Greek

8. **Aegina** (ee·JY·nuh).
9. **Milos** (MEE·laws).

ship and asked to see the victims. Trembling with
fear, they stood up at the prow, with Theseus beside
them. At once a quarrel started. When King Minos
saw that there were fifteen and not fourteen of them,
he said he would keep one of them as his slave. And
he picked out Eriboia,[10] the most beautiful of the
girls, and touched her pale cheek with his hand as if
she were already his slave. She screamed to Theseus
to help her.

Theseus leaped up and stood chin to chin with
King Minos and said, "She is no slave but a noble's
daughter. If you touch her again I shall throw you
into the sea."

---

10. Eriboia (ehr·ih·BOY·uh).

Never before had anyone spoken to King Minos like that.

"Who are you that dare insult me so?" said King Minos, white with anger.

"I am Theseus, son of King Aegeus."

"I am the warlord of Cnossus,[11] king of the islands," said Minos. "Immortal Zeus,[12] the king of the gods, is my father." And stretching out his hands to heaven, he called on Zeus to confirm it with a flash of lightning.

At once the whole face of the sky was split with lightning, and there was a great drum roll of thunder.

"I have the blood of Poseidon,[13] the sea god, in my veins," said Theseus. "He will give me whatever help I need."

"Then fetch this," said King Minos. He threw his gold signet ring into the sea, and it sank at once.

Theseus climbed on to the stern rail and dived into the sea, deep down to the watery halls of Poseidon, the sea god. And a hundred dolphins, rolling and plunging, brought him to the palace of the Nereids,[14] the daughters of Ocean, who were shining with the splendor of fire. Thetis,[15] the loveliest of the sea nymphs, dressed him in a purple robe and gave him a jewelled crown. Meanwhile her sisters swam everywhere to find the golden ring. At last they found it in a cranny of rock and, in front of Poseidon the sea god, they gave it to Theseus. Then

When letters were sealed with hot wax, the writer used a *signet* /sig′·nit/ ring to make an impression in the wax. An unbroken seal indicated that the letter had not been opened by anyone.

11. Cnossus (NAHS·uhs).
12. Zeus (ZOOS).
13. Poseidon (puh·SY·duhn).
14. Nereids (NUR·ee·ids)
15. Thetis (THEE·tis).

he sped towards the sea roof, a long trail of bubbles
marking his path back to the ceiling of light. When
he broke the surface, the young men and girls hauled
him eagerly aboard. They were amazed to see him
dressed in a robe even more splendid than King
Minos's and not even wet. And when he handed
Minos the golden ring, how they shouted for joy!

As for Minos, he said not a word, but went back to his ship and returned to harbor.

In those days Cnossus was one of the great cities of the world. The nearby port of Heracleion[16] was crowded with shipping, with trading boats from Egypt and Asia as well as the King's own fleet. People had come from all over the island to see the Athenian[17] strangers. They stared at them as they disembarked and marched up the road to the palace.

Disembarked means *went ashore.*

And what a palace it was! It spread right over the hill. The halls and galleries and countless rooms were built of huge blocks of stone, framed in cypress wood cut from the forests inland. The wooden columns tapered downwards and were painted russet with blue capitals.[18] There was a grand staircase four stories high, lit by wells of light and thus protected from the hot summer sun and freezing winter winds.

Russet is brownish-orange.

As Theseus entered the hall at the foot of the staircase, he was startled to see a huge black bull in front of him. It had gold horns and white nostrils, red-rimmed eyes and a fierce mouth. At once he thought of the Minotaur. He drew his sword and waited for the charge.

"The beast is harmless," laughed King Minos. "Sheathe your sword."

"Sheathe your sword" means *"put your sword back into its case."*

Then Theseus saw it was only a painting on the wall, and he too laughed.

It was the custom for King Minos to entertain his Athenian guests to dinner; they were not shut in the

---

16. Heracleion (ee·RAH·klee·awn).
17. Athenian (uh·THEE·nee·uhn).
18. capitals: in this story, the upper parts of columns or pillars.

Labyrinth till the following day. The cups and dishes were all of solid gold; and the food was lavish and magnificent. Yet Theseus and his companions did not feel hungry. They were haunted by the thought of what lay in store for them next day.

Lavish means *expensive* and *plentiful*.

In the middle of the dinner they were puzzled by a sudden growl of thunder that seemed to come from underneath their feet. King Minos was quick to explain it.

"The Minotaur is hungry tonight," he said. "Perhaps he has smelled human flesh and cannot wait till morning."

Then the floor began to tremble and the foundations of the palace quivered and shook.

"The Minotaur is trying out his paces," said the King. "His temper does not improve with waiting. But why should we cut short our entertainment to please him?"

King Minos clearly enjoyed his guests' dismay. Not so his daughter, Ariadne,[19] who admired Theseus's dignity and calm. She asked about his exploits on the road to Athens and listened entranced while he told her about them. She could not bear to think of the miserable death that awaited him and his companions next morning. So she decided to help him.

After the dinner she took Theseus to the Hall of Distaffs, where she did her weaving. The walls were bright with deep blue dolphins and starfish and spiky sea urchins painted against a pale blue ground, all lit with a soft light.

"Tomorrow I must wrestle with death," said Theseus.

"I can help you win and escape safely," said Ariadne. "Daedalus,[20] the master craftsman who built the Labyrinth, once told me how to find the way out."

She went to her spindle and picked up a ball of wool.

"As soon as you are inside the door, tie the loose end of the wool to the lintel," she said, "and unwind the ball as you go. Do not let it out of your hand or you will never find the way back. When you meet the Minotaur, seize him by the horn and stab him."

"But we are allowed no weapons," said Theseus.

---

19. **Ariadne** (ahr·ee·AD·nee).
20. **Daedalus** (DED·uh·luhs).

"Take this dagger and hide it in your tunic." She gave it to him; the hilt was of solid gold and the iron point sharp as a needle.

"Tomorrow I shall owe my life to you," said Theseus. "Dearest princess, what can I do for you in return?"

"Make me your wife and take me back to Greece," said Ariadne, and the tears welled up in her eyes. "I am lonely and unhappy here. The palace is full of soldiers; the talk is of nothing but wars and fighting. And at night the monster bellows so loudly that I cannot sleep. I beg you to take me away."

"With all my heart," said Theseus, much moved by her beauty and goodness. And he took her in his arms and kissed her.

A *tunic* is a loose, sleeveless garment worn by the ancient Greeks and Romans.

The *hilt* (line 2) is the handle of a sword or a dagger.

141

Next morning the palace guards locked Theseus and his companions in the Labyrinth. The huge iron door shut behind them with a clang that echoed through the dark twisting passages, the numberless corridors. And when the last echo had faded, there was a dreadful stillness.

"You have nothing to fear," said Theseus. "I shall keep my promise. Wait here till I return."

He had hidden Ariadne's dagger under his cloak. And to light him on his way, he had the jewelled crown which Thetis had given him. He fastened one end of the ball of wool to the lintel above the door and set off into the darkness. Crouching by the door, his companions watched the splash of light on the walls till he turned a corner and vanished; then they listened in the pitch darkness to the echo of his footsteps fading into the distance.

On and on down the endless corridors went Theseus, hour after hour, unwinding the wool as he walked. The stone walls were ice cold and slimy; they glistened wet in the light of the jewels. Sometimes he stopped to look for signs of the monster, to listen for its footsteps.

He had come to a place where the corridor branched into three when he suddenly heard the sound of heavy breathing. He put down the ball of wool and gripped the hilt of his dagger. He peered round and turned his head slowly while the jewels on his crown, shining like a torch, floodlit the darkness.

The Minotaur was lying in the mouth of the third passage, curled up, asleep. The monstrous bull's head with its golden horns and white nostrils was nodding

over a human chest. Roused by the light, it opened
its eyes, red-rimmed and bloodshot, and for a whole
minute blinked at Theseus. Suddenly it let out so
great a bellow that it seemed as if the walls had
crumbled and fallen in. High above in the palace
Ariadne heard it as she sat weaving in her room, and
the distaff fell from her hand. The trees in the forest
trembled and a great wave rolled ashore and rocked
the ships in harbor.

Then the creature scrambled upright. It lowered
its head and, snorting smoke from its fiery nostrils,
charged. There was no room for Theseus to step

aside, but he remembered what Ariadne had told him to do. He reached up with his left hand, caught hold of a horn and wrenched the head backwards. With his right hand he plunged the dagger into its neck. The beast groaned and slumped forward on top of him, almost smothering him as they fell. For a long moment they rolled and wrestled on the stony floor. Then the Minotaur's muscles went limp and slack and it never moved again.

Theseus struggled to his feet. He picked up what was left of the ball of wool, and winding it up as he went, groped his way back to the mouth of the Labyrinth where his companions were waiting. They cheered when they saw him and kissed his hands.

But he silenced them at once, for they were not out of danger yet. "We must stay here till night-fall, till the guards are sure we are dead," he told them. "Then Ariadne will unlock the door and let us out."

At last they heard the key grate in the lock and the door creak open. The stars were shining as they tiptoed out into the warm night. He called softly to Ariadne. "I have killed the Minotaur," he whispered. He slipped her hand into his and they hurried down to the harbor, with the seven young men and the seven girls behind them.

The ship was waiting. They hoisted sail and cast off their moorings and steered past the sleeping ships. So that King Minos could not pursue them, they scuttled one of the ships in the harbor mouth to block the way out. Then joyfully they made for the open sea.

With his companions as witnesses, while the wind
filled the sail and tugged at the rigging, Theseus
made Ariadne his wife. And as a pledge that he
would love her all his life, he gave her his jewelled
crown and set it on her head, where it sparkled in
the darkness as brightly as the stars.

Ask the students to
research the rest of
the myth to find out
about Ariadne's un-
happy end.

Questions

1. Some heroes are fortunate: they have "outside help." What "outside help" did Theseus have?

2. What did Theseus do that made him a hero?

3. If Theseus were alive today, what is one deed he might do to show that he is still a hero?

4. Look back in the story to find the underlined words below. Then choose the best answer to each question.

   a. Is a lintel a vegetable for making soup, a small piece of thread, or a support at the top of a door? (See page 142.)

   b. In this story is scuttled what Theseus did when he sank a ship, what Ariadne did when she made thread, or what happens when you stumble? (See page 144.)

Activity **Critical/relating to experience** *Drawing labyrinths.*

A *labyrinth* is a maze or a network of confusing paths. On a large sheet of paper, draw a diagram for a labyrinth. (Make sure only one path is the exit and the other paths are "dead ends.") Then ask a friend to try an escape route from your labyrinth by tracing the way to get out of it. Give your friend a time limit of forty-five seconds.

BOOKSHELF

The Bat-Poet by Randall Jarrell. Macmillan, 1964.
A young bat becomes aware of nature's beauty.
He is inspired to create poems about his experiences and to share his poems with a chipmunk.
Reading Level Average

Chitty-Chitty-Bang-Bang, the Magical Car by Ian
Fleming. Random House, 1964. Commander Crackpot restores an old racing car and finds it has
the power to fly, float, and chase robbers. **Reading Level** Challenging

A Gift of Magic by Lois Duncan. Little, Brown, 1971.
Each of the Garrett children has a special talent,
but Nancy's gift is extrasensory perception. **Reading Level** Average

The Mightiest of Mortals: Heracles by Doris Gates.
Viking Press, 1975. Heracles, the super strong,
half god, half human son of Zeus, is forced to
perform twelve labors in order to gain immortality. **Reading Level** Average

Adventures with the Giants by Catherine F. Sellew.
Little, Brown, 1950. These stories of the adventures
of the Norse gods include Thor's great battle with
the giants. **Reading Level** Challenging

Miss Osborne-the-Mop by Wilson Gage. William
Collins/World, 1963. Jody hates her new glasses
until she discovers that while wearing them she can
change people and objects into something else
and back again. **Reading Level** Average

The Piemakers by Helen Cresswell. J. B. Lippincott,
1967. The Roller family of Danby Dale in England
have been piemakers for generations. But never
before have the Rollers made such an enormous
meat pie—a pie to feed two thousand people, including the King. **Reading Level** Challenging

3 Never Give Up

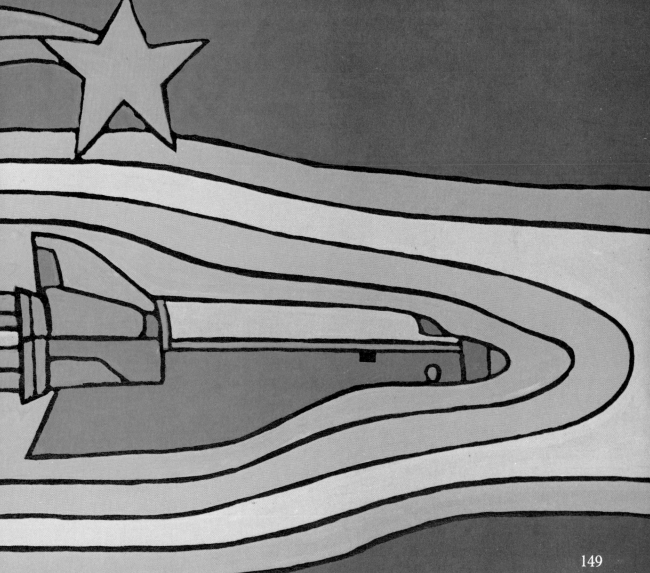

Objectives ● To recognize the importance of friendship and a shared interest to characters in a story. ● To identify obstacles overcome by a story character. ● To compare personal experiences and feelings with those in a story. ● To extend a story by dramatizing additional scenes.

Synopsis of the Story Davy, Sam's elderly friend, has had a heart attack. Because of their friendship and mutual love of baseball, Sam decides to get Davy a special gift—a baseball autographed by their heroes, the Brooklyn Dodgers. Sam scrapes together the money for a baseball and for bus fare and admission to the ballpark. After several attempts to get autographs, he is almost thrown out of the park by an angry usher. At last Sam reaches Dodger star Jackie Robinson, who listens to his story and helps him get an autographed ball.

Reading Level Easy

Something for Davy

From the novel *Thank You, Jackie Robinson*

by Barbara Cohen

Illustrated by Lyle Miller

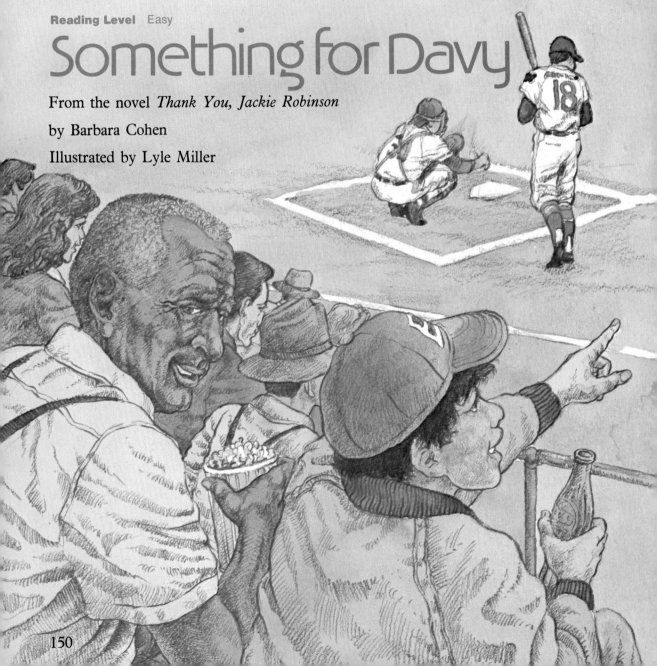

150

Background   The Brooklyn Dodgers were a
National League team at the time of this story
(1948). Jackie Robinson, second baseman,
was the first Black ballplayer in the major
leagues and he was elected to the Baseball
Hall of Fame in 1962. Other Dodger players
mentioned in the story include Eddie Miskis
(infielder); Carl Erskine and Preacher Roe
(pitchers); Roy "Campy" Campanella
(catcher); Gil Hodges (first baseman);
Pee Wee Reese (shortstop); Bill Cox (third
baseman); Carl Furillo, Duke Snider, and
Marv Rackley (outfielders).

Introducing the Story   *What are your
favorite hobbies, sports, or interests? Do you
have friends who share your interest? What
kinds of things do you do together that
center around that interest? In* Something for
Davy, *Sam is a real baseball fan, and so is his
friend Davy. As you read the story, think
about the many obstacles Sam manages to
overcome to do something special for Davy.*

Word to Know

  autograph: to write one's name on some-
    thing (page 152); a person's name writ-
    ten in his or her own handwriting (page
    163).

*After his father died, Sam Greene was lonely. With
his mother busy running the family's New Jersey inn
and his sisters busy with their own interests, Sam spent
long hours alone with his radio, listening to what he
loved most—major league baseball games.*

*Then Davy came to be the new cook at the inn,
and Sam and Davy discovered they loved the same
things—baseball, the Brooklyn Dodgers, and Jackie
Robinson, the Dodgers' star player in that year of
1947. Though Sam and Davy were fifty years apart
in age, they became great friends, talking endlessly of
baseball and going to the Dodgers' games together.*

*Davy's heart attack two years later was a terrible
shock for Sam. Not only was his best friend in the
hospital, but—because he wasn't a family member—
Sam wasn't even allowed to visit Davy. When he
heard that Davy was asking to see him, Sam made a
decision. If he couldn't see Davy in person, at least he
could do something to help Davy get well. As Sam tells
the story, "I'd had it. I was going to do something
spectacular. I was going to make him better all by
myself. It would be like magic."*

In 1974, the novel
*Thank You, Jackie
Robinson* was one of
the Library of Con-
gress Children's
Books of the Year
and was on the Ameri-
can Library Associa-
tion Notable Children's
Books list.

That afternoon I got on my bike and rode down-town. I went into Muldoon's Sporting Goods and bought a brand new Spalding regulation baseball. It cost one sixty-five. I couldn't count on catching one at the ball park. In all the time Davy and I had gone to the games that had never happened to us. It probably never would, if we went to a thousand million games. I had to take matters into my own hands, and then rough the ball up a little bit and persuade the players to autograph it, even if I hadn't caught it.

The day after that was Friday. I collected my allowance and got my mother to give me my three dollars and fifty cents that was in the safe.

"I think that's too much to spend on a present for Davy," Mother said. "A dollar would be plenty."

"Mother!" I exclaimed. I was shocked. "If I had a thousand dollars it wouldn't be too much to spend."

"Davy wouldn't want you to spend all your money on him. You know that."

"*I* want to spend all my money on Davy," I said. "Davy never has to know."

"It's your money, but I think you're crazy. You don't need to spend money to show love."

"It's the only way," I said. "The hospital won't let me in to see him."

"It's your money," she repeated, shaking her head, but then she gave it to me.

The next day, Saturday, was of course the busiest day of the week at the inn. Even during July and August, the slow months, Saturday was sometimes busy. I was lucky. On this particular Saturday there was a wedding reception. What with Davy sick and the new cook not quite up to preparing a whole banquet, my mother had to be in six places at once. She really didn't have time to worry about us. It was one of those days when she just wanted us to disappear somewhere and not bother her until it was time for my sister Sara and me to help dish out the meal. I obliged. I told her I was going over to my friend Mickey's house and that I would stay there for dinner, but I'd come home before dark. If she had time to think about it, she might have wondered why I spent so much time at Mickey's lately, but she didn't have time to think about it.

I suppose I could have told my mother where I was going. She might have been perfectly willing to let me go. She might have given me money for it.

But I couldn't be sure. A mother who worried so much about our crossing the highway after sunset might not want us to go all the way to Ebbets Field by ourselves. I couldn't risk her telling me not to go. So I just went.

I had gone into the kitchen real early in the morning, before anyone else was up, and made myself a couple of egg-salad sandwiches. I had them and my money and the baseball in its little cardboard box. I walked the mile and a half to the bus station because there'd be no place to leave my bike if I rode there. I took the bus into New York City and I took a subway to Ebbets Field. I didn't have to ask anyone anything, except the bus driver for a ticket to New York City and the man in the subway booth for change of a quarter.

There was one thing I'd learned from Sara, and that was that if you know how to read you can do anything. Right in the middle of the subway was this big map of the subway system and Ebbets Field was marked right on it in large black letters. BMT, Brighton Local, downtown, get off at the station near Ebbets Field. I didn't even have to change trains.

You could see flags flying above the ball park when you climbed up out of the subway station. You had to walk three blocks and there you were. Inside it was as it always had been, as bright and green as ever, remote from the sooty streets that surrounded it, remote from all the world. In the excitement of being there, I almost forgot about Davy for a moment. I almost forgot why I had come. But then, when the Cubs' pitcher, Warren Hacker, began to

154

warm up, I turned to Davy to ask him if he thought Shotton was going to give Jackie's sore heel a rest that day. But Davy wasn't there, and I remembered.

I thought maybe I'd better start trying right away. My chances were probably better during batting practice than they would be later. I took my ball out of its box and stashed the box underneath my bleacher seat. Then I walked around to the first-base side and climbed all the way down to the box seats right behind the dugout. I leaned over the rail. Billy Cox was trotting back to the dugout from home plate, where Erskine had been throwing to him.

I swallowed my heart, which seemed to be beating in my throat, and called out, "Billy! Hey, Billy!" waving my ball as hard and high as I could. But I was scared, and my voice wasn't very loud, and I don't think Billy Cox heard me. He disappeared into the dugout.

Marv Rackley came out of the dugout and then
Carl Furillo. I called to them too, but they didn't
seem to hear me either.

This method was getting me nowhere. I had to
try something else before the game began and I'd
really lost my chance. I looked around to see if there
were any ushers nearby, but none was in sight. It
was kind of early and the place hadn't really started
to fill up yet. I guess the ushers were loafing around
the refreshment stands.

I climbed up on the railing and then hoisted myself onto the roof of the dugout. That was something
you could not do at many places besides Ebbets
Field. That was one of the few advantages of such a
small ball park. Of course, you know, you couldn't
go see Ebbets Field now if you wanted to. They tore
it down and put an apartment building there.

I could have stood up and walked across the dugout roof to the edge, but I figured if I did that an
usher surely would see me. I sneaked across the roof
on my belly until I came to the edge and then I
leaned over.

It was really very nice in the dugout. I had always
kind of pictured it as being literally dug out of the
dirt, like a trench in a war. But it had regular walls
and a floor and benches and a water cooler. Only
trouble was, there were just a couple of guys in there—
Eddie Miksis, and Billy Cox whom I'd seen out on
the field a few minutes before.

I was disappointed. I had certainly hoped for
Campy's signature, and Gil Hodges', and Pee Wee

Reese's, and of course Jackie Robinson's. But I figured Davy would be thrilled with Miksis and Billy Cox, since their names on a ball would be more than he'd ever expected. And anyway a few more guys might come <u>meandering</u> in before I was through.

But no matter how hard I swallowed, my heart was still stuck in my throat. "Eddie!" I called. "Eddie! Billy!" Hardly any sound came out of my mouth at all.

And then all of a sudden I heard a voice calling real loud. Whoever it was didn't have any trouble getting the sound out of *his* mouth. "Hey you, kid, get down off that roof," the voice said. "What do you think you're doing?" I sat up and turned around. An angry usher was standing at the foot of the aisle, right by the railing, screaming at me. "Get yourself off that roof," he shouted. "Right now, or I'll throw you out of the ball park."

I scrambled down fast as I could. Boy, was I a mess. My chino pants and my striped jersey were absolutely covered with dust and grime from that roof. I guess my face and arms weren't any too clean either. I looked like a bum.

"I'm going to throw you out anyway," the usher said, "because you don't have a ticket."

I got real mad when I heard him say that. People had been throwing me out of places all week long and I was plenty sick of it. Especially since I certainly did have a ticket.

"You can't throw me out," I shouted back at him. "I've got as much right to be here as you have." I had suddenly found my voice. I was scared of the

ball players, but this usher didn't frighten me one
bit. I pulled my ticket stub out of my pocket. "See?"
I said, thrusting it into his face. "I certainly do have
a ticket."

He made as if to take it out of my hand. I guess
he wanted to look at it close, to make sure it was a
stub from that day and not an old one I carried
around in my pocket for emergencies. But I pulled
my hand back.

"Oh, no, you don't," I said. "You can't take this ticket away from me. You won't give it back to me and then you'll throw me out because I don't have a ticket!"

"You crazy, kid?" he asked, shaking his head. "This is what I get for working in Ebbets Field. A bunch of crazy people. Next year I'm applying for a job at the Polo Grounds."

The *Polo Grounds* was the home of the New York Giants, the Dodgers' rivals.

"Go ahead," I said, "you traitor. Who needs you?" I turned away from him and leaned over the rail.

"I better not see you on that roof again," the usher said. "I'll have my eye out for you—and so will all the other ushers."

"Don't worry," I said.

Then I felt his hand on my shoulder. "As a matter of fact, kid," he said, "I think I'll escort you to your seat where you belong. Up in the bleachers where you can't make any trouble."

Well, right then and there the whole enterprise would have gone up in smoke if old Jackie Robinson himself had not come trotting out onto the field from the dugout that very second. "Hey, Jackie!" I called. "Hey, Jackie!" in a voice as loud as a thunderbolt. I mean there were two airplanes flying overhead right that minute and Jackie Robinson heard me anyway.

He glanced over in the direction he could tell my voice was coming from, and I began to wave frantically, still calling "Jackie! Hey, Jackie!"

He lifted up his hand, gave one wide wave, and smiled. "Hey, kid," he called, and continued on his way to the batting cage. In another instant he'd

have been too busy with batting practice to pay any attention to me.

"Sign my ball!" I screamed. "Sign my ball!"

He seemed to hesitate briefly. I took this as a good omen. "You gotta," I went on frantically. "Please, please, you gotta."

"He don't gotta do nothing," the usher said. "That's Jackie Robinson and everyone knows that he don't gotta do nothing."

I went right on screaming.

"Come on, kid," the usher said, "we're getting out of here." He was a big hulking usher who must have weighed about eight hundred pounds, and he began pulling on me. Even though I gripped the cement with my sneakers and held onto the rail with my hand, he managed to pull me loose. But he couldn't shut me up.

An *omen* is a sign that something is going to happen.

161

"Please, Jackie, please!" I went right on screaming.

It worked. Or something worked. If not my screaming, then maybe the sight of that monster usher trying to pull me up the aisle and scrungy old me pulling against him for dear life.

"Let the kid go," Jackie Robinson said when he got to the railing. "All he wants is an autograph."

"He's a fresh kid," the usher said, but he let me go.

"Kids are supposed to be fresh," Jackie Robinson said.

I thrust my ball into Jackie Robinson's face. "Gee, thanks, Mr. Robinson," I said. "Sign it, please."

"You got a pen?" he asked.

"A pen?" I could have kicked myself. "A pen?" I'd forgotten a pen! I turned to the usher. "You got a pen?"

"If I had," the usher said triumphantly, "I certainly wouldn't lend it to you!"

"Oh, come on," Jackie Robinson said. "Don't be so vindictive. What harm did the kid do, after all?"

Vindictive means *revengeful.*

"Well, as it happens, I don't have one," the usher replied smugly.

"Wait here," I said. "Wait right here, Mr. Robinson. I'll go find one."

Jackie Robinson laughed. "Sorry, kid, but I've got work to do. Another time, maybe."

"Please, Mr. Robinson," I said. "It's for my friend. My friend, Davy."

"Well, let Davy come and get his own autographs," he said. "Why should you do his dirty work for him?"

"He can't come," I said. The words came rushing out of me, tumbling one on top of the other. I had to tell Jackie Robinson all about it, before he went away. "Davy can't come because he's sick. He had a heart attack."

"A heart attack?" Jackie Robinson asked. "A kid had a heart attack?"

"He's not a kid," I explained. "He's sixty years old. He's my best friend. He's always loved the Dodgers, but lately he's loved them more than ever."

"How did this Davy get to be your best friend?" Jackie Robinson asked.

So I told him. I told him everything, or as near to everything as I could tell in five minutes. I told him how Davy worked for my mother, and how I had no father, so it was Davy who took me to my first ball game. I told him how they wouldn't let me into the hospital to see Davy, and how we had always talked about catching a ball that was hit into the stands and getting it autographed.

Jackie listened silently, nodding every once in a while. When I was done at last, he said, "Well, now, kid, I'll tell you what. You keep this ball you brought with you. Keep it to play with. And borrow a pen from someone. Come back to the dugout the minute, the very second, the game is over, and I'll get you a real ball, one we played with, and I'll get all the guys to autograph it for you."

"Make sure it's one you hit," I said.

What nerve. I should have fainted dead away just because Jackie Robinson had deigned to speak to me. But here he was, making me an offer beyond my wildest dreams, and for me it wasn't enough. I had to have more. However, he didn't seem to care.

"O.K.," he said, "*if* I hit one." He had been in a little slump lately.

"You will," I said, "you will."

And he did. He broke the ball game wide open in the sixth inning when he hit a double to left field, scoring Rackley and Duke Snider. He scored himself when the Cubs pitcher, Warren Hacker, tried to pick him off second base. But Hacker overthrew, and Jackie, with that incredible speed he had, ran all the way home. Besides, he worked two double plays

Deigned means thought fit.

A *slump* is a period when baseball players are not hitting or playing as well as they normally do.

with Preacher Roe and Gil Hodges. On consecutive
pitches, Carl Furillo and Billy Cox both hit home
runs, shattering the 1930 Brooklyn home-run record
of 122 for a season. The Dodgers scored six runs,
and they scored them all in the sixth inning. They
beat the Cubs, 6–1. They were hot, really hot, that
day and that year.

But I really didn't watch the game as closely as I had all the others I'd been to see. I couldn't. My mind was on too many other things—on Jackie Robinson, on what was going to happen after the game was over, on that monster usher who I feared would yet find some way of spoiling things for me, but above all on Davy and the fact that he was missing all of the excitement.

And then I had to worry about getting hold of a pen. You could buy little pencils at the ball park for keeping box scores, but no pens. It was the first—and last—time in my life I walked into a ball park without something to write with. And I didn't see how I could borrow one from someone, since in all that mess of humanity I'd never find the person after the game to return it to him. Unless I took the guy's name and address and mailed it back to him later.

It didn't look to me like the guys in the bleachers where I was sitting had pens with them anyway. Most of them had on tee shirts, and tee shirts don't have pockets in them for pens. I decided to walk over to the seats along the first-base line to see if any of those fans looked more like pen owners. I had to go in that direction anyway to make sure I was at the dugout the second the ball game ended. I took with me my ball in its box.

On my way over I ran into this guy hawking soft drinks and I decided to buy one in order to wash down the two egg-salad sandwiches I had eaten during the third inning.

This guy had a pen in his pocket. As a matter of fact, he had two of them. "Look," I said to him, as I

A *box score* is a play-by-play record of a baseball game.

166

paid him for my soda, "could I borrow one of those pens?"

"Sure," he said, handing it to me after he had put my money into his change machine. He stood there, waiting, like he expected me to hand it back to him after I was done with it.

"Look," I said again, "maybe I could sort of buy it from you."

"Buy it from me? You mean the pen?"

"Yeah."

"What do you want my pen for?"

"I need it because Jackie Robinson promised me that after the game he and all the other guys would autograph a ball for me." Getting involved in all these explanations was really a pain in the neck.

"You don't say," the hawker remarked. I could tell he didn't believe me.

"It's true," I said. "Anyway, are you going to sell me your pen?"

"Sure. For a dollar."

I didn't have a dollar. Not anymore. I'd have to try something else. I started to walk away.

"Oh, don't be silly, kid," he called to me. "Here, take the pen. Keep it." It was a nice pen. It was shaped like a bat, and on it, it said, "Ebbets Field, Home of the Brooklyn Dodgers."

"Hey, mister, thanks," I said. "That's real nice of you." It seemed to me I ought to do something for him, so I added, "I think I'd like another soda." He sold me another soda, and between sipping first from one and then from the other and trying to watch the game, I made very slow progress down to the dugout.

I got there just before the game ended in the top of the ninth.

The Dodgers didn't have to come up to bat at all in that final inning, and I was only afraid that they'd all have disappeared into the clubhouse by the time I got there. I should have come down at the end of the eighth. But Jackie Robinson had said the end of the game. Although my nerve had grown by about seven thousand percent that day, I still didn't have enough to interrupt Jackie Robinson during a game.

I stood at the railing near the dugout, waiting, and sure enough, Jackie Robinson appeared around the corner of the building only a minute or two after Preacher Roe pitched that final out. All around me people were getting up to leave the ball park, but a lot of them stopped when they saw Jackie Robinson come to the rail to talk to me. Roy Campanella, Pee Wee Reese, and Gil Hodges were with him.

"Hi, kid," Jackie Robinson said. He was carrying a ball. It was covered with signatures. "Pee Wee here had a pen."

"And a good thing, too," Pee Wee said, "because most of the other guys left the field already."

"But these guys wanted to meet Davy's friend," Jackie Robinson said.

By that time, Preacher Roe had joined us at the railing. Jackie handed him the ball. "Hey, Preacher," he said, "got enough strength left in that arm to sign this ball for Davy's friend here?"

"Got a pen?" Preacher Roe asked.

I handed him the pen the hawker had given me.

I was glad I hadn't gone through all the trouble of getting it for nothing.

"Not much room left on this ball," Roe said. He squirmed his signature into a little empty space beneath Duke Snider's and then he handed me both the pen and the ball.

Everybody was waving programs and pens in the faces of the ballplayers who stood by the railing. But before they signed any of them, they all shook my hand. So did Jackie Robinson. I stood there, clutching Davy's ball and watching while those guys signed the programs of the other fans.

Finally, though, they'd had enough. They smiled and waved their hands and walked away, five big men in white uniforms, <u>etched</u> sharply against the bright green grass. Jackie Robinson was the last one into the dugout and before he disappeared around the corner, he turned and waved to me.

Something that is *etched* stands out from the background.

I waved back. "Thank you, Jackie Robinson," I called. "Thanks for everything." He nodded and smiled. I guess he heard me. I'm glad I remembered my manners before it was too late.

When everyone was gone, I looked down at the ball in my hands. Right between the rows of red seaming, Jackie Robinson had written, above his own signature, "For Davy. Get well soon." Then all the others had put their names around that.

I took the ball I had bought out of the box and put it in my pocket. I put the ball Jackie Robinson had given me in the box. Then I went home.

Discussion Questions *Find parts of the story that tell how Sam feels about Davy.* ("If I had a thousand dollars it wouldn't be too much to spend"—page 153; "He's my best friend"—page 163.) *Find parts of the story that tell how Davy feels about Sam.* ("Davy wouldn't want you to spend all your money on him"—page 153; "I had no father, so it was Davy who took me to my first ball game"—page 164.)

Enriching Activities   1. *Oral extension/ improvisation.* Have the students discuss what might have happened after the story ended, and choose volunteers to act out these scenes: Sam comes home and tells his mother where he's been; Davy calls Sam to thank him; Sam and his sister discuss what to say in a thank-you note to Jackie Robinson. **2.** *Question writing.* Have the students write three questions they would like to ask a favorite sports star or famous person.

Questions

1. Sam wanted "something for Davy." What was it?
   1. Literal/recall   An autographed baseball. (pages 152, 163)

2. To get "something for Davy," Sam had to solve problems. Arrange the following problems in the order in which they appeared in the story.
   a. to ask the ball players for a favor
   b. to get a regulation baseball
   c. to get a pen
   d. to get money for the game
   e. to get to Ebbets Field
   f. to get to the dugout on time

   2. Literal/recall b. (page 152), d. (page 152), e. (page 154), a. (pages 156–164), c. (pages 166–167), f. (pages 167–168).

3. Two times in the story Sam "lost his voice." But another time, he "found his voice." For each of these times, write what happened to cause Sam to lose or find his voice, and tell how Sam felt.

   3. Interpretive/ inference   Sam lost his voice when he called to Billy Cox (pages 156, 158) and Eddie Miskis (page 158) because he felt scared. Sam found his voice when he argued with the usher and when he called and talked to Jackie Robinson (pages 158, 160). He felt angry with the usher and frantic and desperate with Robinson.

Activity

"Bit players" in a television play or a movie are characters who have small parts. There are bit players in "Something for Davy," too. List two bit players in the story who make a big difference in Sam's day. Then write one or two paragraphs about a bit player in your own life—someone who may have made an important difference to you. Provide details describing the person's actions, appearance, and speech. Such details will make the person more real to your readers.

Critical/relating to experience *Writing.* Possible answers: the hawker; the usher; Jackie Robinson. Students might write about such people as a piano teacher, a coach, an athletic teammate, or a pen pal.

Today Song

A poem by Robert McGovern

Objectives ● To recognize the meaning of a poem. ● To note that the repetition in a poem creates emphasis.
Introducing the Poem *Why might a person think about yesterday?* (Possible answers: to recall a happy experience; to consider how things might have been different.) *Why might a person think ahead to tomorrow?* (Possible answers: to plan actions; to look forward to a pleasant experience.) *Before you read this poem, think for a moment about today. Think of what you expected to happen today. Then think of how you will feel about today if you look back upon it tomorrow.*

Two days are never quite the same—
Yesterday's then, tomorrow is when.
If today is good, I'll remember it then
When now is when, and when was then,
Good morning.

Discussion Questions *Why do you think the words* when *and* then *are in the poem?* (The poem is about the past, present, and future.) *What does the poem say?* (Help the students try to paraphrase lines three and four: If today is good, I'll remember it tomorrow, when today becomes yesterday and tomorrow becomes today.)

Enriching Activity *Cartoons.* Have the students draw cartoons of a good day and a bad day in the life of a character. Encourage them to draw facial expressions and to write dialogue in balloons.

Illustrated by Marie-Louise Gay

Objectives • To identify conflict and resolution in a story. • To recognize the use of dialect in a story. • To identify what makes a story character interesting and likable.

Synopsis of the Story When Beth Lambert first meets her collie puppy, she hugs it, names it Friendly, and—ah-choo! Beth finds out that she is allergic to the puppy and must return it to the kennel. Beth tries two other puppies—a chihuahua and a poodle—with the same results. Painfully,

Beth begins to accept the disappointment of not having a puppy to care for. Then she is swept up in the excitement of the birth of her brother Benjamin.

Background The novel *Philip Hall likes me. I reckon maybe* was a Newbery Honor Book in 1975 and a Children's Choice in 1974. In 1974 it was also one of the Library of Congress Children's Books of the Year and was on the American Library Association Notable Children's Books list.

I Never Asked for No Allergy

From the novel *Philip Hall likes me. I reckon maybe.* by Bette Greene

Illustrated by Diane de Groat

Reading Level Easy

Lately, things have been changing for Beth Lambert. Her best friend, Philip Hall, has been spending most of his time with other friends, and Beth's family is too busy getting ready for a new baby to think much about her. What Beth wants right now is something special—something just for her. And if that something special just happened to be a dog, *well, Beth Lambert wouldn't mind that at all!*

Introducing the Story *Who knows what hay fever is? (Hay fever is a disease caused by an allergy to certain pollens.) Many people have allergies and must avoid the things that give them rashes or make them sneeze and wheeze. How would you feel if you found out that you were allergic to something you really like? (Angry, disappointed; you might feel that having an allergy is unfair.)*

This story is about Beth, a girl who wants a puppy very much. From the title, what do you think happens? (She finds out she has an allergy.) Read and find out if Beth's problem is solved.
Word to Know
  allergic rhinitis: Refer students to the footnote, page 180.

Mr. Barnes stopped the school bus along the side of the highway just at that spot where the dirt road leading to our farm meets the blacktop. First Philip Hall got off. Then I jumped off in front of the faded black-and-white sign at the intersection which read:

1 mile

↑

Lambert Farm
good turkeys
good pigs

As I took a flying leap across the frozen drainage ditch that separated the road from the field, I heard Philip calling me.

"Hey, Beth!" He was still standing on the blacktop just where the bus left him. "You oughtna be going through the field. You might step into an ice puddle."

175

Of all days to have to stop and start explaining things to Philip Hall. But at any other time I'd be thinking that he wouldn't be fretting about my feet if he didn't really like me. Now would he? "Frosty feet ain't nothing," I told him, "when you have a spanking new puppy waiting to meet you."

"What if Mr. Grant wouldn't swap a collie dog for one of your pa's turkeys?" asked Philip, grinning as though he hoped it was so.

"That's all you know! When I left the house this morning, my pa was picking out six of our fattest turkeys for swapping." I turned and began running across the field.

"Well, one collie dog is worth more than six of your old turkeys," called Philip.

I kept on running, pretending not to hear. And, anyway, everybody loves to eat turkey. Don't they?

When I reached the rise in the field, I could see our house a nice pale green. As I came closer, I could see my mama on the porch. She was hanging work-worn overalls across the porch clothesline. I tiptoed up behind her and threw my arms around her.

"Ohhh!" She jumped. "What you mean scaring me clear out of my wits, girl?"

"Where is he?" I asked. "Where's the collie?"

She put on her I'm-not-fixing-to-listen-to-any-nonsense face and said, "I don't know nothing about no collie."

"Did Pa make the swap? Did he?"

"Get out of here, girl. Go on into the kitchen."

"Tell me if Pa got the collie," I pleaded. "Now did he?"

Her mouth was still set into that no-nonsense way of hers, but it was different with her eyes. Her eyes were filled up with pure pleasure. "And I told you," she said, "to get on into the kitchen, didn't I?"

Suddenly I understood. I threw open the screen door and, without waiting to close it gently behind me, ran in a straight line through the living room and into the kitchen.

176

And then I saw him. There in a cardboard carton next to the cookstove was a reddish-brown puppy with a circle of white fluffy hair ringing his neck and spilling down to his chest. I dropped to my knees and showed my open palms. "Hi, puppy. Beautiful little collie puppy."

"He's beautiful, sure enough," said Ma from behind.

The collie just looked at me for a few moments. Then he got to his feet and trotted over.

"And you're friendly too," I said, patting his back. "Hey, that would be a good name for you."

"Friendly," said Ma, smacking her lips like she was word tasting. "That's a right good name."

I gave Friendly a hug and a kiss. "I will now name you— *ah-choo!*" I tried again. "I will now name—*AHHHHhhhh-choo!!*"

Ma shook her head the way she does when she catches me at mischief. "You done gone and got yourself a cold, now, didn't you?"

"*AHHHHhhhhh-ha-ha-ha-choo!* I now name you Friendly," I said at last.

By bedtime I was sneezing constantly and water kept pouring from my sore, itchy eyes. But, thank goodness, all my sneezing didn't seem to bother Friendly, who slept peacefully in his cardboard carton at the foot of my bed.

I could hear my folks in the kitchen talking about what they were always talking about these days—names for our soon-to-be-born baby. When they finally tired of that topic, Ma said, "Beth got me worried. All them wheezing sounds coming from her chest."

"I seen Doc Brenner in town this afternoon," said Pa. "He asked me to kill and clean one of our twenty-pound birds. Said he'd stop by this evening to pick it up."

"When he comes by," said Ma, "ask him to kindly take a look at our Beth."

I climbed out of bed to take off my raggedy tail of a nightgown and put on the one that Grandma had given me last Christmas. She had made it out of a sack of Fairy Flake flour, but she dyed it a bright, brilliant orange. It was nice.

Friendly started to bark.

"Don't you be frightened, little Friendly. It's only me, only Beth."

While I patted my new pet, I told him how glad I was that he had come to live with us. "You're going to like it here, you'll see. I'm going to bring all my friends to meet you. Philip Hall, Susan, Bon—*ahh-choo-whoo! Ahh choo!* Bonnie, Ginny, Esther. You're going to like all my friends, Friendly, but you're going to like me best of all . . . I reckon maybe."

Ma called out, "Is you out of bed, Beth?"

I jumped back into bed before answering. "No ma'm. I'm right here. Right here in bed."

I kept my eyes open, waiting for the doctor to come, but after a while my eyelids came together. Sleep stood by waiting for me to fall . . . fall asleep . . . sleep . . . sleep.

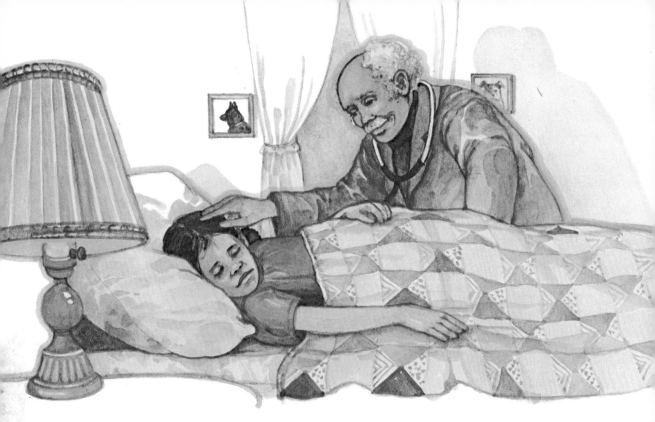

"Let me take a look at my old friend, Beth," said a big voice.

My cheeks were being patted. "Doctor's here, Beth honey," Ma was saying.

I pulled myself up to sitting and looked into the face of Dr. Brenner, who said, "This won't hurt," as he placed a stethoscope to my chest.

"Just breathe naturally," he said. He listened quietly without saying a word. Then he took the stethoscope from his ears. "I heard some wheezing sounds coming from your chest. Tell me, how do your eyes feel?"

"They feel like I want to grab them out of their sockets and give them a good scratching. They're so . . . so itchy."

"Uh-hun," answered Dr. Brenner, as though he knew all about itchy eyes. "Beth, can you remember when all this sneezing and wheezing began?"

"Yes, sir," I told the doctor. "It all started when I met Friendly."

Friendly must have heard his name called 'cause he jumped out of his carton and jogged floppily on over.

"Hi, little Friendly, little dog."

I picked him up and gave him a hug and a kiss. *"AHHHHhh-choo! Ah-choo!"*

"Beth," said Dr. Brenner, running his fingers through his silver hair. "I'm sorry to do this, but I'm going to have to tell you something. Something you're not going to like hearing. I believe you have an allergy to Friendly."

"Oh, no sir, I don't!" I cried. "I don't have one, honest. I never asked for no allergy. Why, I don't even know what that means."

Dr. Brenner took my hand. "It simply means that Friendly's dog hair is making you sick. And, furthermore, it means that he must be returned to wherever he came from."

"But Friendly is *my* dog. He belongs to me. And he's never *never* going to go back to that kennel!" I felt tears filling up my eyes. "I love Friendly. Friendly loves me."

"I know you love each other," agreed Dr. Brenner. "But all this sneezing, wheezing, and red eyes is your body's way of telling you something."

I shook my head no.

Doc Brenner nodded his head yes. "Bodies don't need to say fancy words like allergic rhinitis[1] — or any words at all, Beth. When your throat is dry, you don't wait to hear the word *water* before taking a drink. And do you really need the school's lunch bell to ring before you know when it's time to eat? Well, now your body is saying something just as important. Listen to it!" he said, cupping his hand around his ear. But the only sound in the room was the hissing noise coming from my own chest.

When the morning sun came flooding through my bedroom window, my eyes opened and I remembered about the allergy. Was it real or only a dream?

"Friendly," I called. "Come here, little Friendly."

But Friendly didn't come and I didn't hear him either. I jumped to the foot of my bed. The cardboard box was empty. They've

---

1. **allergic rhinitis** (uh•LUHR•jik ry•NY•tis): a sensitivity to something that causes sneezing and a painful, red swelling inside the nose.

taken him back to Mr. Grant's kennel!

I was just about to shout out for Friendly when outside the kitchen window I heard my brother Luther's and my sister Anne's voices: "Get that ball, Friendly. Friendly, you going to get that ball?"

Ma laughed. "That dog ain't fixing to do nothing he ain't a mind to do."

I went out the kitchen door still wearing my orange night-gown and sat down on the back steps next to her. She put her arm around me and gave me a quick squeeze. "How you feeling, honey babe?"

I thought about her question. My chest felt as though it was still filled up with old swamp water while my head carried around last night's headache. Finally, I gave my answer, "I'm OK, Mama. I reckon."

"After you come home from school, I want you to take a little nap. Never mind them chores. Just put your head down on the pillow and nap. 'Cause you spent half the night crying into your pillow."

"About what the doctor said... about taking Friendly back to the kennel. We're not going to listen to that, are we?"

She looked past me, out to where Luther and Anne were playing with Friendly. "Life don't always be the way we want it to be. Life be the way it is. Ain't nothing we can do."

"You *can't* take him back!" I shouted. "Besides, Mr. Grant probably's eaten up all the turkeys."

"If he did, he did," answered Ma.

"You don't understand," I said, bringing my voice back down to size. "I *need* Friendly! Luther was three and Anne was two when I was born so they had me, but I never had nothing little and soft to—"

"And I told you," she said, "that life be the way it be. Ain't nothing we can do. But if you misses that school bus, there is something I can do. I can take a switch to you. So *get!*"

At school I felt better and worse. Better because I didn't sneeze or wheeze and even my eyes stopped itching and watering. And worse because tonight, after supper, Friendly was going back to Mr. Grant's kennel.

If only I had some magic. One time I remembered my teacher, Miss Johnson, pointing to shelves of books and saying that they held many secrets. Could one of her books hold the secret of making the allergy go and the dog stay?

At recess, she stood on a three-step ladder to bring down a heavy book from the top shelf.

"This book may have the secret we're looking for," she said, pointing to a page. "Right here," she whispered, the way people do when they're telling secrets. "It says that people who have an allergy to long-haired dogs, like the collie, might not have an allergy to a short-haired dog, like the chihuahua."

At the kennel I held Friendly close to me while Pa explained about the allergy to Mr. Grant. "You are welcome to swap," he said, reaching out for Friendly.

"Wait!" I said. "A person has got to say good-bye, don't they?" I looked into Friendly's eyes and wondered how I could make him understand. "I never wanted to get rid of you, Friendly. I only wanted to get rid of the aller—*Her-her-choo!*—of the allergy."

He licked my ear almost as if to tell me not to worry because any dog as friendly as Friendly would get along just fine.

Again Mr. Grant reached out, only this time I gave him my Friendly. As he took him away, I heard him say, "Rest of the collies going to be mighty happy to see you again."

When he returned, Friendly wasn't with him. "An allergy sure is a bothersome thing," said Mr. Grant. "Reason I know that is because I've had an allergy ever since I was about your age."

It was so hard to believe. "You got yourself an allergy to collies too?" I asked.

"Nope." Mr. Grant pointed to the bend in his suntanned arm. "Tomatoes—that's what gets my allergy going. One tomato and my arm breaks out like a strawberry patch."

"Tomatoes don't bother me a bit," I said proudly.

"Reckon that's what an allergy is," said Mr. Grant. "It's what don't bother some folks, bothers other folks a whole lot."

When we stopped in front of the chihuahua's run, a tiny fellow came rushing to the gate, barking. "That's the dog for me," I said.

On the drive back home I held the chihuahua in my lap while my folks went back to trying to pick out a baby name. I was hoping they'd find a better name for the baby than they found for me.

When Pa turned off the highway onto the dirt road leading to our farm, the puppy jumped off my lap. He stood on his toes, pressing his nose against the truck's window. I hollered, "Looky there! Look at Tippietoes!"

"Ohhhh," said Ma, turning her head. "Now ain't that something?

And what a fine name for him too."

I put my hands against the little dog's cheeks and gave him a kiss between the eyes. "I now name you—*ah-ah*—I now name you—*ah-ah-ah-choo!*"

"Oh, *no!*" said Ma and Pa at exactly the same time.

But finally I was able to say, and say proudly, "I now name you Tippietoes."

By the time I crawled into bed, my eyes were red and itchy. My nose was sneezy and my chest was wheezy. Ma stood at my doorway. "Tippietoes going to sleep next to the cookstove tonight, but tomorrow evening we're going to take him back."

I shook my head no. "Mama, don't say that. I don't care nothing about no little allergy. Cross my heart I don't. All I care about is my little dog. My own little Tippietoes."

"Girl, you ain't talking nothing but a heap of foolishness. I ain't about to let you walk around sick. Not as long as I'm your mama, 'cause I ain't that kind of mama. Now you get yourself to sleep."

At first recess, I told Miss Johnson about having an allergy, not just to long-haired dogs but to short-haired ones too.

"Maybe I can find still another secret in that book," she said, bringing down the big book again. She fingered through a lot of pages before she finally began to read aloud: "People who have an allergy to both long-haired and short-haired dogs might not have an allergy to poodles, as they are the only dogs that never shed hair."

Pa explained to Mr. Grant what I had learned from the book. "So we'll be much obliged if you'll kindly swap Tippietoes here for one of your poodles."

"Fine with me," said Mr. Grant, reaching for Tippietoes.

"Wait!" I said, holding onto the little one for another moment. "A person still has to say good-bye." I patted his chin. He licked my fingers. "Good-bye, little boy, little Tippietoes. I'm sorry you couldn't be my dog."

I closed my eyes as I gave him over to Mr. Grant, who took him away. When he came back he said, "Come along, folks. Let me introduce you to my poodles."

We followed him until he stopped at the gate of a chain-link fence. "Poodles may be just the right dog for a girl with an allergy," he said, pointing to two white dogs that looked more like fluffy powder puffs than real dogs. "Because they never have dandruff or a doggy odor. And the book is right. They never shed a single hair."

He unhooked the gate and I walked in saying, "This time I'm going to be lucky. This time I *hope* I'm going to be lucky."

"Hope so," said Ma and Pa at exactly the same moment.

Both poodles walked over to say hello. They were quite polite. I bent down and one of the puppies came closer. "Is it you?" I asked him.

He took one step closer, resting his fluffy little head in my hand. I whispered, "I'm going to take real good care of you."

Inside the crowded cab of the pickup truck, I held the poodle puppy on my lap as Pa turned on the headlights and started for home. My patting must have relaxed the little dog 'cause he closed his eyes and went to sleep.

After a while Ma said, "I think we ought to name the baby after my great-aunt Alberta."

Pa's nose crinkled. "What you want to name our baby after her for?"

Ma's nose climbed. "Ain't she my grandma's sister? The oldest living member of my family?"

"That nosy old lady!" said Pa.

"Aunt Alberta ain't one bit nosy," Ma corrected. "What she is, is interested. I'm disappointed in you, Mr. Eugene Lam—"

"Have you all noticed," I asked, hoping that my interruption would stop an argument from starting, "that I haven't sneezed even one time?"

Ma smiled. "Ain't it the truth."

"And Puffy will never have to go back to Mr. Grant's," I said.

"Puffy?" asked Pa, surprised.

"Don't you see," I asked, "how he's all puffy like cotton candy?"

Ma turned to look at Pa. "Beth has thought up three good names for three dogs while we is still fussing over one name for one baby."

Puffy opened his eyes and looked around. "You're here, Puffy," I said, putting my face into his white fluffiness. "And you're always going to be . . . my . . . my—*choo*! My—*ahhhhhhh-ey*!"

"Don't go telling me I heard what I think I heard," said Ma, fixing her eyes on the ceiling of the truck.

"It ain't what you think," I said quickly. "I really—*ahhh-choo! Ah-choo-who!* I really think I'm catching Billy Boy Williams's cold. He had one at school today. Sneezed all over the place—choo, choo, choo, choo, like that! Spreading his germs about."

Pa drove the truck over to the side of the road and turned off the engine. "Beth, I is sorry to disappoint you. I know how much you wanted a pup, but there ain't nothing I can do."

"If you take him back," I warned, "I ain't never going to live home again. For the rest of my life I'm going to live in the kennel with Puffy."

My mama patted my hand. "In this life you got to be happy about the good things and brave about the bad ones."

"I don't want to be brave," I shouted. "All I want is my little dog."

Pa started up the truck, made a U-turn on the highway, and headed back toward the kennel. "Ain't nothing in this wide world we can do," he said, shaking his head.

The next morning I asked Miss Johnson to bring down the book again. But after a while we stopped reading. It didn't have any more secrets to tell. I walked away 'cause I didn't have a single word for a single solitary soul. But later in the afternoon I told her, "I guess it's nobody's fault. But I reckon I'm learning to be brave about things I don't like."

"And I want you to know," said Miss Johnson, taking off her glasses, "that I think you're learning very well."

When the school bus stopped in front of our sign, I jumped off and with a running leap crossed the ditch.

"How come you shortcutting through the field again?" called Philip Hall. "Ain't no dog waiting for you today."

"Guess I know that," I said, wondering how I could have forgotten. And yet for some reason I really was in a hurry to get home.

When I reached the rise, I could see the outline of my mother. But it didn't look like her, not exactly. After I passed the vegetable garden, I could see that it wasn't her. It was . . . my grandmother.

I started running my fast run. "Grandma, Grandma! Hello!"

"Howdy there, Beth babe," she called back.

I ran into her arms as she closed them around me. "How come you're here? All the way from Walnut Ridge?"

Grandma smiled. "I came to see my new grandbaby. Born this very morning, a few minutes after nine."

"Where are they?" I asked.

"Shhhhh," she said, pointing to the inside of the house. "They are both real fine, but they're resting just now."

I asked, "Is it a . . . is it a brother?"

"A brother for you, a grandson for me," she said, hugging me some more.

I danced a circle around her. "My own little brother. He's going to be fun to take care of and fun to play with. Sometimes boys are almost as much fun to play with as girls. I've noticed that."

"Reckon I've noticed that too," said Grandma, joining my dance.

"What's my brother's name?"

Grandma stopped dancing. "Your folks ain't come to no decision on that," she said.

"Don't fret about that," I told her. "I happen to be good at names."

Then I heard Pa calling from inside the house, "Beth, come on in and meet up with your brother."

I closed the screen door quietly behind me the way I always remember to do when there is a visitor in the house. Pa stood at the door of his and Ma's bedroom and waved me on. "I want you to see something real pretty," he said.

Ma was sitting up in bed, propped up by two pillows. As I came closer, I saw something in her arms that I had never seen there before. A baby.

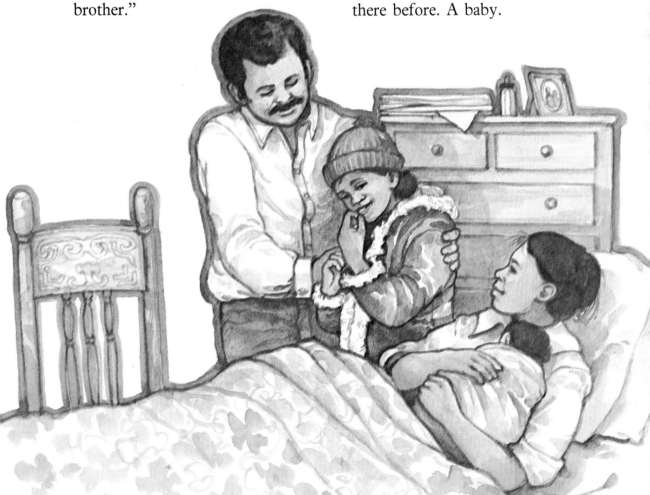

Ma said, "Fold your arms."

"Like this?" I asked.

"Just like that," she said, placing my soft little brother in my arms.

"Ohhhhh," I said, touching my lips to his warm head. "You are a beautiful baby brother. Baby brother Benjamin."

"Benjamin?" asked Ma. "Benjamin? *Benjamin!*—Oh, yes. That's it. That's the name!"

Pa smiled. "Benjamin is a good strong name for a boy."

"Finally," said Grandma, coming into the room. "A name for the baby."

I put my face next to Baby Benjamin's and breathed in deep. I didn't sneeze. "You're always going to be our Baby Benjamin," I whispered in his ear. "And anyway, Mr. Grant wouldn't know what to do with a real baby."

Discussion Questions *Name three ways the grown-ups in the story try to help Beth.* (Miss Johnson looks in books to find other breeds of dogs; Mr. Grant agrees to exchange the puppies; Beth's parents let Beth try three different puppies.) *Find the words Beth's mother says to help Beth accept her disappointment.* ("Life don't always be . . . ."—page 182; "In this life, you gotta be happy about the good things . . . ."—page 187.)

Enriching Activities   1. *Art/research.* Ask the students to draw pictures or find magazine photographs of different breeds of dogs. Then have the students describe the breeds' characteristics below their pictures.
2. *Problem solving.* Have the students work in pairs to propose conflicts, such as wanting to practice a noisy instrument early in the morning, and then work out resolutions to the problems. Each pair can write about the problem as a letter to an imaginary newspaper and give a reply in a class question and answer column.

Questions

1. Sometimes you want something, but something else gets in the way. There is a *conflict.* What was Beth's conflict? What solved the conflict?

2. Why did Beth and her family decide to get a poodle? Did the idea work? Please explain.

3. What did Beth learn from her troubles?

4. If you could talk to Beth about getting a pet, what kind of pet would you recommend?

5. Here are three things that people say in "I Never Asked for No Allergy." What is another way to say each one?
   a. "You oughtna be going . . ."
   b. "I reckon maybe . . ."
   c. "Life don't always be . . ."

Activity

Dear Reader,

I heard that you like a character in a story. Her name is Beth Lambert. Well, I have decided to write a book. Please give me advice about how I can make my main character as interesting as Beth Lambert.

Interpretive/extrapolation *Letter writing.* Urge the students to think about Beth's personality and her character traits that attracted them to her. Tell them to base their letters on their opinion of Beth and to suggest new traits the author might add.

Thank you,
An Author

1. Literal/recall Beth's allergy prevented her from keeping a puppy. (pages 180–187) She got a baby brother instead. (page 188)
2. Literal/recall Poodles do not shed hair, so Beth might not be allergic to them. The idea did not work; Beth was allergic to the poodle. (pages 185–186)
3. Interpretive/inference She learned to accept things she did not like. (page 188)
4. Interpretive/extrapolation Accept any kinds of pets that would *not* affect Beth's allergy, such as a goldfish or a bird.
5. Interpretive/inference a. "You shouldn't be going . . . ." (page 175); b. "I think maybe. . . ." or "I think perhaps. . . ." (page 178); c. "Life isn't always. . . ." (page 182).

Objectives ● To identify characters' motives and feelings. ● To relate a story character's experience to personal experience. ● To list steps for a process explained in a narrative (expository writing). ● To interpret expository writing through pantomime.

Synopsis of the Story Twelve-year-old Miguel Chavez is trying to prove that he is ready for an adult's work on his family's sheep ranch. During shearing, Miguel is given the job of hanging the sack for wool and packing the fleeces into it. To his horror, Miguel falls into the huge sack and can't get out. He is so embarassed that he does not call for help and even refuses his father's ef-

Reading Level Easy

THE WORST MORNING

From the novel . . . *and now Miguel* by Joseph Krumgold
Illustrated by Don Bolognese

Each summer in New Mexico the days become very hot, and the lowland grass dies. It is then that the men of the Chavez[1] family drive their sheep high into the Sangre de Cristo[2] Mountains, where the grass stays green. For several years young Miguel[3] Chavez has been waiting for the time when his father will allow him to join the summer journey. During the past year, twelve-year-old Miguel has tried to show that he is ready to make the journey by working as hard as the adults. When a group of sheep become lost, it is Miguel who finds them and brings them safely home. And when sheep-shearing days begin, Miguel is given more responsible jobs than ever before. Miguel begins to hope that he is accepted, at last, as a working member of his family. Then comes the worst morning. Here is how Miguel tells about it.

---

1. **Chavez** (CHAH•bays).
2. **Sangre de Cristo** (SAHN•gray THAY KREES•toh).
3. **Miguel** (mee•GEHL).

Just to look at, the morning was all right. Or
even, to tell the truth, it was a nice morning. The
sun was shining and the shadows were long and
heavy when we came out of the house. The sky
was blue and big like there was more of it around
than usual, more clear sky thin as deep water all
around. Over the mountains there were clouds
looking like a flock of clouds grazing around up
there, big and little ones. And over the house,
there were a couple of little ones, tramp clouds,
like orphans. The Sangre de Cristo Mountains,
they looked closer than I ever saw them before.

I felt good that morning when we all went out
to finish the shearing. When we all walked out together, my grandfather told me to hang up the
bag for the wool. The rest of the unshorn sheep
had to be herded from the fields, where they
had grazed all night, into the corral. All the other
hands had to go out to round them up and bring
them in. So it was up to me, my grandfather

Hands (line 19) are
people hired to work
on a ranch.

A *corral* (line 18) is a
fenced area for keep-
ing animals.

said, to hang up the big sack. Me, that is, and
Uncle Eli.[4]

I was glad to do this because hanging the sack,
after all, is an important job which you don't ask
anyone at all to do and which I had never been
asked to do before. I knew how it worked, though,
from watching.

First, Uncle Eli and I, we got this iron hoop, like
a hoop off a barrel only thick and solid, and this

---

4. Eli (AY•lee).

hoop we put around the top outside the opening of the sack. Then we turned over the cloth of the sack, which is burlap, we turned it over the hoop all the way around. All that's left is to take some nails, which you use like they were pins, to fasten the turned-over burlap to the rest of the sack so that the hoop is all covered over and it can't fall off.

Once you do this, it's very easy to hang the sack. All you do then is to go up on the wall of the shed where is nailed this square wooden frame and drop the bottom of the empty sack through the frame. But the opening of the sack can't go through because the hoop is bigger than the wooden square and it rests on the square letting the sack hang down at its full length, six or seven feet. That's all there is to it.

But once we got the sack hung up, Uncle Eli said, "Stay up there, Miguelito.[5] We'll get started and sack up these fleeces from yesterday."

Down below there was a bin into which the fleeces are put by the men who tie them up, my father and grandfather. A dozen or so were left over from the afternoon before, covered by a tarpaulin to keep them from the wet and the dew during the night. Eli took off the tarp and started to hand up the fleeces to me standing high up where I was, on the wooden frame on top of the sack. I dropped the fleeces into the sack, one after another, as Eli handed them to me.

Have the students note the steps for hanging the sack. The suggested **Enriching Activity** (page 205) asks students to pantomime this process.

Miguelito is an affectionate name for Miguel.

A *tarpaulin* (or *tarp*) is a large plastic or canvas sheet used to protect things from moisture.

---

5. **Miguelito** (mee·gay·LEE·toh).

195

By this time the first bunch had been herded into the yard in front of the shearing shed, the clippers were working, the shearing was started. And through the window that is in the back of the shed more fleeces were already starting to come into the bin where Eli was. He kept handing them up to me. I kept dropping them into the sack.

I saw that my big brother Blasito[6] was sweeping with the broom, which was the job I did the day before. So I just stayed up on top there, sacking the wool. If anything, this is even a more important kind of work than sweeping, to stand way up on top there to take the fleeces the shearers had cut and my father had tied, and sack them up so we could take them to the buyer, Mr. Morrison. I never thought I'd be doing this for years yet. But no one said I shouldn't, so there I was up on top, sacking the wool. And by this time the fleeces were coming through the window pretty fast, and no one took any notice who was doing the work as long as it was getting done. Eli didn't have any more time to hand me the fleeces. He started throwing them up to me.

It was easy to catch them. And it was nothing at all to drop them in the sack. But this is not the important part of sacking the wool.

The important part is that the wool has to be packed tight. It must be stamped down so hard and solid that the sack gets to look like one big round sausage. It is not difficult to do. You wait

6. **Blasito** (blah·SEE·toh).

until the fleeces pile up and then you step in the middle of the bag and stamp up and down and jump with all your might until the wool is hard beneath your feet. You don't have to be afraid the bag will tear. It's made out of the best burlap, the strongest kind, and can hold even the biggest men, who are usually the ones that do the sacking.

So there I was up on top. Fleeces flying up from Uncle Eli. Everybody as busy and working as fast as they could, like on the day before. And soon the woolly fleeces filled up the sack to the very top. I stepped in the middle to stamp them down. And it was like the whole world gave way from right under my feet.

I dropped slowly down to the bottom of the sack. One long drop, and then a soft bump. There had not been enough fleeces to hold me up, not enough soft wool. I just went down, slow, and there was nothing to do. The sides of the bag, the burlap, were hard and rough with nothing to catch, not even with fingernails. Like going down a smooth tunnel standing straight up. There was no way to save myself. And yell, I couldn't yell. How could I yell and tell everyone what a fool I was to be falling that second into the bag which was for the wool?

I didn't yell.

I didn't breathe.

Outside nothing stopped. The clippers went on. And the gasoline engine went on. The sheep went on bawling like before. One lamb there was who kept crying louder than all the others, again and again. From the shearers there came a shout, "Sheep up, sheep up!" Someone laughed. And there was one somewhere singing. It was a song called "Chiapanecas"[7] which is also a dance. They played it at the fiesta. The singing came from far away, outside there. All these noises, I heard them in the same second. I myself made no noise. Not even to breathe.

I looked up. As if I was climbing up the rough cloth with my eyes, I looked up all the little criss-crosses of the cloth, and at the end I reached the top. Way up, high above me, I saw the sky, still

Bawling means *calling* or *crying out.*

The shearers hollered *"Sheep up"* when they were ready to shear another group of sheep.

A *fiesta* is a public celebration with music and dancing.

---

7. **Chiapanecas** (chee·ah·pah·NAY·kahs).

blue like this morning but no longer big and wide.
An eye, a round eye it was, way up at the end of
the tunnel, still blue and with one tramp cloud, an
orphan cloud.

I breathed. And then a shadow went past the
eye. It was a fleece. And right away another. Eli,
without looking, he was still throwing fleeces up to
me and I wasn't there. The fleeces were going
right over the top of the bag. Another came and
another. And no one to catch them. I stretched

my hands, high, high, knowing I couldn't stretch high enough but stretching up anyway if only to beg they should stop. But over it came, another shadow. I grabbed at the bag around me, wishing I was a cat with claws. But there was nothing, the cloth was too tight and hard to grab. And still it came, another fleece sailing over the opening of the bag way up above.

There was a shout. "Miguel!"

Someone yelled. "What are you doing with the fleeces, Eli? Throwing them away?"

"Eli!"

"What?" That was Eli. "What's wrong? Well, what do you know! Miguel! Where is he? Miguel!"

The fleeces stopped. And everywhere, shouts. For me, Miguel.

"Ai, Miguel!" *Ai,* pronounced /äē/, is a signal of distress.

"Miguel, where are you?"

"Where'd he go, Miguel?"

"Miguel!"

"Did you see Miguel?"

"Hey Miguel, Miguel! Speak up! Miguel!"

I didn't say anything. I wished only that my name was something different from Miguel. Alexander, Joe, Babaloo—anyone, except me.

"Miguel!"

It was my big brother Blasito who thought of it first. "Maybe he fell into the bag?"

Said one of the shearers, "Yeah, you better look in the bag."

Eli yelled, "Miguel, are you in there? Answer me, Miguel!"

"He's in there all right." It was Salph, the big, round shearer. "How do you like that? The boy fell in the bag."

"What do you think?" Everyone started to laugh, they roared. "Miguel's in the bag!"

Then I heard Johnny Marquez.[8] The man I thought was my friend. Mr. Marquez. Johnny was laughing harder than all the rest.

"Did you ever see anything like that Miguel?" He hit somebody on the back. I could hear it. "He gets tired of being a big man up there. So he jumps back into the sack and goes to sleep."

They screamed and yelled and laughed at how funny this was. There were also other jokes. When I looked up again it was just in time to see the face of my father come into the round blue hole way up there, above my head.

"He's here all right!" yelled my father. He looked down at me again. "What in Heaven's name, Miguel, do you think you're doing down there?"

I was breathing. That's all. But there was no need to tell him this.

"Is this any time to start playing games, hide and seek, like you were a little boy?"

When he said this I stopped breathing again.

He put down his hand. It hung there, big fingers and a big thumb, right in front of my nose.

"Come on, Miguel, let me get you out of this!" The thumb and one of the other fingers, they

___
8. **Marquez** (MAHR·kays).

snapped. They made a loud noise, one, two, three times. "Miguel! Give me your hand. Up!"

I went back to breathing. But I didn't take the hand. Even when the fingers snapped again, loud and angry. I didn't want to go up. I wanted to stay down here, where there was a shadow and it was dark.

Out there it was bright and blue and the sky was big, and if I went up everyone could see from all around that it was me, Miguel. I could only stay down here, at the bottom of this tunnel. The fingers snapped again, and still I didn't move. The only thing I wanted now was that when I got pulled out I should be somebody different from who I was—Alexander, or Joe, or Babaloo. Not me, Miguel.

My father was angry. "Give me your hand, Miguel, or I'll pull you out by the <u>scruff</u> of your neck. Now come on! Up!"

The big finger, upside down, shook at me. I put up my hands and took the hand hanging there in front of my nose. As soon as I did, my father grabbed me by the wrist.

"Games," he said. "At a time like this."

He lifted me up into the bright day. He dropped me over the side. I fell into the dirt at the bottom of the sack. Up above my father yelled, "Gabriel, get over here! And get those fleeces out of the rubbish. Come on, hombres,[9] we got a day's shearing yet to do."

The *scruff* is the back of the neck.

---

9. **hombres** (OHM·brays).

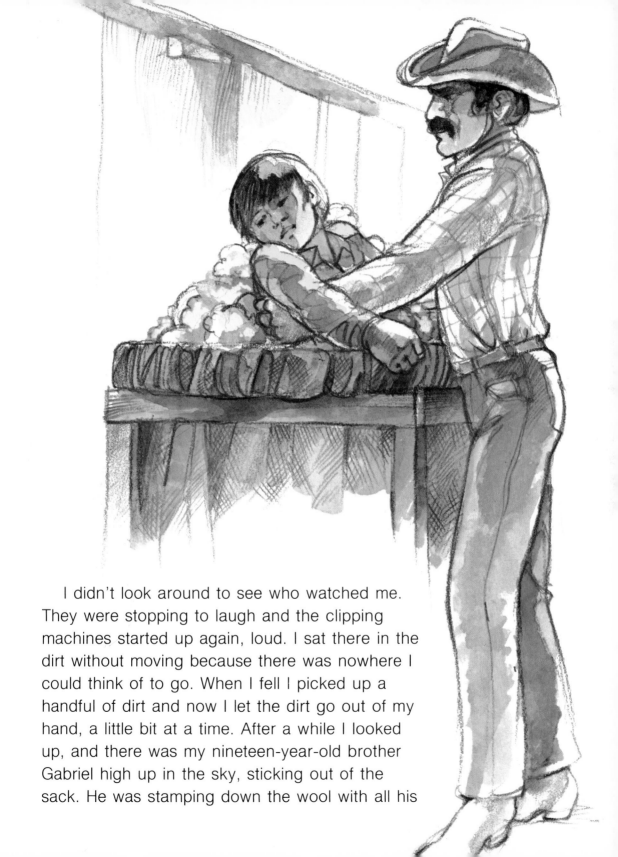

I didn't look around to see who watched me.
They were stopping to laugh and the clipping
machines started up again, loud. I sat there in the
dirt without moving because there was nowhere I
could think of to go. When I fell I picked up a
handful of dirt and now I let the dirt go out of my
hand, a little bit at a time. After a while I looked
up, and there was my nineteen-year-old brother
Gabriel high up in the sky, sticking out of the
sack. He was stamping down the wool with all his

might, and at the same time he caught the fleeces that Eli was throwing up to him. He turned round and round up there, pushing down the wool solid and tight the way it should be, Gabriel with all the blue and the clouds behind him.

Whatever dirt there was left in my hand, I threw it away.

I made myself small and I got up. I walked away from the shearing shed across the yard, without looking back. No one called me to look back, and there was no one I wanted to see.

Discussion Questions *After falling into the sack, what might Miguel have done to show that he was mature?* (He could have called for help, told his father he would be more careful, and gone back to work.) *Why do you think he did not do this?* (He was too embarrassed; he thought he had failed completely by making one mistake.) *Why do you think the world looks so beautiful to Miguel in the first paragraph of the story?* (He is going to help with the sheep shearing.) *How did it look to him at the end?* (The sky and clouds seemed far away; he felt very small.)
Enriching Activity *Writing directions.* Have several students work together to list and number the steps involved in putting up a sack and packing the fleeces (see pages 194–197). Other students might work alone or in pairs to write the steps for such tasks as wrapping a package, baking a cake, or making a bed. These lists can then be used for a game of charades.

Questions

1. What happened to Miguel to cause him to feel embarrassed?

2. Why was Miguel embarrassed instead of scared or angry?

3. Why was Miguel's father angry with Miguel instead of glad that Miguel was rescued?

4. The story explains how to do something. What does it explain how to do?

5. Here are four pairs of words from the story. Explain how the words in each pair are related to each other.
   a. fleeces—shearers
   b. Chiapanecas—fiesta
   c. burlap—crisscrosses
   d. wool—sack

1. Literal/recall He fell into a burlap sack and couldn't get out. (page 198)

2. Interpretive/inference Possible answer: he felt that the mishap showed he wasn't mature enough to do the job he had been given. (pages 201–203)

3. Interpretive/inference Possible answer: he was angry because Miguel had been careless and acted foolishly. (page 202)

4. Literal/recall How to hang the burlap sack and how to pack the fleeces. (pages 194–197)

5. Vocabulary a. Shearers clip fleeces from sheep. (page 196) b. Chiapanecas is a song or dance performed at a fiesta. (page 198) c. Burlap cloth is woven in crisscrosses. (page 198) d. The shorn wool was dropped into the sack. (page 196)

Activity **Critical/relating to experience** *Drawing/writing/acting.*

When Miguel is a year older, the sheep shearing time may be happier for him. Think back. What was difficult for you a year ago that is easier now? How can you best tell about the experience?

Draw your experience or write about it—or be ready to act it out for your classmates.

Running Away

A poem by Karla Kuskin

Running away
From the rest of today
Running away
From you
Running away
From "Don't do that"
From all of the things
I must constantly do.
I feel too tall
I feel too old
For a hundred helpings of being told.
Packing my head
Taking my feet
Galloping down the familiar street.
My head is a bird.
My heart is free again.
I might come back
When I feel like me again.

206

Illustrated by Nancy Schill

About KARLA KUSKIN

"Running Away," like many of Karla Kuskin's poems, came from a childhood memory. One day when she was nine, she got mad at her mother and decided to run away. "I was going to stay away until they were really scared," she writes, "maybe a week." She got no farther than the nearby woods. "Suddenly there was a very large spider web right in front of me," she remembers. "There was a very large spider in it. I've always been afraid of spiders so I went home."

Karla Kuskin, who was born in New York City, has written more than twenty books of poetry. Some, like *James and the Rain,* tell complete stories in verse. Others are collections of separate poems. She has illustrated all but one of her books herself.

Karla Kuskin grew up hearing her parents and teachers read poetry aloud to her. Even when she didn't understand all the words, she loved the sounds they made. Today, she often teaches young people about poetry. Sometimes she asks them to write poems of their own. "You can write about anything," she believes. "You can write about things or feelings. When I have feelings that make me sad or angry I try to write them down to get them outside myself."

Books of Poetry by Karla Kuskin

Near the Window Tree: Poems and Notes   (Harper & Row, 1975)
Any Me I Want to Be: Poems   (Harper & Row, 1972)

Characters to Remember

Think about some favorite characters in stories you have read. Were they brave? determined? clever? honest? wicked? These are all *traits*. A character's traits are what make that character stand out in your mind. They are what make a character someone you are likely to remember.

A character's traits may be learned from what that character says. What traits do you detect in Beth from what she says in the following section from the story "I Never Asked for No Allergy"? In this scene, Beth is saying good-bye to her dog, Friendly, because she is allergic to him.

At the kennel I held Friendly close to me while Pa explained about the allergy to Mr. Grant. "You are welcome to swap," he said, reaching out for Friendly.

"Wait!" I said. "A person has got to say good-bye, don't they?" I looked into Friendly's eyes and wondered how I could make him understand. "I never wanted to get rid of you, Friendly. I only wanted to get rid of the aller—*Her-her-choo!*—of the allergy."

Caring, sensitive, concerned—these are traits you may have observed in Beth from what she says.

Objectives • To identify traits of story characters through actions, dialogue, and description. • To write a descriptive paragraph that reveals a character's traits.
Introducing the Lesson *Think about some favorite characters in stories you have read. Which story character would you most like to know? Why? We're going to read about some of the characters who appear in this book. As you read, think about how the* authors have made these characters *"come alive" for the reader.*

Read aloud the excerpts on pages 208–209. For each excerpt, have the students find the sentences that show the character traits discussed in the text. In the first excerpt, for example, Beth's *concern* is shown in the sentence "I looked into Friendly's eyes and wondered how I could make him understand." (Continued on next page.)

A character's traits also may be learned from what the author tells us. Here is the way author Natalie Babbitt describes Egan as he begins to climb the mountain in the story "The Megrimum."

. . . Egan was half an hour ahead by that time. And he was young and strong, alone—and determined.

Later in that story, the traits of being *strong* and *determined* are shown in what Egan does—in his actions.

Egan, deep in the mist, heard nothing. He wandered up the final stony slope toward the top like a sleepwalker lost in dreams. . . . And then he stopped, chilled suddenly out of his trance. Just ahead there came a noise as of an animal thrashing about, and the low rumble of a voice.

He crept forward, grasping the nearly forgotten stick tightly, and his heart pounded. The Megrimum! At last, the Megrimum! Slay it, perhaps—perhaps; but at least he would see it.

More thrashing in the weeds ahead. "Owanna-ooowanna," the voice seemed to murmur.

Closer and closer crept Egan and then he saw it dimly, all flailing arms, rolling about on the ground.

209

You've seen that a character's traits can be shown in several ways—through the words and actions of the characters themselves and through the words of others. Now read some paragraphs about other characters from the stories in this book. Match the characters with one or more of the traits in the list on this page. Choose only those traits that describe the characters in the examples given here. You may want to use some traits more than once, but not all the traits need to be used. Add new ones if you need them.

Character Traits

cheerful	outspoken	wise	determined	curious
sensible	thoughtful	cautious	sensitive	caring
brave	careful	kind	honest	practical
funny	friendly	adventurous	bold	dignified

1. Mr. Wigg in "Laughing Gas"

"I'd better explain, I think," Mr. Wigg went on calmly. "You see, it's this way. I'm a cheerful sort of man and very disposed to laughter. You wouldn't believe, either of you, the number of things that strike me as being funny. I can laugh at pretty nearly everything, I can."

And with that Mr. Wigg began to bob up and down, shaking with laughter at the thought of his own cheerfulness.

210

2. Lucy in "Lucy's Adventure"

Lucy felt a little frightened, but she felt very inquisitive and excited as well. She looked back over her shoulder and there, between the dark tree trunks, she could still see the open doorway of the wardrobe and even catch a glimpse of the empty room from which she had set out. (She had, of course, left the door open, for she knew that it is a very silly thing to shut oneself into a wardrobe.) It seemed to be still daylight there. "I can always get back if anything goes wrong," thought Lucy. She began to walk forward, *crunch-crunch,* over the snow and through the wood towards the other light.

3. Katharine in "The Tournament"

"I wish I could fight ten times as well as you, you bully! Yah!" were the words that the valiant Sir Kath spoke upon the field. It was a cry of pure temper. . . . What followed would have to be seen to be believed. Katharine came down like several wolves on the fold.

Knowing a character's traits may help you describe that character to someone else. Imagine that you've been asked to introduce your favorite book character to your class. Write one paragraph in which you introduce the character. Before you write, make a list of the traits you may want to mention.

Metaphor

A poem by Eve Merriam

Introducing the Poem *In a metaphor, poets compare two different things by saying that one thing is another. Read this poem to see why it is called "Metaphor."*

Discussion Questions *What two things are being compared in this poem?* (Morning and a new sheet of paper.) *How can morning be a new sheet of paper?* (You have the chance to do new things with each morning and with each sheet of paper. Help the students paraphrase their understanding of the poem.)

Morning is
a new sheet of paper
for you to write on.

Whatever you want to say,
all day,
until night
folds it up
and files it away.

The bright words and the dark words
are gone
until dawn
and a new day
to write on.

Enriching Activity *Writing metaphors.* Have the students write metaphors for such subjects as a shooting star, a telephone, or a new friend.

212

Illustrated by Sharon Harker

BOOKSHELF

All It Takes Is Practice by Betty Miles. Alfred A. Knopf, 1977. Peter and Stuart learn that being real friends can mean taking risks and standing up for one's beliefs. **Reading Level** Average

The Great Gilly Hopkins by Katherine Paterson. T. Y. Crowell, 1978. Gilly Hopkins, just settled in her third foster home, is already trying her "guaranteed-to-drive-you-crazy-techniques" on her new foster mother, Maime Trotter. But in Mrs. Trotter, Gilly has finally met her match. **Reading Level** Average

Cockleburr Quarters by Charlotte Baker. Prentice-Hall, 1972. Dolph rescues a blind dog and her eight puppies, but he needs help when one of the pups dies and another becomes sick. **Reading Level** Average

The Hundred Penny Box by Sharon Bell Mathis. Viking Press, 1975. As Michael listens to the stories of Great-Great-Aunt Dew, he counts out the pennies in her old, beat-up box—one for each year of her life. **Reading Level** Easy

The Wheel on the School by Meindert DeJong. Harper & Row, 1954. The people of Shora, a small Dutch fishing village, believe that storks bring good luck. To attract a stork to their school, Lina and her friends start a long search for a wagon wheel a stork could use as a nesting place. **Reading Level** Easy

Child of the Owl by Laurence Yep. Harper & Row, 1977. With her mother dead and her father in the hospital, Casey comes to live with her grandmother in San Francisco's Chinatown. **Reading Level** Challenging

4 Facing the Unknown

Dinky

A poem by Theodore Roethke

Objectives ● To identify what a character in a poem might represent. ● To extrapolate other actions of a poem's character. ● To draw an imaginary being.

Introducing the Poem   *Imagine a mysterious being who follows you around, losing your possessions, getting you into trouble, making you uncomfortable. Who would be mean enough to do that? It must be . . . Dirty Dinky! See what trouble Dirty Dinky causes in this poem.*

O what's the weather in a Beard?
It's windy there, and rather weird,
And when you think the sky has cleared
    —Why, there is Dirty Dinky.

Suppose you walk out in a Storm,
With nothing on to keep you warm,
And then step barefoot on a Worm
    —Of course, it's Dirty Dinky.

As I was crossing a hot hot Plain,
I saw a sight that caused me pain,
You asked me before, I'll tell you again:
    —It *looked* like Dirty Dinky.

Last night you lay a-sleeping? No!
The room was thirty-five below;
The sheets and blankets turned to snow.
    —He'd got in: Dirty Dinky.

You'd better watch the things you do.
You'd better watch the things you do.
You're part of him; he's part of you
    —*You* may be Dirty Dinky.

216

Discussion Questions *What things does Dirty Dinky get blamed for in this poem?* (Cloudy skies, stepping barefoot on a worm, freezing in bed.) *What does the last line of the poem mean?* (Beware, you may be Dirty Dinky, the cause of your own problems.) *If you were to make up some verses to add to the poem, what things might Dirty Dinky do?*

Enriching Activity *Drawing/painting.* Have the students paint or draw what they think Dirty Dinky looks like. Post the pictures on a bulletin board so the students can compare their perspectives.

Illustrated by Glen Iwasaki

Objectives ● To recognize the style and elements of a folk tale. ● To list the sequence of events in a story. ● To extrapolate story events and character motives.
Synopsis of the Folk Tale In return for making her family rich, the youngest daughter of a poor farmer goes away with a White Bear. The Bear is kind to her and provides her with everything she desires. One night, she discovers that the Bear is really a handsome prince under a spell. Because she discovers his secret, he must go to a far-distant land and marry a wicked princess. The broken-hearted girl seeks him

East O' the Sun and West O' the Moon

A Norwegian folk tale

Reading Level Average

Illustrated by Katie Thamer

A *husbandman* is a farmer.

Explain that folk tales often use turned-around sentences such as "Kind and good children they were." After they complete the story, have the students pick out other sentences with this structure.

Once on a time there lived a poor husbandman who had so many children that none had food or clothing enough. Kind and good children they were, but the kindest was the youngest daughter.

'Twas on a Thursday evening late in the fall of the year. The weather was wild outside. Rain fell and the wind blew till the walls of the cottage shook. There they all sat around the fire, busy with this thing and that. But all at once, something gave three taps on the windowpane—tap! tap! tap! The father went out to see what it was, and, when he got out of doors, what should he see but a big, White Bear.

"Good evening to you," said the Bear.

"The same to you," said the man.

"Will you give me your youngest daughter?" said the Bear. "If you will, I'll make you as rich as you are poor tonight."

in a long and difficult journey. Finally she reaches East o' the Sun and West o' the Moon, where she helps free the prince, and the wicked princess is destroyed.

Introducing the Folk Tale *A folk tale is a story that has been told for generations. Many folk tales, such as* Snow White *or* Rumpelstiltskin, *were written just as they were told. In this folk tale, a young girl makes a terrible mistake and, as a result, must do something that no one else has ever done. As you read, think about what the story teaches us.*

Well, the man would be glad to be rich. But give up his daughter? No, that he wouldn't, he said. But the White Bear said, "Think it over. Next Thursday night I'll come back and then you can give me your answer."

So the father went into the house and told them all that had happened. Now when the lassie heard how she could lighten the poverty of her parents and brothers and sisters, she said at once she would go. Let her family beg never so hard, go she would, she said. I can't say her packing gave her much trouble. She washed and mended her rags and made herself ready to start.

Next Thursday evening the White Bear came. She got on his back with her bundle and off they went through the woods.

"Are you afraid?" said the Bear.

"No, not at all," said the lassie.

So she rode a long, long way till they came to a great steep hill. The White Bear knocked on the face of the hill, a little door opened, and they entered a castle, with rooms all lit up and gleaming, splendid with silver and gold. There, too, was a table laid. It was all as grand as could be. Then the White Bear gave the lassie a bell and told her to ring when she wanted anything.

Well, after she had eaten, she thought she would go to bed. Scarcely had she lifted the bell when she found herself in a room with a bed as fair and white as any one could wish to sleep in. But when she had put out her light she heard someone enter the room next to hers, and there someone stayed until dawn.

Night after night the same thing occurred. Not a single human being did the lassie see through the day, but, when all the lights were out, someone would enter the room next to hers and sleep there until dawn. But always before the daylight appeared, whoever it was was up and off, so as never to be seen.

Things went on well for a while. But all day long the lassie had not a soul to talk to except for the White Bear and she knew not whether it was man or beast who slept in the next room at night. So at last she grew silent and sorrowful. Then the White Bear came and said, "What troubles you, my lassie? Here you have everything a heart can wish. You have only to ring the bell and whatever you want is brought to you."

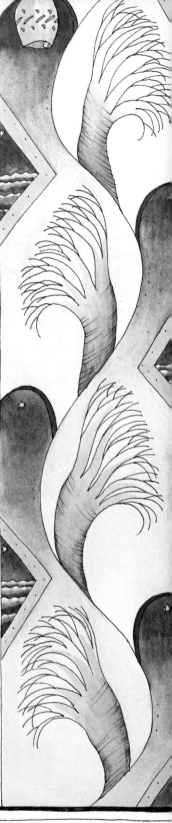

"Nay then," said the lassie. "I am lonely. Who is it that sleeps in the room next to mine?"

At that the Bear begged her to ask no such questions. "Trust me," he said. "Don't try to find out and in due time you will know."

Now the lassie was grateful to the Bear and fond of him. But in spite of what he said, she grew more and more sorrowful and more and more lonely. Who was it that shared the castle with her? Who was it? Who was it? Who was it? She was forever thinking of that one thing alone. All day long and all night long she wondered and fretted. Still for a long, long time she obeyed the Bear and did not try to find out. But at last she could stand it no longer. In the dead of night she got up, lit a candle, and slipped softly into the next room.

There asleep on a bed the lassie saw the loveliest Prince one ever set eyes on. Slowly she crept up to him, bent over, and kissed him. But as she did so, three drops of hot tallow fell from her candle onto his shirt and awoke him.

"Alas! What have you done?" he cried. "Now you have spoiled all that was gained by the months you were faithful to me. Had you held out only this one year, you would have set me free. For an evil queen has cast a spell upon me, so that I am a white bear by day and a man only at night. A year of good faith and you would have saved me. Now all is over between us. Back I must go to the castle *East o' the Sun and West o' the Moon.* There I must marry a princess with a nose three ells long. She must now be the wife for me."

The lassie wept, but there was no help for it. Go
he must, he said. Then she asked if she mightn't
go with him.

No, she mightn't, he said.

"Tell me the way there, then," said she, "and I'll
search you out over all the world, no matter how
hard is the journey."

"But there is no way to that place," cried the
Prince. "It lies *East o' the Sun and West o' the Moon.*
That is all I can tell you."

Next morning when the lassie awoke, both Prince and castle were gone. There she lay on a little green patch in the midst of the gloomy, thick wood. By her side lay the same bundle of rags which she had brought with her from home.

When she had rubbed the sleep out of her eyes and wept at her loss of the Prince, she set out on her journey. She walked for many days, until she came to a lofty crag under which an old woman sat tossing a golden apple. Her the lassie asked if she knew the way to the castle that lay *East o' the Sun and West o' the Moon*. But the old woman answered:

"All I know about it is that it lies *East o' the Sun and West o' the Moon* and thither you'll come late or never. But go on to my next neighbor. Maybe she will be able to tell you more." Then she gave the lassie her golden apple. "It might prove useful," she said.

So the lassie went on a long, long time till she came to another crag, under which sat another old woman with a golden carding-comb.[1] Her the lassie asked if she knew the way to the castle that lay *East o' the Sun and West o' the Moon*. But this old woman likewise knew nothing about the matter.

"Go on to my next neighbor," she said. "Maybe she can tell you." And she gave the lassie the carding-comb and bade her take it with her.

So the lassie went on and on, a far, far way and a weary, weary time till at last she came to another

---

1. **carding-comb:** a tool used to comb and untangle sheep's wool so the wool can be spun into yarn.

crag under which sat another old woman spinning
with a golden spinning wheel. Her too she asked
if she knew the way to the castle that lay *East o' the
Sun and West o' the Moon.* It was the same thing
over again. She knew nothing, but this old woman
said:

"Go to the East Wind and ask him. Maybe he
knows those parts and can blow you thither." Then
she gave the lassie her golden spinning wheel, and
bade her take it with her.

So the lassie toiled on many days before she got to the East Wind's house. At last she did get there, and then she asked the East Wind if he could tell her the way to the Prince who dwelt *East o' the Sun and West o' the Moon*. Yes, the East Wind had often heard tell of the Prince and the castle, but he didn't know the way, for he had never blown so far.

"If you will," he said, "I'll take you to my brother, the West Wind. Maybe he knows, for he's much stronger than I. Just get up on my back and I'll carry you thither."

Yes, she got on his back, and I should just think they went briskly along till they came to the West Wind's house. Then the lassie asked the West Wind if he knew how to get to the castle *East o' the Sun and West o' the Moon*.

"Nay," said the West Wind. "So far I've never blown. But if you'll get on my back, I'll carry you to our brother the South Wind. He has flapped his wings far and wide. Maybe he can tell you."

So she got on his back and travelled to the South Wind, and wasn't long on the way. And the lassie asked the South Wind if he knew the way to the castle *East o' the Sun and West o' the Moon*.

"Well, I've blustered about in most places in my time," answered the South Wind, "but so far I've never blown. Just get up on my back, and I'll carry you to my brother, the North Wind. He is the strongest of all of us, and if he doesn't know where it is, you'll never find anyone to tell you."

So she got on his back, and away he went.

When they got to the North Wind's house, he was so wild and cross that they felt his cold icy puffs when they were a long way off. "What do you want?" he roared in a voice that made them shiver. Then the lassie asked the North Wind if he knew the way to the castle *East o' the Sun and West o' the Moon.*

"Yes!" roared the North Wind. "I know well enough! Once in my life I blew an aspen leaf thither. I was so tired I couldn't blow a puff for ever so many days after. If you really wish to go so far and aren't afraid to come along, I'll take you on my back and see if I can blow you thither."

Yes, with all her heart! She must and would get there if she could possibly do it. And as for fear, no matter how madly he went, she wouldn't be afraid at all.

Early next morning they started. The North Wind puffed himself up and made himself so stout 'twas gruesome to look upon him. Off they went through the air, as if they would never stop till they got to the end of the world. Down below a storm raged.

They tore on and on—no one can believe how far they went—and all the time they still went over the sea. The North Wind got more and more weary, and so out of breath he could scarcely puff. His wings drooped and drooped, till he sunk so low that the crests of the waves went dashing over his heels.

"Are you afraid?" asked the North Wind.

No, she wasn't afraid.

But they weren't very far from the land, and the North Wind still had strength enough to throw her up on the shore. Now at last she was under the windows of the castle which lay *East o' the Sun and West o' the Moon.*

All through the day the lassie saw no one. But toward night she began to play with her golden apple, tossing it into the air. At that, out came Long-nose, who was going to marry the Prince.

"What do you want for your apple?" she asked.

"It's not for sale," answered the lassie. "But if I may visit the Prince, I will give it to you for nothing."

That she might, said Long-nose, and snatch! she seized the apple. But before Long-nose let the lassie in, she gave the Prince a drink that put him fast asleep, so though the lassie called him and shook him, she could not wake him up. Then along came Long-nose and drove her out again.

Next day the same thing happened. So long as it was light, the gloomy old castle was still as death and no one even looked out of it. But at nightfall signs of life awoke, and when the lassie began to card with the golden carding-comb, out came Long-nose to buy it.

"It's not for sale for gold or money," answered the lassie. "But if I may visit the Prince, you shall have it." Now when the lassie went up this time she found the Prince fast asleep as before, and all she called, and all she shook, she couldn't wake him up. Then along came Long-nose and chased her out again.

So the next night the lassie sat down under the castle window and began to spin with her golden spinning wheel. Long-nose must have the spinning wheel too. So in went the lassie once more. But this time, the Prince's servants had told him how a beautiful lassie had come and wept over him and called him two nights running. So, when Long-nose gave him his night drink, he poured it out secretly on the floor, and the lassie found, to her joy, that his eyes were wide open. Then she told him the whole long story of how she had made the far, far journey and the Prince wept and smiled and had great joy of her coming.

"You've got here just in the nick of time," cried he, "for tomorrow's to be my wedding. Be waiting at the gate and you'll see what you will see."

Well, the wedding was to be the next night in the dark, for neither Long-nose nor the trolls who had been invited could endure the daylight. But when the time came, the Prince announced:

"Ere I marry, I'll see what my bride can do. Here is my wedding shirt, but on it are three spots of tallow. I'll have no other for a bride save her who can wash it clean."

"No great thing to do," said Long-nose. So when the moon stood high, shining over the treetops, she hung a caldron of boiling lye in a clearing in the woods. Thither came running, tumbling, scolding, a whole pack of trolls, red-eyed, ugly, a hideous sight to see. First Long-nose began to wash. She washed as hard as she could. But the more she rubbed and scrubbed the bigger grew the spots. "Oh, you can't wash! Let me try!" a troll woman cried, and wash, wash, wash—every one in turn scrubbed away on that shirt. But the more they washed, the blacker and uglier grew the shirt, till at last it was black all over as if it had been up the chimney.

"Ah!" cried the Prince. "You're none of you worth a straw. I'll have none of you for my bride. Why look! Outside the gate there sits a beggar lass. I'll be bound she knows how to wash better than your whole pack. Come in, lassie!" he shouted.

So in came the lassie, and almost before she had taken the shirt and dipped it in the water, it was white as the driven snow.

"You are the lassie for me!" cried the Prince. Then the trolls rushed raging upon him, but ah! while they had been washing, the night had slowly waned. Just then the sun came up. The moment it pierced the mist and gloom and shone directly on Long-nose, she burst, like an empty bubble. The whole pack of trolls uttered horrid shrieks and hurried away toward the castle, but it was no use at all. The instant the sun struck them squarely, they every one of them vanished.

As for the Prince and Princess, they took hold of hands and ran away as far as they could from the castle that lay *East o' the Sun and West o' the Moon.*

Questions

1. How can you tell that this folk tale is meant to be told by a storyteller?

2. Suppose you are telling this story to someone. You'll need to remember who helped the lass find her prince. List those who helped her, in the order in which they appear in the story.

3. Did the lass ever see her family again? Tell what you imagine happened *after* the story's end.

4. When the lass wanted to know who was sleeping in the next room, the storyteller said, "Who was it? Who was it? Who was it?" What did the storyteller mean?
   a. That the lass kept asking everyone she met.
   b. That the lass said the words three times for magic.
   c. That the lass wanted desperately to know.

1. Interpretive/ inference   The teller refers to him or herself as "I" (page 220); sentences are repeated or interrupted (page 222).
2. Literal/recall An old woman with a golden apple (page 224), an old woman with a golden carding comb (page 224), an old woman with a golden spinning wheel (page 225), East Wind (page 226), West Wind (page 226), South Wind (page 226), and North Wind (page 227).
3. Interpretive/ extrapolation Possible answer: the girl and the prince were married and lived in the castle in the hill with her parents.
4. Interpretive/ inference   c. (page 222)

Activity

Imagine that you have taken a journey *East o' the Sun and West o' the Moon* and want to tell the story of your adventures. Write an opening paragraph for your story. Try to interest people in what will happen next.

Interpretive/ inference and **Critical/relating to experience** *Story writing.*

Direction

A poem by Alonzo Lopez

I was directed by my grandfather
To the East,
    so I might have the power of the bear;
To the South,
    so I might have the courage of the eagle;
To the West,
    so I might have the wisdom of the owl;
To the North,
    so I might have the craftiness of the fox;
To the Earth,
    so I might receive her fruit;
To the Sky,
    so I might lead a life of innocence.

Illustrated by Katrina Taylor

About ALONZO LOPEZ

Most Native American stories, poems, and songs have been passed along by word of mouth for several thousand years. Many Native American peoples regard this kind of artistic expression as an essential part of everyday life, special ceremonies, and religious experience. Such traditional literature has always depended upon participation and performance for its very existence. For this reason as well as many others, most Native Americans required no written alphabet. But in recent years, ways have been devised to represent in written form the several hundred complex Native American languages. Native American writers who wish to do so, can now express themselves in their traditional languages.

Alonzo Lopez, a member of the Papago tribe in Arizona, is one Native American poet who chooses to write in English. Mr. Lopez studied writing, drama, dance, and Native American crafts at the Institute of American Arts in Santa Fe, New Mexico. Later he attended Yale University for a year, and then transferred to Wesleyan University in Connecticut, where he studied the Navajo language, helped organize an American Indian Festival, and worked to start a class in Native American poetry. While attending Wesleyan University he made recordings of his own Papago language. He had to learn to read and write Papago to do this, and he said, "It is fun but I never knew that speaking my own language could be so difficult. It seems so unusual to see it written and try to read it, when I'm so used to speaking it only."

Mr. Lopez's poems appear in a book of poems by young Native Americans called *The Whispering Wind.* Like "Direction," his writing often reflects the richness of his cultural heritage.

Objectives ● To recall a story's sequence of events. ● To identify characters' motives. ● To identify situations that are humorous to others, but not to those involved. ● To invent imaginative games.

Synopsis of the Story On Halloween night, April, Melanie, Elizabeth, and Marshall head for the vacant lot where they sometimes play the Egypt Game. There they begin the Great Ceremony of the Celebration of the Return to Egypt. When two boys intrude on their ritual, April and Melanie fear the boys will tell others about the Egypt Game and ruin the fun. So Elizabeth invites the boys to join them in return for a vow of secrecy.

Background In 1968, the novel *The Egypt Game* was a Newbery Honor Book and was in "Fanfare," the *Horn Book*'s honor list. In 1967, it was one of the Library of Congress Children's Books of the Year and was on

THE RETURN TO EGYPT

From the novel *The Egypt Game* by Zilpha Keatley Snyder

Illustrated by Angela Adams

Reading Level Challenging

the American Library Association Notable Children's Books list.

Introducing the Story *Perhaps you and your friends have imagined yourselves as space explorers or as castaways on a desert island. Why are these games exciting?* (Possible answer: they give people a chance to be important characters in dangerous, suspenseful situations.) *Why might friends not want others to know about their game?* (Possible answer: others might laugh at them and spoil the game.) *This story is about three girls and a boy who play a game about ancient Egypt. Let's see how they keep their game a secret.*

Words to Know

  pharaoh: Refer the students to the footnote, page 237.

  omen: Refer the students to the footnote, page 238.

  sacrifice: an offering to a god. (page 243)

You could say that the Egypt Game began that summer in the library where April and her friend Melanie read all the books about Egypt. But it really began one September day in a weed-grown lot behind a junk store. It was in that secret and forgotten place that April, Melanie, and Melanie's four-year-old brother, Marshall, found the statue of Nefertiti.[1] Finding the statue was only the beginning of the magic. Soon, the three friends had transformed the old lot into Egypt and themselves into Egyptians. Marshall became the young pharaoh,[2] Marshmosis. And their new friend, a shy fourth-grader named Elizabeth, reigned as Egypt's queen, Neferbeth.

Sparked by April's daring and imagination, the Egypt gang invented chants and ceremonies, and made offerings to the gods of goodness and evil. They played their secret game as often as they dared, but only in the daytime, when it was safe. They had not been to Egypt for a while when Halloween came—and their chance for a nighttime visit.

---

1. **Nefertiti** (NEF·ur·TEE·tee): a queen of ancient Egypt.
2. **pharaoh** (FAY·roh): a ruler of ancient Egypt.

The trick-or-treat group was a milling mob of devils, witches, tramps, and monsters. Mr. Barkley, who always acted as if being the father of six-year-old twin boys was almost more than he could stand, looked positively exhausted; and even Mr. Kamata's sturdy smile was beginning to wilt. Outside the Casa Rosada apartment house, a black cat, a mechanical man, a Little Red Riding-Hood, two tramps, and four ancient Egyptians joined the already unwieldy group.

When the crowd turned up Elm Street where there were good houses to visit, the Egyptians began to drop to the rear of the group where it would be easier to get away. That meant they were the last ones up to each home, and sometimes most of the good stuff was already taken; but they hardly noticed. They were too busy looking for an omen.[3]

At the last house before they turned off Elm Street, the Egypt gang started up the front walk and collided with two other trick-or-treaters who also seemed to be hanging behind the main group—a monster and a walking pile of boxes. "Hey," the monster said, "it's Ross and February. What are you supposed to be?"

The rubber monster mask completely covered the speaker's head, but the voice was familiar; and besides, the sixth-grade boys were the only ones who called April, February. Then the walking boxes said, "Hey man! It's a whole herd of Egyptians." He poked Marshall in the stomach and said, "Hi there, King Tut."

"Okay, Mr. Wise-Guy Alvillar," Melanie said. "I know who you are." She turned to April with an exasperated shrug. "It's Kamata and Alvillar."

Ken Kamata and Toby Alvillar were just about the most disgusting boys in the sixth grade, in a fascinating sort of way. They were best friends and always together, and everybody always voted for them for everything and wanted to be on their team. But not April and Melanie. April and Melanie always told each other that Ken and Toby were just ordinary (ugh) boys, and it was stupid the way everybody treated them so

---

3. **omen** (OH•muhn): something that is seen as a sign of what is going to happen.

special. April and Melanie just couldn't figure out what people saw in them.

Of course, Toby had a special talent for getting people off the hook by making the teacher laugh. Just when Mrs. Granger was really building up a head of steam over something, Toby would make some little remark and Mrs. Granger would start choking and have to turn her back. Sometimes she'd try to pick things up where she left off, but all that lost momentum made a big difference.

Ken *was* sort of cute in a way. He had a clean-cut all-American look about him, and he walked with a high-school swagger. Toby was thinner, with big ears that stuck out of his shaggy hair and enormous brown eyes that were always up to something, like a pair of TV screens turned on full blast. But right now you couldn't see what either one of them really looked like at all.

Ken had a man's old overcoat on over a pillow-padded hunch-back, and (wouldn't you know it) rubber monster hands and feet, too, as well as the mask. Ken's father sold a lot of real estate and he could afford expensive stuff like that. Toby was the box man. He had a small box over his head, with a plastic-wrap-covered opening shaped like a TV screen to look out through. The rest of him was covered with all sorts of other boxes all strung together and painted black and covered with pasted-on ads out of papers and magazines.

"Boy! Are you two in character," April said. "A monster and a pile of junk."

"I'll have you know that I represent the New American," Toby said haughtily. Then he grinned. "It was my dad's idea. He says it's a new art form he just invented."

Toby's dad was a graduate student at the university. He was also a sculptor who made statues out of all kinds of junk.

"An art form!" April said. "Well, all I can say is—"

"Don't," Toby interrupted. "You'd just show off your ignorance."

"Come on, Tobe," Ken said. "We're getting left behind."

"Yeah, you little kids ought to keep up with the group better," Toby said, as he started off up the sidewalk. "You're liable to get hurt."

"Little kids!" Melanie yelled after him. "Look who's talking!"

Marshall ran after Toby and gave him a shove on the rear of his biggest box. "We're not little kids," he said. "We're Egyptians."

Toby swiveled his TV head around and surveyed the damage. "Hey, watch it!" he said.

April and Melanie didn't believe in encouraging Toby by laughing at him, but that was too much. By the time the Egyptians got over their convulsions of giggles, Ken and Toby had disappeared around the corner, and the lady whose walk they were on was calling to ask if they wanted some treats or not.

After that Melanie suggested that maybe they'd better stay up with the group a little better or the fathers would notice and start watching them. But even when they were trying, it wasn't easy to catch up because their costumes were such a success. At almost every house they had to be admired and questioned and other members of the family had to be called to see them—particularly Elizabeth and Marshall. Everyone thought Elizabeth and Marshall were just "darling," and "adorable," and they had to be admired and fussed over before the Egyptians could take their treats and leave.

At last, at one house they had to wait while the man got his flash camera out to take their picture, and when they finally got away and rushed down the stairs the big group of trick-or-treaters had completely disappeared.

There they were, all alone on the dimly lit sidewalk and it was suddenly very quiet. They ran down the block to the corner where they could look all four ways, but still there wasn't a person in sight. They were still just standing there looking around and wondering what to do, when suddenly Melanie pointed at the horizon. "Look," she said. "A shooting star!"

"A shooting star!" Everybody repeated it in whispered unison as if they'd been rehearsed. Then everybody looked at April. She nodded. "The secret omen," she said slowly, making every syllable heavy with significance. Marshall started turning around and around, smelling the air.

Looking around one last time to be sure no one was watching, the girls grabbed Marshall out of his tailspin and started down the sidewalk in the direction that they had come. They scurried down two blocks without seeing a soul, turned the corner, and a moment later ducked into the alley that led to Egypt.

If the secret and mysterious land of Egypt was fascinating in the daytime, it was doubly so at night. Dimly lit by a distant street light, two flashlights, and a jack-o'-lantern, it was almost too fascinating to bear. April told everyone to wait just inside the fence while she tiptoed forward and lit the cone of incense on the altar of Set[4] and the two candles

that stood before the goddess Isis.[5] Then she motioned everyone forward.

"The Great Ceremony of the Celebration of the Return to Egypt has begun!" she chanted, and all four Egyptians prostrated themselves before the egg crate and the bird bath.

April and Melanie rose to their knees from their deep bows before the double altars of Egypt. Over the heads of Elizabeth and Marshall they exchanged a glance that said, "Okay. What's next?" Melanie reached over absently to help Marshall with his pharaoh's crown, which had slipped down over his eyes while he was touching his forehead to the floor. Suddenly her eyes lit up with an "I have it" expression. She gave the crown a final tug down over Marshall's ears and turned to face the altar of Set. She raised her arms and April quickly followed suit.

"The gods are angry at us for being gone so long," she chanted.

---

4. **Set:** in Egyptian mythology, the animal-headed god of darkness, night, and evil.

5. **Isis** (EYE·sis): an important goddess in Egyptian mythology. Her name is the Greek form of the ancient Egyptian *hieroglyph* (picture writing) meaning *throne*. Often Isis is pictured with the hieroglyphic sign of the throne on her head.

"The gods are angry," April repeated. A quick glare at Elizabeth and Marshall got them going.

"The gods are angry," they parroted.

Melanie nodded and continued with her inspiration. "The gods demand that we make a <u>sacrifice</u> so that we may be forgiven." She looked over at April, and April nodded delightedly.

"The gods demand that we make a horrible and bloody sacrifice," April took up Melanie's theme with relish.

"A horrible and bloody sacrifice," Melanie agreed.

"A horrible and bloody sacrifice," Marshall and Elizabeth repeated dutifully, but Elizabeth's voice quavered a little and Marshall leaned over and poked his sister.

"What sort of bloody?" he demanded in a whisper.

But now April was off and away, and Melanie was following. "The gods will tell us what the sacrifice must be," April said. "We must approach the altar one at a time and touch the Crocodile Stone, the sacred symbol of Set. We must touch the sacred symbol of Set and wait for a message about the sacrifice. Then we will decide whose message is the best."

April went first. She approached the egg crate using the correct Egyptian walk, which was done by walking with your shoulders sideways, arms held out from the body and bent sharply at the wrist. In front of the altar she bowed deeply with her head tucked between her upraised arms, and then placed her finger tips on the Crocodile Stone. She stood for a minute with her face turned upward. Melanie poked the other kids and motioned for them to watch closely.

When April stalked back to them looking wildly secretive, Melanie walked up to the altar and followed her example, doing exactly the same things. Then came Elizabeth's turn and finally Marshall's. Then they all sat down in a circle on the floor.

As soon as everyone was seated, Elizabeth raised her hand and shook it frantically. She was looking excited and pleasantly surprised with herself. She had just had a terribly daring idea and she couldn't wait to tell it.

"All right, Elizabeth first," Melanie said. "Okay, April?"

April nodded. "Go ahead, Neferbeth," she said, "but put your hand down, for heaven's sake. You're not in school, you're a lady pharaoh."

Elizabeth snatched her hand down and suggested eagerly that Set's message was that they should stick their fingers with a needle and write him a letter in their own blood.

April and Melanie exchanged surprised and appreciative glances, and Elizabeth beamed proudly. She didn't think it was necessary to mention that her teacher had just read *Tom Sawyer* to the class— and just possibly Set had had a little help from Mark Twain.[6]

However, there was one small detail—nobody had a needle. Elizabeth looked crushed. "Don't feel bad, Bethy," Melanie said. "It was a neat idea."

"I'll say," April agreed. "It was a terrific idea."

"It was a dumb idea," Marshall muttered. "When you stick your finger you get infested."

"Infected," Melanie corrected. "You go next, April."

April made a trance-like face. "When I stood before the altar," she chanted, "I heard the voice of the Crocodile god. He said the object to be sacrificed must be something very dear to us. It must be something we hate to part with. Otherwise it won't count. The Crocodile god has told me that we must sacrifice—" she pointed dramatically, "—Security!"

"NO!" Marshall shouted, jumping up and hugging his stuffed octopus, Security, to his chest.

---

6. **Mark Twain:** American author (1835–1910). It was his book, *The Adventures of Tom Sawyer,* that gave Elizabeth the idea mentioned in the story.

"NO! NO! NO!" With every shout he stamped his foot. All three girls were around him in a moment, shushing and begging him to keep still. He shushed, but he went over to the edge of the shed and stood with his back to them.

"All right, Marshall. We won't sacrifice Security. Will we, April?" Melanie said.

April went into a quick trance with her fingers to her forehead. "The gods have changed their minds," she announced in a moment. "They say they don't want Security. But just don't *yell* like that any more. Somebody will hear us, and we'll get caught."

"Somebody already heard us," Marshall muttered darkly.

"What do you mean, somebody already heard us?" Melanie gasped. But Marshall only shrugged and said nothing more.

"Come on back to the circle," Melanie coaxed. "We take it all back about Security. Besides, it's your turn to say what the message was."

Marshall allowed himself to be led back to the circle, but his chin was still sticking out, and he was glaring at April. He put his hand to his forehead the way

April had done and then jerked it away. "Let's sacrifice April," he suggested.

That gave everybody the giggles, and finally Marshall broke down and smiled, too. Then it was Melanie's turn. Melanie said that she had read about some people who cut off their fingers as sacrifices. At that point even April looked shocked, and Elizabeth almost fainted. But Melanie only laughed. "I didn't mean we should do *that*," she said. "It just gave me an idea. We could pull out some hairs—and maybe cut off some fingernails."

"No scissors," Elizabeth reminded with just a touch of satisfaction.

"We could bite them off," April suggested. "I do it all the time."

A few minutes later a small fire of twisted paper was burning in the mixing bowl fire-pit, and the high priestesses (and junior high priest) of Egypt were parading in a circle before the altar. They were walking in the Egyptian manner— one shoulder forward, arms bent at the wrist—except from time to time when they had to chew off another fingernail. Now and then one or another would approach the altar, bow and drop a scrap of humanity on the flames; a hair or two or a shred of fingernail.

It was just about the best ceremony they'd ever had, and it was a shame to end it; but Melanie was just thinking that perhaps it was time to leave when suddenly she heard Elizabeth give a gasp of pure terror. Following Elizabeth's gaze, Melanie was horrified to see a huge misshapen figure teetering on the top of the high board fence. The figure teetered wildly in the dim light, and then sprang forward to land in a horrible threatening crouch, right in the middle of Egypt.

When the shapeless inhuman figure sprang into the middle of the storage yard, the four Egyptians could only clutch each other in panic, too shocked for the moment to even scream. April had just managed to get her mouth open to yell for help, when suddenly Marshall pointed and said, "Look." A second figure was appearing over the top of the fence.

This second invader, who was having some difficulty climbing over the wire at the top of the fence, had a strangely angular look about him. Strangely angular— and strangely familiar. In all four Egyptians, frozen fear boiled at once into a choking mixture of anger and relief. In April it over-flowed in stuttering sputter. "You-you d-d-dirty f-f-finks!" she yelled.

On top of the fence Toby finally managed to get his boxy legs free of the barbed wire. He jumped down, losing his TV head in the process. Then, as the four badly shaken Egyptians turned loose of each other and tried to regain their dignity, the monster and the box-man leaned on each other and choked with fiendish laughter.

They laughed leaning on each other and standing up—bending over as if they were in pain—and finally collapsed, sitting flat on the ground. Then, while the four members of the Egypt gang stared at them in helpless fuming anger, they just sat there, leaning against each other's backs, still shaking with gradually weakening seizures.

"Man—oh—man!" Toby gasped finally. "I've got to quit laughing. My stomach's killing me."

"Sheesh! Me too," Ken said. "I'm dying." Ken fell over backward and just lay there, holding his stomach and saying "Sheesh" weakly from time to time. But Toby crossed his legs and leaned forward with his chin on one hand and stared at the angry Egyptians.

"Hey, February," he said finally. "How do you say panic button in Egyptian?"

April clenched her fists and took a step forward. Toby started to scramble to his feet—he'd seen April in action before. But Melanie and Elizabeth grabbed her and held her back.

"Turn loose," April said. "I'm going to punch him in the nose."

"There's no use doing that," Melanie whispered. "That won't do any good. We can't keep them from telling on us by punching them in the nose."

After a moment's consideration April nodded. "Okay. Turn loose. I won't punch them. At least not till we find out what they're going to do." She unclenched her fists and all three girls approached the enemy. Left behind, Marshall sat down on the edge of the temple floor in a good position to watch everything that might happen. Both the boys were standing now, watching the girls warily.

"Well," Melanie began. "Are you going to tell on us, or not?"

"Tell on you?" Ken said. "What makes you think we'd do a thing like that?"

"Of course not," Toby said. "We don't go around finking on people." The girls glanced at each other in surprised relief. "However," Toby continued, "this is not a matter of plain and simple finking. Letting you Egyptians get away with all this secret stuff just might be considered—like, unpatriotic, or something."

"Hey, you're right," Ken said. "Maybe we ought to tell the FBI."

"Maybe we should. Or maybe we could just make an official

report on the whole scene—like, for current events tomorrow morning.'' Toby stalked to the middle of the yard in what was obviously meant to be the Egyptian walk. Then he faced the group, cleared his throat, and in a phony voice he said, '''What's Happening in Egypt'—a very official report by Tobias Alvillar, Secret Agent.''

Toby was pretty funny all right, but no one laughed but Ken. April was thinking a horrible thought. If they knew about the Egyptian walk, how much else did they know? Up until then she'd been thinking that the fence was too high to look over—and they couldn't have seen very much while they were scrambling over it. She ran to the loose board and looked out into the alley. When she pulled her head back in, Melanie guessed the awful truth before she heard it.

Taking Melanie aside, April whispered, ''There are boxes piled up out there. They could have been watching forever! Shall I punch them *now?*''

Melanie shrugged hopelessly. ''Go ahead if you want to. But it won't do any good. I think we might as well—leave the country, or something.''

Elizabeth had followed Melanie and listened to April's horrible news. Now all of a sudden she said, ''I have an idea.''

Both the bigger girls looked surprised. Elizabeth wasn't the kind of person you expect to come up with ideas in an emergency. But the situation was desperate so April and Melanie listened.

When Elizabeth finished whispering, April shook her head gloomily. ''It'll never work,'' she said.

''Well, we may as well try it,'' Melanie said. ''It can't make things any worse.''

The enemy watched cautiously as the girls returned to face them. For a few seconds April and Melanie couldn't think of a way to get started, and the five of them just stood there staring at each other. Melanie spoke first.

''We don't have permission to be here from our folks or any-body.''

Toby grinned. ''So what else is new?'' he said.

April's fists clenched but she forced herself to open them. ''We'll be in terrible trouble if you tell on us,'' she said in as pitiful a voice as she could manage. To her amazement she noticed that the look the two boys exchanged was just the tiniest bit confused. And Kamata and Alvillar were two guys who weren't easy to confuse. Warming to her theme, she went on, "We'll probably get beaten and everything."

There was no doubt about it, the enemy had faltered for a few moments, but they managed to regroup.

"We're crying," Ken said. "See the tears."

"Yeah. We'll come to your funerals," Toby said.

Just then Elizabeth pushed her way between April and Melanie. Everyone looked at her in surprise—she'd probably never spoken to a sixth-grade boy before in her life, but now she looked as if she meant to. "Please," she said, in a feathery little voice. "Please don't tell on us, and we'll let you play, too."

April cringed. It was such a corny, baby thing to say. She had a crazy urge to grab Elizabeth and drag her out of wisecrack range, before she got hurt. But seconds passed and nobody pounced. April unsquinched her eyes. Strangely enough, the boys were looking confused again. More confused than ever. Elizabeth was looking shyly hopeful, like an unspanked puppy.

Then Ken blinked his eyes like someone coming to after a whack on the head. "Come on, Tobe, let's get out of here," he said.

And then, to no one in particular, "Maybe we won't *fink* on you guys. You never can tell. Maybe we just won't be in the mood for finking. Huh, Tobe?" But Toby only nodded absently. Ken picked up Toby's TV head and jammed it into his hands. "Come *on,* Tobe," he said. "We've got to get back before my dad misses me."

But Toby appeared to be thinking. He nodded again slowly and then walked around the girls to the temple. He looked for a moment at each altar and then around the yard. When he came back his eyes had a faraway look.

"Okay," he said. "Okay. We don't rat, and we get to join the game. Is it a deal?"

"Join the game!" Ken said. "This game? Are you kidding? We could make a deal about using the yard—like for—" he paused and glanced around, "—four-square or handball or something, but—" He caught a glimpse of Toby's face, and his voice trailed off. Toby was lit up like a pinball machine. Ken shrugged philosophically. "Okay," he said. "So we're Egyptians. It figures."

From then on things happened fast. Toby made everybody take a solemn oath not to tell where they'd been, even if they'd been missed and people started asking questions. Then, there was a brief crisis over getting Toby out of the yard. He wouldn't fit through the hole in the fence with his boxes on, and the big box the boys had used for climbing over was too big and heavy to throw into the yard. He couldn't take his costume off because he didn't think he could get back into it without his dad's help, and it wouldn't be wise to rejoin the trick-or-treat group in pieces. Finally he lay down on the ground and had everybody stomp on him, more or less gently (less, in the case of April who was still mad) until the boxes were flattened enough to squeeze through the hole. Afterwards, they tried to square him back up, but he never did look quite the same.

As soon as they'd carried off the boxes the boys had piled up to climb on, they started off after the trick-or-treat group. Fortunately Ken knew the line of march, and since they didn't stop at any houses, it wasn't too long until they caught up. They even had time to collect a few more treats before it was time to go home.

Discussion Questions *Why was playing the Egypt Game on Halloween night especially exciting?* (Possible answers: people were in costume; it was considered dangerous to go to a vacant lot at night; they had never played the game at night before.) *What might happen when Ken and Toby join the game?* (Possible answers: the boys might think of exciting new adventures for the Egyptians; they might demand to be pharaohs in the game.)

Enriching Activities 1. *Creative games.* Have small groups of students make up games like the Egypt Game, such as the Game of the Pioneers or the Pirate Game, and explain how they might be played. **2.** *Radio play.* Ask volunteers to read the narration and the parts of the children in the story; then have the students tape record the story as a radio play. Choose one or two students to create sound effects; for example, they might drop books on the floor when Toby falls over the fence.

Questions

1. Literal/recall c. (page 240); d. (page 242); f. (page 243); b. (page 247); a. (page 250); e. (page 253).
2. Interpretive/inference Possible answers: they liked the girls; Toby especially wanted to join the game. (page 253)
3. Vocabulary a. parroted (page 243); b. omen (page 238).

1. Give the order of these happenings.
    a. April says that the Egyptians will be in trouble if they are discovered.
    b. The Egyptians are frightened by invaders.
    c. The Egyptians make fun of Ken and Toby's costumes.
    d. The Egyptians go to their secret place.
    e. The Egyptians have two new members.
    f. The Egyptians decide on a sacrifice.

2. Why did Ken and Toby change their minds and decide *not* to tell the secrets of the Egyptian group?

3. Which word below each sentence means about the same as the underlined words?
    a. The Egypt group <u>repeated</u> what the leader said.
        infested   parroted   prostrated

    b. The Egypt group looked for a <u>sign to tell them what to do.</u>
        omen   panic button   scene

Activity

Critical/relating to experience *Writing newspaper columns.*

Some things that happen are funny—*if* they happen to somebody else. Write a paragraph that could go into a school newspaper column called *Not-So-Funny* describing such a happening.

About ZILPHA KEATLEY SNYDER

Zilpha Keatley Snyder receives many letters asking her why she became a writer. In response, she tells of her California childhood in the country. She spent her time with animals and with books. "I think I read almost a book a day during my childhood," she says, "and loved every minute of it. . . . As soon as it occurred to me that books were written by ordinary human beings, I decided that was the kind of human being I'd like most to be." That happened when Zilpha Keatley Snyder was eight, and from then on she considered herself a writer.

Zilpha Keatley Snyder married, raised three children, and taught elementary school for nine years before she returned to her writing. While teaching, she met many wonderful students whose personalities and ideas inspired her. All six of the main characters in *The Egypt Game* are based on the boys and girls she taught.

Mrs. Snyder loves to write because it gives her the opportunity to "make things up." She chooses to write for boys and girls aged nine to fourteen because, she says, "they are magical people."

More Books by Zilpha Keatley Snyder

Black and Blue Magic   (Atheneum, 1972)
The Headless Cupid   (Atheneum, 1975)
The Famous Stanley Kidnapping Case   (Atheneum, 1979)

What a Fright!

Two limericks

Objectives ● To identify the characteristics of a limerick. ● To select and read aloud a favorite limerick. ● To write a limerick.

Introducing the Poems *Limericks are short poems about funny people and unlikely situations. In these limericks, even ghosts are funny!*

Discussion Question *How is the form the same in both limericks?* (Like all limericks, each has five lines; they have the same rhythm; lines 3 and 4 are shorter; lines 1, 2,

Khartoum is the capital city of Sudan, a region in North Africa.

A skeleton once in <u>Khartoum</u>
Asked a spirit up into his room;
    They spent the whole night
    In the eeriest fight
As to which should be frightened of whom.

—Anonymous

and 5 rhyme; lines 3 and 4 rhyme. Point out that both poems identify character and place in the first line.)

Enriching Activities **1.** *Oral reading.* Have each student select and read aloud two or three limericks from a collection such as Edward Lear's *The Book of Nonsense* (Garland, 1976). **2.** *Creative writing.* Ask the students to suggest character and place names that they would like to use in a limerick. Then have them suggest two or three words that rhyme with the place names. Have the class work together to create an original limerick, using the words they have chosen. Tell the students to choose words that have several rhyming possibilities for the ends of lines 1 and 3.

Kew is a town in the southeastern part of England, famous for its gardens.

Wailed a ghost in a graveyard at Kew,
"Oh, my friends are so fleeting and few,
For it's gravely apparent
That if you're transparent
There is no one who knows if it's *you!*"

Point out that *gravely* is a pun.

—Myra Cohn Livingston

Illustrated by Marie-Louise Gay

Objectives ● To identify conflict and resolution in a story. ● To extrapolate events after a story. ● To name imaginary places in ordinary settings. ● To infer details of setting by drawing a story map.
Synopsis of the Story While exploring a large country house with her brothers and her sister, Lucy steps into a wardrobe and finds herself in a strange, magical land.

There she meets a faun named Mr. Tumnus who invites her to tea. Lucy enjoys her visit until Mr. Tumnus admits that he has been planning to kidnap her for the White Witch. Lucy persuades him to let her escape and is relieved when she steps through the wardrobe into the old house.

Reading Level Average

Lucy's Adventure

Two chapters from the novel

The Lion, the Witch and the Wardrobe

by C. S. Lewis

Illustrated by Emanuel Schongut

A fantasy story is often full of things that seem impossible to imagine. If the story is a good one, it makes the reader believe in it even so. One of the most popular fantasies ever written is C. S. Lewis's The Chronicles of Narnia. *This collection of stories fills seven books. The tale that follows is from the first book in the series.*

Background The novel *The Lion, the Witch, and the Wardrobe* was one of the American Library Association Notable Children's Books in 1950.

Introducing the Story *An old mysterious house would seem to be a great place to explore on a rainy day. The children in "Lucy's Adventure" enjoy their explorations until Lucy discovers something incredibly strange. See if you would be as brave as Lucy.*

 ## Lucy Looks into a Wardrobe

Once there were four children whose names were Peter, Susan, Edmund, and Lucy. This story is about something that happened to them when they were sent away from London during the war because of the air raids. They were sent to the house of an old Professor who lived in the heart of the country, ten miles from the nearest railway station and two miles from the nearest post office. He had no wife and he lived in a very large house with a house-keeper called Mrs. Macready and three servants. (Their names were Ivy, Margaret, and Betty, but they do not come into the story much.)

He himself was a very old man with shaggy white hair, which grew over most of his face as well as on his head, and they liked him almost at once. But on the first evening when he came out to meet them at the front door, he was so odd-looking that Lucy (who was the youngest) was a little afraid of him, and Edmund (who was the next youngest) wanted to laugh and had to keep on pretending he was blowing his nose to hide it.

As soon as they had said good night to the Professor and gone upstairs on the first night, the boys came into the girls' room and they all talked it over.

"We've fallen on our feet and no mistake," said Peter. "This is going to be perfectly splendid. That old chap will let us do anything we like."

"I think he's an old dear," said Susan.

"Oh, come off it!" said Edmund, who was tired and pretending not to be tired, which always made him bad-tempered. "Don't go on talking like that."

"Like what?" said Susan. "And anyway, it's time you were in bed."

"Trying to talk like Mother," said Edmund. "And who are you

to say when I'm to go to bed? Go to bed yourself."

"Hadn't we all better go to bed?" said Lucy. "There's sure to be a row if we're heard talking here." A *row* is an argument.

"No there won't," said Peter. "I tell you this is the sort of house where no one's going to mind what we do. Anyway, they won't hear us. It's about ten minutes' walk from here down to that dining room, and any amount of stairs and passages in between."

"What's that noise?" said Lucy suddenly. It was a far larger house than she had ever been in before and the thought of all those long passages and rows of doors leading into empty rooms was beginning to make her feel a little creepy.

"It's only a bird, silly," said Edmund.

"It's an owl," said Peter. "This is going to be a wonderful place for birds. I shall go to bed now. I say, let's go and explore tomorrow. You might find anything in a place like this. Did you see those mountains as we came along? And the woods? There might be eagles. There might be stags. There'll be hawks."

"Badgers!" said Lucy.

"Snakes!" said Edmund.

"Foxes!" said Susan.

But when next morning came, there was a steady rain falling, so thick that when you looked out of the window you could see neither the mountains nor the woods nor even the stream in the garden.

"Of course it *would* be raining!" said Edmund. They had just finished breakfast with the Professor and were upstairs in the room he had set apart for them— a long, low room with two windows looking out in one direction and two in another.

"Do stop grumbling, Ed," said Susan. "Ten to one it'll clear up in an hour or so. And in the meantime we're pretty well off. There's a wireless and lots of books." A *radio*.

"Not for me," said Peter, "I'm going to explore in the house."

Everyone agreed to this and that was how the adventures began. It was the sort of house that you never seem to come to the end of, and it was full of unexpected places. The first few doors they tried led only into spare bedrooms, as everyone had expected that they would. But soon they came to a very long room full of pictures and there they found

a suit of armor. After that was a room all hung with green, with a harp in one corner; and then came three steps down and five steps up, and then a kind of little upstairs hall and a door that led out onto a balcony, and then a whole series of rooms that led into each other and were lined with books—most of them very old books and some bigger than a Bible in a church. And shortly after that they looked into a room that was quite empty except for one big wardrobe, the sort that has a looking glass in the door. There was nothing else in the room at all except a dead bluebottle on the windowsill.

"Nothing there!" said Peter, and they all trooped out again—all except Lucy. She stayed behind because she thought it would be worthwhile trying the door of the wardrobe, even though she felt almost sure that it would be locked. To her surprise it opened quite easily, and two mothballs dropped out.

Looking inside, she saw several coats hanging up—mostly long fur coats. There was nothing Lucy liked so much as the smell and feel of fur. She immediately stepped into the wardrobe and got in among the coats and rubbed her face against them, leaving the door open, of course, because she knew that it is very foolish to shut oneself into any wardrobe. Soon she went further in and found that there was a second row of coats hanging up behind the first one. It was almost quite dark in there and she kept her arms stretched out in front of her so as not to bump her

face into the back of the wardrobe. She took a step further in—then two or three steps—always expecting to feel woodwork against the tips of her fingers. But she could not feel it.

"This must be a simply enormous wardrobe!" thought Lucy, going still further in and pushing the soft folds of the coats aside to make room for her. Then she noticed that there was something crunching under her feet. "I wonder is that more mothballs?" she thought, stooping down to feel it with her hands. But instead of feeling the hard, smooth wood of the floor of the wardrobe, she felt something soft and powdery and extremely cold. "This is very queer," she said, and went on a step or two further.

Next moment she found that what was rubbing against her face and hands was no longer soft fur but something hard and rough and even prickly. "Why, it is just like branches of trees!" exclaimed Lucy. And then she saw that there was a light ahead of her; not a few inches away where the back of the wardrobe ought to have been, but a long way off. Something cold and soft was falling on her. A moment later she found that she was standing in the middle of a wood at nighttime with snow under her feet and snowflakes falling through the air.

Lucy felt a little frightened, but she felt very inquisitive and excited as well. She looked back over her shoulder and there, between the dark tree trunks, she could still see the open doorway of the wardrobe and even catch a glimpse of the empty room from which she had set out. (She had, of course, left the door open, for she knew that it is a very silly thing to shut oneself into a wardrobe.) It seemed to be still daylight there. "I can always get back if anything goes wrong," thought Lucy. She began to walk forward, *crunch-crunch,* over the snow and through the wood towards the other light.

In about ten minutes she reached it and found that it was a lamppost. As she stood looking at it, wondering why there was a lamppost in the middle of a wood and wondering what to do next, she heard a pitter-patter of feet coming towards her. And soon after that a very strange person stepped out from among the trees into the light of the lamppost.

 ## What Lucy Found There

He was only a little taller than Lucy herself and he carried over his head an umbrella, white with snow. From the waist upwards he was like a man, but his legs were shaped like a goat's (the hair on them was glossy black) and instead of feet he had goat's hoofs. He also had a tail, but Lucy did not notice this at first because it was neatly caught up over the arm that held the umbrella so as to keep it from trailing in the snow. He had a red woolen muffler round his neck and his skin was rather reddish too. He had a strange, but pleasant little face with a short pointed beard and curly hair, and out of the hair there stuck two horns, one on each side of his forehead. One of his hands, as I have said, held the umbrella. In the other arm he carried several brown paper parcels. What with the parcels and the snow it looked just as if he had been doing his Christmas shopping. He was a Faun. And when he saw Lucy he gave such a start of surprise that he dropped all his parcels.

"Goodness gracious me!" ex-claimed the Faun.

"Good evening," said Lucy. But the Faun was so busy picking up his parcels that at first he did not reply. When he had finished he made her a little bow.

"Good evening, good evening," said the Faun. "Excuse me—I don't want to be inquisitive—but should I be right in thinking that you are a Daughter of Eve?"

"My name's Lucy," said she, not quite understanding him.

"But you are—forgive me—you are what they call a girl?" asked the Faun.

"Of course I'm a girl," said Lucy.

"You are in fact Human?"

"Of course I'm human," said Lucy, still a little puzzled.

"To be sure, to be sure," said the Faun. "How stupid of me! But I've never seen a Son of Adam or a Daughter of Eve before. I am delighted. That is to say—" and then he stopped as if he had been going to say something he had not intended but had remembered in time. "Delighted, delighted," he went on. "Allow me to introduce myself. My name is Tumnus."

"I am very pleased to meet you, Mr. Tumnus," said Lucy.

"And may I ask, O Lucy, Daughter of Eve," said Mr. Tumnus, "how you have come into Narnia?"

"Narnia? What's that?" said Lucy.

"This is the land of Narnia," said the Faun, "where we are now; all that lies between the lamppost and the great castle of Cair Paravel on the eastern sea. And you—you have come from the wild woods of the West?"

"I—I got in through the wardrobe in the spare room," said Lucy.

"Ah!" said Mr. Tumnus in a rather melancholy voice, "if only I had worked harder at geography when I was a little Faun, I should no doubt know all about those strange countries. It is too late now."

"But they aren't countries at all," said Lucy, almost laughing. "It's only just back there—at least—I'm not sure. It is summer there."

"Meanwhile," said Mr. Tumnus, "it is winter in Narnia, and has been for ever so long, and we shall both catch cold if we stand here talking in the snow. Daughter of Eve from the far land of Spare Oom where eternal summer reigns around the bright city of War Drobe, how would it be if you came and had tea with me?"

"Thank you very much, Mr. Tumnus," said Lucy. "But I was wondering whether I ought to be getting back."

"It's only just round the corner," said the Faun, "and there'll be a roaring fire—and toast—and sardines—and cake."

"Well, it's very kind of you," said Lucy. "But I shan't be able to stay long."

"If you will take my arm, Daughter of Eve," said Mr. Tumnus, "I shall be able to hold the umbrella over both of us. That's the way. Now—off we go."

And so Lucy found herself walking through the wood arm in arm with this strange creature as if they had known one another all their lives.

They had not gone far before they came to a place where the ground became rough and there were rocks all about and little hills up and little hills down. At the bottom of one small valley Mr. Tumnus turned suddenly aside as if he were going to walk straight into an unusually large rock, but at the last moment Lucy found he was leading her into the entrance of a cave. As soon as they were inside she found herself blinking in the light of a wood fire. Then Mr. Tumnus stooped and took a flaming piece of wood out of the fire with a neat little pair of tongs, and lit a lamp. "Now we shan't be long," he said, and immediately put a kettle on.

Lucy thought she had never been in a nicer place. It was a little, dry, clean cave of reddish stone with a carpet on the floor and two little chairs ("one for me and one for a friend," said Mr. Tumnus) and a table and a dresser

and a mantelpiece over the fire
and above that a picture of an old
Faun with a gray beard. In one
corner there was a door which
Lucy thought must lead to Mr.
Tumnus' bedroom, and on one
wall was a shelf full of books.
Lucy looked at these while he
was setting out the tea things.
They had titles like *The Life and
Letters of Silenus* or *Nymphs and
Their Ways* or *Men, Monks and
Gamekeepers; a Study in Popular
Legend* or *Is Man a Myth?*

"Now, Daughter of Eve!" said
the Faun.

And really it was a wonderful
tea. There was a nice brown egg,
lightly boiled, for each of them,
and then sardines on toast, and
then buttered toast, and then toast
with honey, and then a sugar-
topped cake. And when Lucy was
tired of eating the Faun began to
talk. He had wonderful tales to tell
of life in the forest. He told about
the midnight dances and how the
Nymphs who lived in the wells and
the Dryads who lived in the trees
came out to dance with the Fauns;
about long hunting parties after the
milk-white Stag who could give you
wishes if you caught him; about
feasting and treasure-seeking with

the wild Red Dwarfs in deep mines and caverns far beneath the forest floor; and then about summer when the woods were green and old Silenus on his fat donkey would come to visit them, and sometimes Bacchus himself, and then the streams would run with wine instead of water and the whole forest would give itself up to jollification for weeks on end. "Not that it isn't always winter now," he added gloomily. Then to cheer himself up he took out from its case on the dresser a strange little flute that looked as if it were made of straw and began to play. And the tune he played made Lucy want to cry and laugh and dance and go to sleep all at the same time. It must have been hours later when she shook herself and said,

"Oh, Mr. Tumnus—I'm so sorry to stop you, and I do love that tune—but really, I must go home. I only meant to stay for a few minutes."

"It's no good *now,* you know," said the Faun, laying down his flute and shaking his head at her very sorrowfully.

"No good?" said Lucy, jumping up and feeling rather frightened. "What do you mean? I've got to go

269

home at once. The others will be wondering what has happened to me.'' But a moment later she asked, ''Mr. Tumnus! Whatever is the matter?'' for the Faun's brown eyes had filled with tears and then the tears began trickling down his cheeks, and soon they were running off the end of his nose; and at last he covered his face with his hands and began to howl.

''Mr. Tumnus! Mr. Tumnus!'' said Lucy in great distress. ''Don't! Don't! What is the matter? Aren't you well? Dear Mr. Tumnus, do tell me what is wrong.'' But the Faun continued sobbing as if his heart would break. And even when Lucy went over and put her arms round him and lent him her handkerchief, he did not stop. He merely took the handkerchief and kept on using it, wringing it out with both hands whenever it got too wet to be any more use, so that presently Lucy was standing in a damp patch.

''Mr. Tumnus!'' bawled Lucy in his ear, shaking him. ''Do stop. Stop it at once! You ought to be ashamed of yourself, a great big Faun like you. What on earth are you crying about?''

"Oh—oh—oh!" sobbed Mr. Tumnus, "I'm crying because I'm such a bad Faun."

"I don't think you're a bad Faun at all," said Lucy. "I think you are a very good Faun. You are the nicest Faun I've ever met."

"Oh—oh—you wouldn't say that if you knew," replied Mr. Tumnus between his sobs. "No, I'm a bad Faun. I don't suppose there ever was a worse Faun since the beginning of the world."

"But what have you done?" said Lucy.

"My old father, now," said Mr. Tumnus, "that's his picture over the mantelpiece. He would never have done a thing like this."

"A thing like what?" said Lucy.

"Like what I've done," said the Faun. "Taken service under the White Witch. That's what I am. I'm in the pay of the White Witch."

"The White Witch? Who is she?"

"Why, it is she that has got all Narnia under her thumb. It's she that makes it always winter. Always winter and never Christmas; think of that!"

"How awful!" said Lucy. "But what does she pay you for?"

"That's the worst of it," said Mr. Tumnus with a deep groan. "I'm a kidnapper for her, that's what I am. Look at me, Daughter of Eve. Would you believe that I'm the sort of Faun to meet a poor innocent child in the wood, one that had never done me any harm, and pretend to be friendly with it, and invite it home to my cave, all for the sake of lulling it asleep and then handing it over to the White Witch?"

"No," said Lucy. "I'm sure you wouldn't do anything of the sort."

"But I have," said the Faun.

"Well," said Lucy rather slowly (for she wanted to be truthful and yet not to be too hard on him), "well, that was pretty bad. But you're so sorry for it that I'm sure you will never do it again."

"Daughter of Eve, don't you understand?" said the Faun. "It isn't something I *have* done. I'm doing it now, this very moment."

"What do you mean?" cried Lucy, turning very white.

"You are the child," said Mr. Tumnus. "I had orders from the White Witch that if ever I saw a Son of Adam or a Daughter of Eve in the wood, I was to catch them and hand them over to her. And you are the first I ever met. And I've pretended to be your friend and asked you to tea, and all the time I've been meaning to wait till you were asleep and then go and tell *her*."

"Oh but you won't, Mr. Tumnus," said Lucy. "You won't, will you? Indeed, indeed you really musn't."

"And if I don't," said he, beginning to cry again, "she's sure to find out. And she'll have my tail cut off, and my horns sawn off, and my beard plucked out, and she'll wave her wand over my beautiful cloven hoofs and turn them into horrid solid hoofs like a wretched horse's. And if she is extra and specially angry she'll turn me into stone and I shall be only a statue of a Faun in her horrible house until the four thrones at Cair Paravel are filled— and goodness knows when that will happen, or whether it will ever happen at all."

"I'm very sorry, Mr. Tumnus," said Lucy. "But please let me go home."

"Of course I will," said the Faun. "Of course I've got to. I see that now. I hadn't known what Humans were like before I met you. Of course I can't give you up

to the Witch; not now that I know you. But we must be off at once. I'll see you back to the lamppost. I suppose you can find your own way from there back to Spare Oom and War Drobe?"

"I'm sure I can," said Lucy.

"We must go as quietly as we can," said Mr. Tumnus. "The whole wood is full of *her* spies. Even some of the trees are on her side."

They both got up and left the tea things on the table, and Mr. Tumnus once more put up his umbrella and gave Lucy his arm, and they went out into the snow. The journey back was not at all like the journey to the Faun's cave. They stole along as quickly as they could, without speaking a word, and Mr. Tumnus kept to the darkest places. Lucy was relieved when they reached the lamppost again.

"Do you know your way from here, Daughter of Eve?" said Tumnus.

Lucy looked very hard between the trees and could just see in the distance a patch of light that looked like daylight. "Yes," she said, "I can see the wardrobe door."

"Then be off home as quick as you can," said the Faun, "and—c-can you ever forgive me for what I meant to do?"

"Why, of course I can," said Lucy, shaking him heartily by the hand. "And I do hope you won't get into dreadful trouble on my account."

"Farewell, Daughter of Eve," said he. "Perhaps I may keep the handkerchief?"

"Rather!" said Lucy, and then ran towards the far-off patch of daylight as quickly as her legs would carry her. And presently instead of rough branches brushing past her she felt coats, and instead of crunching snow under her feet she felt wooden boards, and all at once she found herself jumping out of the wardrobe into the same empty room from which the whole adventure had started. She shut the wardrobe door tightly behind her and looked around, panting for breath. It was still raining and she could hear the voices of the others in the passage.

"I'm here," she shouted. "I'm here. I've come back, I'm all right."

Some students may wish to read all of *The Chronicles of Narnia* as well as the rest of *The Lion, the Witch, and the Wardrobe.* See page T62 for these titles.

Discussion Questions *When did you first suspect that Tumnus might have a secret?* (When they met, he began to say something but stopped himself.) *When did Lucy first realize that she was in danger?* (When she was ready to leave, Tumnus told her she could not go home.) *What might Lucy see if she returned to Narnia?* (Possible answers: other mythical creatures; the four thrones at Cair Paravel.) *Do you think you would step through the wardrobe as Lucy did? Why or why not?* (Encourage the students to explain whether they feel it would be foolish or courageous.)

Enriching Activities   1. *Story maps.* Have the students draw maps of Narnia and label landmarks and places mentioned in the story. They may want to refer to C. S. Lewis's book, *The Lion, the Witch, and the Wardrobe* (Macmillan, 1970).   **2.** *Improvisation.* Have pairs of students be Mr. Tumnus and another faun. Direct Mr. Tumnus to describe his encounter with Lucy, and his friend to tell why Tumnus should have kidnapped her.

Questions

1. Why did Mr. Tumnus say he was a bad faun?

2. Mr. Tumnus did not know what he should do about Lucy. What was his conflict? How did he solve it?

3. Lucy was firm with Mr. Tumnus, but also kind. Find at least one place in the story that shows this.

4. When the story ends, who is still in trouble? What might happen to help that character?

5. When Peter says ''We've fallen on our feet,'' what does he mean?
   a. Our feet are tired so we should go to bed.
   b. We were lucky.
   c. We were in serious trouble.
   d. We should have looked where we were walking.

1. Literal/recall
He was planning to kidnap Lucy and give her to the White Witch. (page 271)
2. Literal/recall
He likes Lucy and does not want to harm her, but he is afraid of the witch. He lets Lucy go. (pages 271–273)
3. Literal/recall
Possible answers: she tries to comfort him when he cries (page 270); she tells him that he is a good faun (page 271); she forgives him for having planned to kidnap her (page 273).
4. Literal/recall
Mr. Tumnus is still in trouble because he has not brought Lucy to the witch. (page 273) **Interpretive/extrapolation** Perhaps Lucy will return to help Mr. Tumnus.
5. Vocabulary b. (page 259)

Interpretive/extrapolation   *Word play.* You might suggest place names such as Suit of Ar Mor or Londonair Aids.

Activity

Mr. Tumnus was not familiar with Lucy's world. He thought of the *spare room* from which Lucy came as ''the far land of Spare Oom.'' The *wardrobe* he saw as ''the bright city of War Drobe.'' Find words or phrases in the story that would make humorous names of places. Use these words in sentences that show your meaning.

Objectives ● To identify the main idea (theme) of a story. ● To compare story characters. ● To identify sensory details in a description. ● To relate story events to an imaginary personal experience. ● To extrapolate an event based on a story. **Synopsis of the Story** Challenged by a dare, Egan climbs Kneeknock Rise to find the fearful monster, the Megrimum. He knows he faces danger because this same trek was made by his Uncle Ott, who never returned. Though afraid when he hears the moans of the Megrimum, Egan climbs to the mountain top, where he discovers his missing Uncle Ott. When Uncle Ott explains that the moaning sounds are produced by steam from a hot spring and that there is no Megrimum, Egan wants to tell everyone in Instep. Uncle Ott warns Egan that the villagers may not really want to know the truth about their monster.

The Megrimum

Reading Level Average.

From the novel *Kneeknock Rise* by Natalie Babbitt

Illustrated by Arvis Stewart

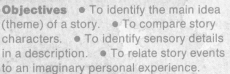

Background In 1971, the novel *Knee-knock Rise* was a Newbery Honor Book and was in "Fanfare," the *Horn Book's* honor list. In 1970, it was one of the Library of Congress Children's Books of the Year and was on the American Library Association Notable Children's Books list.

Introducing the Story *Some people believe the Loch Ness monster is a creature that lives in a lake in Scotland—no one knows for sure. Name some other legendary monsters. (Possible answers: the Abominable Snowman; Bigfoot.) What kind of person might hunt to find such monsters? (Possible answers: someone brave or foolhardy; someone anxious to prove or disprove the legend.) The Megrimum is a monster feared by the villagers of Instep. Egan, the hero of this story, decides to find out if the Megrimum really exists. Join Egan in his climb up Kneeknock Rise by reading "The Megrimum."*

The village of Instep lies at the foot of a huge cliff known as Kneeknock Rise. Though no one has ever seen it, on stormy nights people can hear unearthly moans coming from a creature called the Megrimum, who lives at the top of the Rise. Once a year people come from afar to the Instep Fair, to eat and dance, be entertained, and hear the Megrimum for themselves. When young Egan comes to his first Instep Fair, he finds everyone, including his Uncle Anson and Aunt Gertrude, talking of little else than the fearful monster. Cousin Ada says that the Megrimum has eaten foolish Uncle Ott, who went off some days ago leaving behind his old dog, Annabelle, and some of his verses. Aunt Gertrude claims she saw the Megrimum's horrible face at the window one night. Finally, on a dare from Ada, Egan decides to find out about the Megrimum for himself. He takes Annabelle and begins to climb the Rise.

Aunt Gertrude stood rigid as a post, her hand on her heart, staring at her daughter.

"It's Egan, Papa! Egan," sobbed Ada. "He did it! I teased him, Papa, and he did it. He wouldn't stop."

"*What* did he do, Ada? What did Egan *do?*" cried Uncle Anson, gripping her shoulders firmly.

"Oh, Papa," she gulped, turning her face away from the alarm in her father's eyes. "It's all my fault. I dared him and he's doing it now. He's climbing, Papa. Climbing Kneeknock Rise."

"Merciful heavens!" gasped Uncle Anson, and behind him Aunt Gertrude sagged and dropped in a faint to the floor.

And all the while Egan was climbing. Up and up over rocks and weeds, up between the twisted trees, panting with excitement. From time to time he paused, waiting for Annabelle to catch up with him. The dog's sides were heaving and her tongue dangled sidewise from her jaws, but her stiff old legs churned steadily along and her eyes were bright. Then all at once it began to rain in earnest, blurring the dim light and shellacking the rocks into slippery, treacherous jewels. Egan leaned against a tree trunk to catch his breath and Annabelle dropped down at his feet. He bent over to scratch her ears and then, suddenly, the moaning began. It was loud here, half-way up the Rise, loud and horrifying and desperate.

Shellacking (line 6 from the foot of the page) means *coating a surface so that it is smooth.*

Treacherous (line 5 from the foot of the page) means *dangerous.*

278

Down through the trees it twisted with the wind, a long, unearthly moaning that rose gradually till it wound into a high and hollow wail. Egan stood transfixed with his hand on Annabelle's head and for the first time he was afraid.

Transfixed (line 4) means *motionless*.

The Megrimum was awake at last. In the fields below, the chattering ceased. Faces peered out of tent flaps and windows, serious, frightened, eager. Here and there a man or a child came out into the rain and stood quietly, listening. An old woman dragged a stool from under a little cart and sat clutching an onion, nodding with her eyes tight shut, while the rain wilted her bonnet down around her ears.

But in the village there was frantic activity. Uncle Anson, a lantern bobbing from his hand, was rushing from neighbor to neighbor. "Quick! Quick! To my house at once! Yes, it's my nephew, my wife's sister's child. He's trying to climb the Rise. We've got to stop him. What do you mean, I'm crazy? We can't just let him go!"

Soon a wet and anxious group of men were arguing and shouting before the fire in the little house, while Ada snuffled miserably in a corner and Aunt Gertrude rushed back and forth, making coffee and spilling more than she served.

"But see here, Anson, that boy won't climb all the way up!" said one of the men.

"How do you know he won't?" answered Uncle Anson grimly. "He doesn't live in Instep. He doesn't understand."

"But good lord, man," cried another, "do you realize what you're saying? You're asking us to climb the Rise!"

"I know what I'm asking!" shouted Uncle Anson. "How can you think I don't? But can I let that boy stay out there now? The Megrimum is wide awake. I've never heard it moan so loud."

"Nobody would be fool enough to climb up there," growled another man.

"That boy is fool enough, bless him," said Uncle Anson. "And I know my brother Ott would have climbed in an instant to save him. There's fools and fools, my friend. I'm going. Gertrude, where's my cap? I'm going and I'll go alone if I have to."

"I'll go, then," said one man.

"I, too," said another. "And I'll bring along my bell." And then they were all going, hurrying out into the drenching rain while high above the moaning rose and fell, winding and rippling like ribbon down the night.

But Egan was half an hour ahead by that time. And he was young and strong, alone—and determined. After his first fear, he had clenched his fists and scowled. His early jealousy of the cliff's high pride returned. He searched about him among the trees and found a long, sharp stick.

"Look out up there!" he yelled into the rain. "I'm coming up!"

Off he went again, Annabelle struggling along behind him. And by the time his rescuers were beginning the climb, Egan had come nearly to the top, and the mist that hung there reached out gently and gathered him in.

After they complete the story, have the students reread the passage from "Egan stood uncertainly. . . ." to ". . . by the wizard moon." Ask the students to point out the sound and light imagery in this description. Explain that these details make the setting seem magical and mysterious.

Egan stood uncertainly in the mist. The rain was easing off. There had been no sound from the Megrimum for many minutes now. A mumble of thunder complained from far away and then the clouds parted and the moon rode free. Instantly the mist was luminous, and Egan, with a gasp, felt as if he had suddenly been tucked inside a bubble. Looking up, he saw the moon as a shapeless radiance, like a candle seen through steamy glass. Each drop of moisture in the mist had become a tiny prism, filtering and fanning the dim light into a million pale rainbows of softest color. From a shrouded treetop nearby came the soft, clear notes of a bird's call and, with the faintest of rustles, a small red kneeknock bird floated through the mist ahead of him. Egan held his breath and stared at the magic world around him, a nighttime world bewitched into seeming morning by the wizard moon. Annabelle

stood silent at his feet, and then, all at once, the
old dog stiffened and whined. Nudged in his trance,
Egan bent to soothe her but she pulled away from
his hand, her ears high. She whined again, moved
forward, stopped with tilted head, listening. Then
with a yelp she ran on into the mist and disappeared.
From somewhere up ahead a low groan echoed and
Egan, his stick in his hand, moved slowly after Annabelle, straight toward the very top of Kneeknock Rise.

On the cliffside below, the rescuers paused.

"The storm is over. Look, there's the moon!" said one of the men. "And the Megrimum's been quiet for quite a while now."

"Look here, Anson," said another. "I think we should search around a bit. That boy of yours can't have gone all the way up. He must be somewhere about."

"Perhaps," said Uncle Anson. "We'll divide up and look. But if we don't find him, I'm going on to the top."

With swaying arcs of lantern light washing the dark, the men spread out among the trees along the side of the Rise. Below, in her garden behind the little house, Aunt Gertrude stood wringing her hands. She could hear, faintly, the tinkling of the bell, warning away the Megrimum, and heard as well the

284

distant, muffled voice of her husband calling: "Egan! Egan! Where are you, Nephew? E-e-e-gan!"

Out in the fields, the visitors knew something had happened.

"A boy, you say?"

"What? Climbing up the Rise?"

"A terrible thing—terrible. It called the child, perhaps, called the child to climb."

"Where was the boy's mother, then, to let him run away?"

"They're climbing up to find him. Look—see the lights of the lanterns."

"Brave men, brave men all."

"Never come down again, ever."

Egan, deep in the mist, heard nothing. He wandered up the final stony slope toward the top like a sleepwalker lost in dreams. The heavy air around him, tinted and dim and moist, was growing unaccountably warmer, and a faint, unpleasant smell he could not quite recognize crept into his nostrils. And then he stopped, chilled suddenly out of his trance. Just ahead there came a noise as of an animal thrashing about, and the low rumble of a voice.

He crept forward, grasping the nearly forgotten stick tightly, and his heart pounded. The Megrimum! At last, the Megrimum! Slay it, perhaps—perhaps; but at least he would see it.

More thrashing in the weeds ahead. "Owanna-ooowanna," the voice seemed to murmur.

Closer and closer crept Egan and then he saw it dimly, all <u>flailing</u> arms, rolling about on the ground.

Flailing means *waving wildly.*

285

Another few cautious steps, and then:

"Oh, Anna, Anna, dear old dog!" crooned the voice. There before him, sitting on the ground, was a wild-haired, laughing man who had to be his Uncle Ott, engulfed and struggling happily in the wriggling, wagging ecstasy of Annabelle.

Egan stood with his mouth hanging open. The stick dropped from his hand, and at the sound the man and the dog paused in their greeting and looked toward him. Annabelle trotted over and beamed at him and then turned back.

"Hallo there, boy. Who might you be?" said the man warily.

Egan gulped. "Why, I'm your nephew. Sort of. That is, if you really *are* my Uncle Anson's brother. Are you? Are you Uncle Ott?"

"That's right!" said Uncle Ott in great surprise. "And you—you must be Anson's wife's sister's boy. I guess I've got that right. But what in the name of goodness are you doing up here?"

"I came . . . " Egan paused. "Well, I came to kill the Megrimum." He waited for his uncle to laugh or scold, but Ott did neither. He merely nodded as if it were all quite natural. "But where *is* the Megrimum?" asked Egan. "And why is it so awfully warm up here?"

Uncle Ott stood up and brushed bits of twigs and leaves from his clothes.

"The Megrimum. Yes. I came to find it, too." He paused and looked thoughtfully at Egan and then, in a rush, he said, "Boy, listen to me. There isn't any Megrimum. Never was. It's all been just a lot of—

megrimummery, if you will. It's too bad, that's what it is. Too bad. Come along. I'll show you."

Close to the top of Kneeknock Rise lay a shallow cave. At the mouth of the cave the mist was very thick and as hot as steam, and the strange, unpleasant smell was almost overwhelming.

"Phew!" said Egan. "What in the world is in there? It must be something very rotten and dreadful!"

"No, not at all," said Uncle Ott. "It's only a mineral spring. Sulphur. Nasty, but not unnatural."

"A spring?" puzzled Egan. "But how could it be a spring? Springs aren't hot."

"Sometimes they are," said Uncle Ott. "This cliff must have been a volcano long ago. The water boils

Explain that *sulphur* is a common element in volcanic spring water. When water mixed with sulphur boils, as in a hot spring, a gas, with an unpleasant smell resembling rotten eggs, is formed.

up to the top through a narrow hole, from far under the earth where it's very hot. And that makes this steamy mist. Usually the hole lets the steam through quietly, but when rain seeps into the hot places—more pressure, more steam. And the steam makes the whistling, whining, moaning sound as it shoots out the top of the hole. Just like a boiling kettle. The cave echoes and makes the sound even louder, and that, my dear boy, is the long-feared, long-loved Megrimum."

Egan stood and stared and then all at once he was very pleased. "I knew this old cliff wasn't so wonderful," he said. "Can I go in there and look at the spring?"

Uncle Ott shook his head. "Too hot," he said. "And anyway, there's not much to it. Just a hole in the ground and a lot of hot rocks." He shook his head again and sighed. "Too bad about that. Just a hole in the ground."

They turned away from the cave and walked back to where Annabelle sat waiting for them. "Come down to Instep with me and we'll tell them about it," said Egan. "We can both sleep in your room. I'll sleep on the floor with Annabelle."

"No, no, I think I won't go down to Instep," said Uncle Ott, running his fingers through his wild white hair. "Now that I've got my own dear Annabelle with me—and I do thank you for bringing her up—I guess I'll just go on down the other side."

"Have you been up here all the time?" asked Egan.

"Yes, as a matter of fact I have. I came up thinking I'd be going right back down again, so I didn't bring Annabelle along, and anyway, I was afraid she'd have trouble with the climbing. But when I got up here, the air was so wet and hot—well, it just did wonders for my wheezing. Absolute wonders. See? I can breathe perfectly well!" He took several deep breaths to show that it was true. "It's been a blessing. But now I guess I'll move along."

Egan had a sudden idea. "It was you that night, wasn't it? Tapping at the window?"

Uncle Ott looked embarrassed. "That was too bad. I thought I could get Annabelle to come to

the window and then I could lift her out and take her away with me. But there was Gertrude all of a sudden, screaming, and I had to go away. I felt very bad about scaring her."

"But I don't see why you didn't just come into the house," said Egan. "During the day. And take Annabelle then."

"Because," said Uncle Ott slowly, "I didn't want to have to explain."

Egan was puzzled. "About the Megrimum, you mean?" he asked. "Why not? They're all scared to death of the Megrimum. They'd be happy to hear there isn't one after all."

"Do you think so?" said Uncle Ott. "I really don't know about that. I've been thinking and thinking about that." He looked at Egan sadly. "Is it better to be wise if it makes you solemn and practical, or is it better to be foolish so you can go on enjoying yourself?"

"The king and the fool!" said Egan, suddenly understanding.

"Exactly," said Uncle Ott. "Exactly. I see you've been reading my verses. I've been interested for years in this problem of kings and fools. Now here I am with a perfect example of the question and I really don't know the answer." He sat down on the ground beside Annabelle and stared off into the mist, rubbing his chin. "For me it's always been important to find out the why of things. To try to be wise. But I can't say it's ever made me happier. As for those people down below, they've had their Megrimum for years and years. And I don't know as I want to spoil it all for them. There's always the possibility that they're happier believing. Kind of a nice idea, this Megrimum." He stood up and pulled his jacket close around his chest, breathing the mist deeply. "Yes, it's kind of a nice idea in an odd kind of way," he said. "Do as you like about it. If I knew what was best, I'd certainly tell you, but the fact is I don't. Well, come along, Annabelle. Good-bye, Nephew. A pleasure to have seen you."

He started off and then he paused and stood thinking for a moment. At last he turned and came back. "I've just had another thought on the matter," he said. "It came to me in rhyme. Thoughts often come to me that way—I don't seem to be able to help it:

The cat attacked a bit of string
  And dragged it by the head
And tortured it beside the stove
  And left it there for dead.

"Excuse me, sir," I murmured when
  He passed me in the hall,
"But that was only string you had
  And not a mouse at all!"

He didn't even thank me when
  I told him he was wrong.
It's possible—just possible—
  He knew it all along.

"Well, there it is, for what it's worth. Good-bye." Uncle Ott smiled and then, with Annabelle wagging at his side, he turned and vanished into the mist.

Questions

1. What did the villagers think the Megrimum was?

2. What did Egan find out the Megrimum *really* was?

3. Do you think that Egan should tell the villagers the truth about the Megrimum? Why or why not?

4. Give two reasons why Uncle Ott stayed on Knee-knock Rise with the Megrimum.

5. The author used unusual and interesting language to make this story exciting to read. Which words did the author use to make each of the following descriptions more interesting?
   a. The rain _____ the rocks.

      shellacked   fell on   moistened

   b. The world was bewitched by the _____ moon.

      bright   wizard   cheese-colored

Activity   *Writing.*

Imagine that there is a secret room in your house. No one has ever been in it, but people have said that once each year strange noises can be heard coming from inside the room. Then unusual events begin to happen. Write about an unusual experience you once had when the "noises" began.

About NATALIE BABBITT

Natalie Babbitt's mother was an artist, and at first Natalie followed in her mother's footsteps. She studied art in high school and college. After she married, she and her husband worked on a children's book together. It was called *The 49th Magician*. Her husband wrote the story and she drew the pictures. Later, Natalie herself decided to try writing. "Now I am far more interested in writing than in illustrating," she says.

When Natalie Babbitt began to write *Kneeknock Rise,* she set out to write about the main character in *The 49th Magician*. "It was to have been only a funny story," she says, "but it got away from me." The magician character became a child, and Natalie Babbitt wondered what the child would find at the top of the mountain. "This led to the Kneeknock verse about the other side of the hill," she explains, "and eventually to the Megrimum."

Natalie Babbitt's story ideas begin with her interest in a word or phrase. Then she creates the characters, thinks about the adventures they would have, and begins to write.

More Books by Natalie Babbitt

The Eyes of the Amaryllis   (Farrar, Straus & Giroux, 1977)
The Devil's Storybook   (Farrar, Straus & Giroux, 1974)
The Search for Delicious   (Farrar, Straus & Giroux, 1969)

The Secret Sits

A poem by Robert Frost

Objective ● To note that a poem is a succinct way of expressing an idea.

Introducing the Poem *Robert Frost was a poet who did not waste words. This poem shows how much can be said in a few words.*

Discussion Question *What do you think the poem means?* (Possible answers: that we may never find the answers to questions we wonder about; that our thoughts may go in circles as we think about the unknown and search for the truth.)

Enriching Activity *Art/writing.* Have the students draw a picture or write about something they found mysterious and now understand, or something they still wonder about.

We dance round in a ring and suppose,
But the Secret sits in the middle and knows.

Illustrated by Jan Brett

BOOKSHELF

The Borrowers Aloft by Mary Norton. Harcourt, Brace & World, 1961. Tiny people no taller than a pencil go on a voyage in a teakettle to search for a new home. This is the last book in a series of four.
Reading Level Average

The Children of Green Knowe by L. M. Boston. Harcourt, Brace & World, 1955. In this first book in a series of five, Tolly comes to live with his great-grandmother in an ancient house. His playmates are the same children who lived there two hundred years ago. **Reading Level** Average

The House of Dies Drear by Virginia Hamilton. Macmillan, 1968. Thirteen-year-old Thomas tries to solve a mystery in an enormous mansion that was once a station on the Underground Railroad. **Reading Level** Challenging

Into the Dream by William Sleator. E. P. Dutton, 1979. Paul and Francine are troubled by identical nightmares in which a child's life seems threatened. They work together to end their nightmares and to solve a fantastic riddle. **Reading Level** Average

The Selchie's Seed by Shulamith Oppenheim. Bradbury Press, 1975. For many years Marian has heard the legend of the seal people and her own enchanted family heritage. When she hears the call from the sea, she knows she must answer it. **Reading Level** Average

The Ring in the Prairie: A Shawnee legend edited by John Bierhorst. Dial Press, 1970. Enchanted by the youngest of the star princesses, Waupee cannot rest until he makes her his wife. But a star princess is not meant to live an earthly life. **Reading Level** Challenging

5 To Live With Nature

You have to be careful with snakes—
some are dangerous, and some are
harmless, and you had better know the
difference. Take Old Ben, for example.
That old blacksnake was as harmless
as a kitten.

Objectives ● To enjoy a true story. ● To examine changes in a character's attitude. ● To write about an autobiographical incident. ● To chart the events in a story in chronological order. ● To consider how setting affects a story.

Synopsis of the Story The narrator of the story finds a large, friendly blacksnake and brings it home to the family farm. Eventually everyone becomes fond of Old Ben, who keeps the corncrib free from mice through the summer and fall. One summer day Old Ben is missing. After discovering his track leading to the hogpen, the family sadly realizes that Old Ben has been killed.

Introducing the Story *If you could have any pet you wanted, what would it be? Why? "Old Ben" is a true story about the author's boyhood pet—a blacksnake. Think about how you react to snakes now, and see if this story changes your mind.*

OLD BEN

Reading Level Easy

A short story by Jesse Stuart

Illustrated by John Hamburger

One morning in July when I was walking across a clover field to a sweet-apple tree, I almost stepped on him. There he lay coiled like heavy strands of black rope. He was a big bull blacksnake. We looked at each other a minute, and then I stuck the toe of my shoe up to his mouth. He drew his head back in a friendly way. He didn't want trouble. Had he shown the least fight, I would have soon finished him. My father had always told me there was only one good snake—a dead one.

When the big fellow didn't show any fight, I reached down and picked him up by the neck. When I lifted him he was as long as I was tall. That was six feet. I started calling him Old Ben as I held him by the neck and rubbed his back. He enjoyed having his back rubbed and his head stroked. Then I lifted him into my arms. He was the first snake I'd ever been friendly with. I was afraid at first to let Old Ben wrap himself around me. I thought he might wrap himself around my neck and choke me.

Several varieties of *blacksnake* are found in the United States. They are not poisonous, and they are valuable because they kill rats and mice.

The more I petted him, the more affectionate he became. He was so friendly I decided to trust him. I wrapped him around my neck a couple of times and let him loose. He crawled down one arm and went back to my neck, around and down the other arm and back again. He stuck out his forked tongue to the sound of my voice as I talked to him.

"I wouldn't kill you at all," I said. "You're a friendly snake. I'm taking you home with me."

I headed home with Old Ben wrapped around my neck and shoulders. When I started over the hill by the pine grove, I met my cousin Wayne Holbrook coming up the hill. He stopped suddenly when he saw me. He started backing down the hill.

"He's a pet, Wayne," I said. "Don't be afraid of Old Ben."

It was a minute before Wayne could tell me what he wanted. He had come to borrow a plow. He kept a safe distance as we walked on together.

Before we reached the barn, Wayne got brave enough to touch Old Ben's long body.

"What are you going to do with him?" Wayne asked. "Uncle Mick won't let you keep him!"

"Put him in the corncrib," I said. "He'll have plenty of delicate food in there. The cats we keep at this barn have grown fat and lazy on the milk we feed 'em."

I opened the corncrib door and took Old Ben from around my neck because he was beginning to get warm and a little heavy.

A *corncrib* is a building used for drying and storing corn.

"This will be your home," I said. "You'd better hide under the corn."

Besides my father, I knew Old Ben would have another enemy at our home. He was our hunting dog, Blackie, who would trail a snake, same as a possum or mink. He had treed blacksnakes, and my father had shot them from the trees. I knew Blackie would find Old Ben, because he followed us to the barn each morning.

The first morning after I'd put Old Ben in the corncrib, Blackie followed us. He started toward the corncrib holding his head high, sniffing. He stuck his nose up to a crack in the crib and began to bark. Then he tried to tear a plank off.

"Stop it, Blackie," Pa scolded him. "What's the matter with you? Have you taken to barking at mice?"

"Blackie is not barking at a mouse," I said. "I put a blacksnake in there yesterday!"

"A blacksnake?" Pa asked, looking unbelievingly. "A blacksnake?"

"Yes, a pet blacksnake." I said.

"Have you gone crazy?" he said. "I'll move a thousand bushels of corn to get that snake!"

"You won't mind this one," I said. "You and Mom will love him."

My father said a few unprintable words before we started back to the house. After breakfast, when Pa and Mom came to the barn, I was already there. I had opened the crib door and there was Old Ben. He'd crawled up front and was coiled on a sack. I put my hand down and he crawled up my arm to my neck and over my shoulder. When Mom and Pa reached the crib, I thought Pa was going to faint.

"He has a pet snake," Mom said.

"Won't be a bird or a young chicken left on this place," Pa said. "Every time I pick up an ear of corn in that crib, I'll be jumping."

"Pa, he won't hurt you," I said, patting the snake's head. "He's a natural pet, or somebody has tamed him. And he's not going to bother birds and young chickens when there are so many mice in this crib."

"Mick, let him keep the snake," Mom said. "I won't be afraid of it."

This was the beginning of a long friendship.

Mom went to the corncrib morning after morning and shelled corn for her geese and chickens. Often Old Ben would be lying in front on his burlap sack. Mom watched him at first from the corner of her eye. Later she didn't bother to watch him any more than she did a cat that came up for his milk.

Shelled means separated the kernels from the cobs.

Later it occurred to us that Old Ben might like milk, too. We started leaving milk for him. We never saw him drink it, but his pan was always empty when we returned. We know the mice didn't drink it, because he took care of them.

"One thing is certain," Mom said one morning
when she went to shell corn. "We don't find any more
corn chewed up by the mice and left on the floor."

July passed and August came. My father got used to Old Ben, but not until he had proved his worth. Ben had done something our nine cats couldn't. He had cleaned the corncrib of mice.

Then my father began to worry about Old Ben's going after water, and Blackie's finding his track. So he put water in the crib.

September came and went. We began wondering where our pet would go when days grew colder. One morning in early October we left milk for Old Ben, and it was there when we went back that afternoon. But Old Ben wasn't there.

"Old Ben's a good pet for the warm months," Pa said. "But in the winter months, my cats will have to do the work. Maybe Blackie got him!"

"He might have holed up for the winter in the hay-loft," I told Pa after we had removed all the corn and didn't find him. "I'm worried about him. I've had a lot of pets—ground hogs, crows, and hawks—but Old Ben's the best yet."

November, December, January, February, and March came and went. Of course we never expected to see Old Ben in one of those months. We doubted if we ever would see him again.

One day early in April I went to the corncrib, and Old Ben lay stretched across the floor. He looked taller than I was now. His skin was rough and his long body had a flabby appearance. I knew Old Ben needed mice and milk. I picked him up, petted him, and told him so. But the chill of early April was still with him. He got his tongue out slower to answer the kind words I was saying to him. He tried to crawl up my arm but he couldn't make it.

That spring and summer mice got scarce in the corncrib and Old Ben got daring. He went over to the barn and crawled up into the hayloft, where he had many feasts. But he made one mistake.

He crawled from the hayloft down into Fred's feed box, where it was cool. Old Fred was our horse.

There he lay coiled when the horse came in and put his nose down on top of Old Ben. Fred let out a big snort and started kicking. He kicked down a par-tition, and then turned his heels on his feed box and kicked it down. Lucky for Old Ben that he got out in one piece. But he got back to his crib.

A *partition* is a wall that divides a room into two smaller rooms.

Old Ben became a part of our barnyard family, a pet and darling of all. When children came to play with my brother and sisters, they always went to the crib and got Old Ben. He enjoyed the children, who were afraid of him at first but later learned to pet this kind old reptile.

All snakes, turtles, and lizards are *reptiles*.

Summer passed and the late days of September were very humid. Old Ben failed one morning to drink his milk. We knew it wasn't time for him to hole up for the winter.

We knew something had happened.

Pa and I moved the corn searching for him. Mom made a couple of trips to the barn lot to see if we had found him. But all we found was the rough skin he had shed last spring.

"Fred's never been very sociable with Old Ben since he got in his box that time," Pa said. "I wonder if he could have stomped Old Ben to death. Old Ben could've been crawling over the barn lot, and Fred saw his chance to get even!"

"We'll see," I said.

Pa and I left the crib and walked to the barn lot. He went one way and I went the other, each searching the ground.

Mom came through the gate and walked over where my father was looking. She started looking around, too.

"We think Fred might've got him," Pa said. "We're sure Fred's got it in for him over Old Ben getting in his feed box last summer."

"You're accusing Fred wrong," Mom said. "Here's Old Ben's track in the sand."

I ran over to where Mom had found the track. Pa went over to look, too.

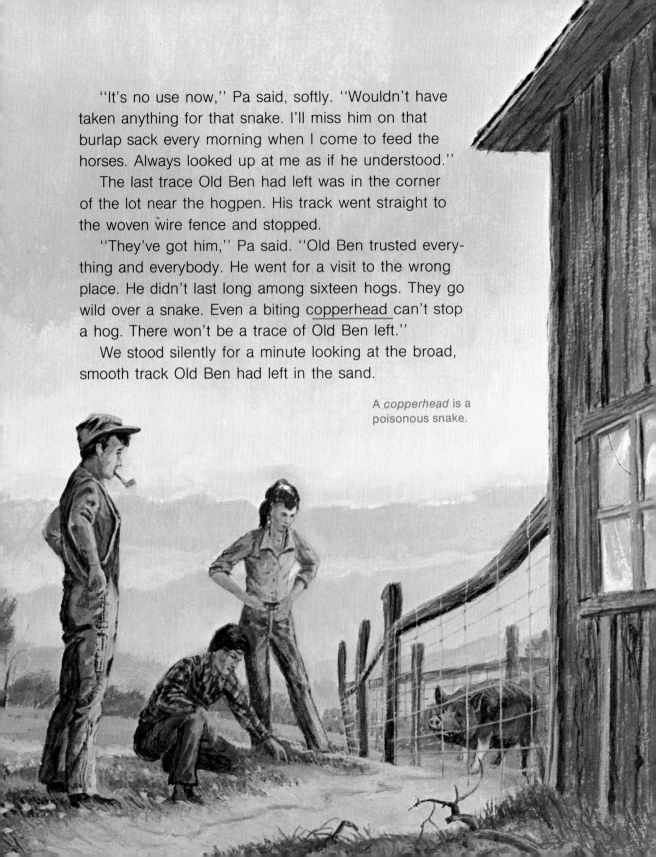

"It's no use now," Pa said, softly. "Wouldn't have taken anything for that snake. I'll miss him on that burlap sack every morning when I come to feed the horses. Always looked up at me as if he understood."

The last trace Old Ben had left was in the corner of the lot near the hogpen. His track went straight to the woven wire fence and stopped.

"They've got him," Pa said. "Old Ben trusted everything and everybody. He went for a visit to the wrong place. He didn't last long among sixteen hogs. They go wild over a snake. Even a biting copperhead can't stop a hog. There won't be a trace of Old Ben left."

We stood silently for a minute looking at the broad, smooth track Old Ben had left in the sand.

A *copperhead* is a poisonous snake.

Discussion Questions *If the narrator lived in a city, how would the story change?* (Possible answer: he might not have found the snake or been able to keep him.) *If you could have a pet snake, would you want one? Tell why or why not.*

Enriching Activities **1.** *Story time line.* Have small groups of students make time lines showing the major events that occurred during the fifteen months that Old Ben was the narrator's pet. Tell the students to include at least six events on their time lines.

2. *Research.* Have each student think of an animal that would make an unusual pet. Ask the students to consult references and prepare brief reports about their animals. Have them list five things that they would have to do to keep the animals as pets and state why their animals would or would not make good pets.

Questions

1. Literal / recall At first they feared the snake or thought that he was dangerous. (pages 299, 302) Later they trusted and liked him. (pages 304, 306)

2. Literal / recall Possible answers: he became affectionate (page 300); he stuck out his tongue as if to answer (page 300); he looked as if he understood Pa's actions. (page 307)

3. Critical / relating to experience Possible answers: it was a good ending because it was realistic; it would have been better if Old Ben had lived because happy endings are more satisfying. (page 307)

4. Vocabulary a. "There he lay coiled like heavy strands of black rope . . . ." b. ". . . the broad, smooth track Old Ben had left in the sand." (page 307)

1. How did people react to Old Ben when they first met him? How did they react to him later?

2. Tell two things that show how Old Ben reacted to people who were friendly to him.

3. The story has a sad ending. Would you rather that it had a happy ending? Why or why not?

4. The author is well known for the simple, yet interesting way in which he retells events from his own life. Find the places in "Old Ben" where he has written the following ideas. Then write the words he has used to make these ideas more interesting.
   a. Old Ben was like a rope. (page 299)
   b. Old Ben left a track in the sand. (page 307)

Activity

Critical / relating to experience *Writing.* If the students cannot think of an incident with nature, suggest that they choose any important, funny, or exciting incident in their lives.

"Old Ben" is based on the *true story* of a pet blacksnake the author once had. A true story or account is called *nonfiction.* The true story of one's own life is called an *autobiography.* Suppose that you are writing about an incident for your autobiography. The incident is about a time when you came upon something in nature, either an enemy or a friend. Write some notes you'll use to help you recall that incident when you write your autobiography.

Riddle

A poem by Elizabeth Coatsworth

What is it cries without a mouth?
What buffets,[1] and yet has no hand?
And, footless, runs upon the waves
To drive them roaring up the sand?

Old as the world, unseen as Time,
Without beginning, without end,
What is it cries and has no mouth,
Wave-wrestler, and the sea gulls' friend?

---

1. **buffets** (BUF•its): to strike over and over.

I Called to the Wind

A haiku by Kyorai /kyorʹ·ī/

Translated by Harry Behn

Objectives (See page 309.)
Introducing the Poem *This poem is a haiku, a traditional form of Japanese poetry that describes an image or event in nature.*

> I called to the wind,
> "Who's there?" . . . Whoever it was
> still knocks at my gate.

A haiku paints a picture in a few words—it has seventeen syllables and is usually written in three lines. Try to picture what happens as you read the poem.
Discussion Questions *What happens in this poem? (A gate swings in the wind.) A haiku describes an event as if it were happening now. Which words give you this feeling? (". . . still knocks.")*
Enriching Activity *Oral reading.* Have the students read aloud some haiku from Harry Behn's *Cricket Songs* (Harcourt Brace Jovanovich, 1964) and *More Cricket Songs,* (Harcourt Brace Jovanovich, 1971).

Illustrated by Christa Keiffer

Wind Is a Ghost

A Dakota poem

Retold by Natalia Belting

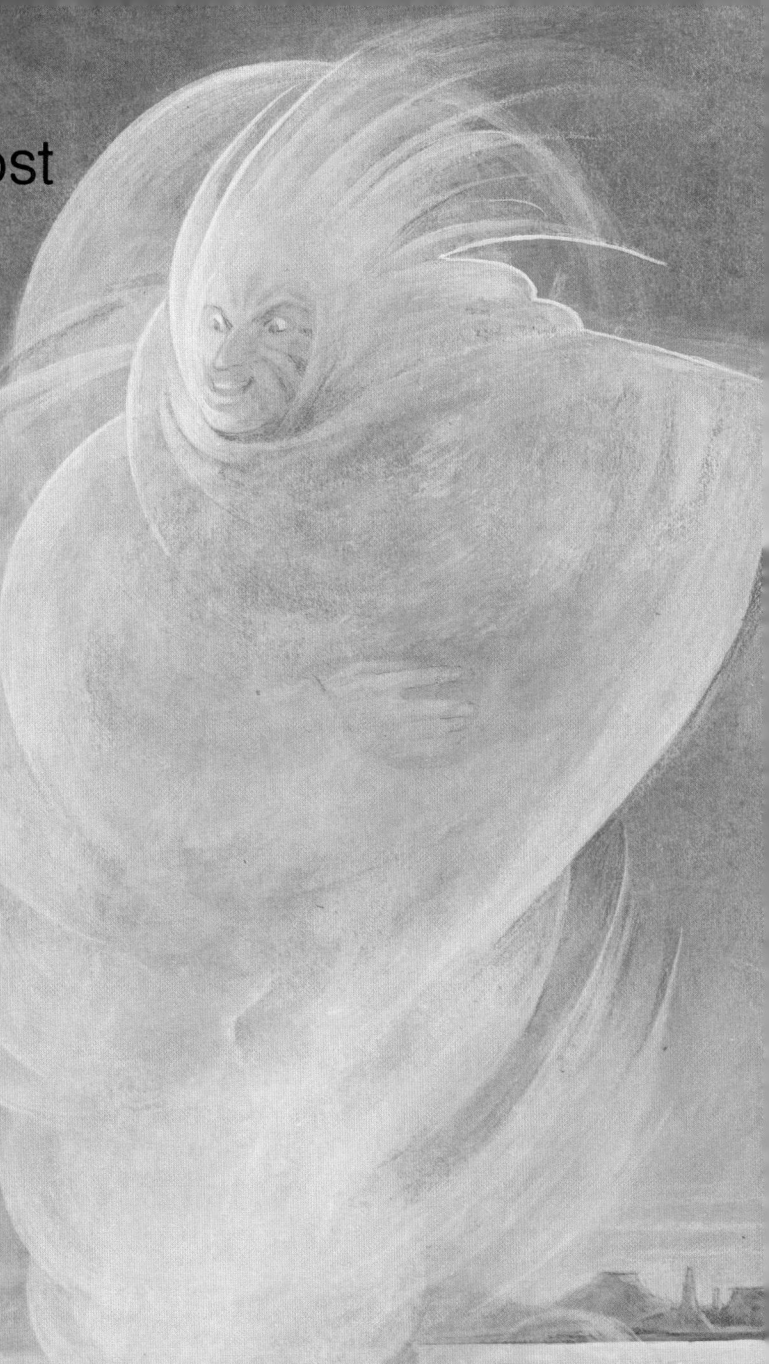

Wind is a ghost
That whirls and turns,
Twists in fleet moccasins,
Sweeps up dust spinning
Across the dry flatlands.

Whirlwind
Is a ghost dancing.

Objectives (See page 309.)

Introducing the Poem *This poem about wind uses a* metaphor. *See if you can tell what it is.*

Discussion Questions *To what does the poet compare the wind?* (A ghost.) *How are the three poems on pages 309, 310, and 311 alike?* (All are about the wind; each uses personification.) *How are they different?* (Possible answers: their forms differ; only one rhymes and has a regular rhythm.)

Enriching Activities **1.** *Music.* Have the students accompany an oral reading of each poem with music (original or recorded) suited to the poem's mood. **2.** *Illustrating poems.* Encourage the students to find a few poems on the same subject, to hand-letter the poems, and to illustrate them with drawings or magazine pictures. The students could bind the poems into small books.

Illustrated by Christa Keiffer

Objectives ● To describe a main character's traits. ● To identify a problem and a solution based on a story's setting. ● To identify *human beings versus nature* as the conflict in a story. ● To dramatize a story scene.

Synopsis of the Story   Bill and his family are aboard a spaceship to one of Jupiter's moons. When the floor of Bill's cabin is punctured by a meteorite, airtight doors swiftly seal off the cabin. Bill stuffs his scout uniform into the hole, calms his panicking bunkmates, and uses a foam-rubber pillow to plug the leak further. As a result, enough oxygen is retained to keep Bill and his bunkmates alive. Soon they are moved to safety, and the hole is patched. Bill receives an official commendation from the captain.

Reading Level   Challenging

Emergency in Space

From the science fiction novel *Farmer in the Sky* by Robert A. Heinlein

Illustrated by Lyle Miller

Some time in the future, the spaceship Mayflower *spins through space toward Ganymede,[1] a moon of the planet Jupiter more than half a billion miles from Earth. The 6,000 Earth people inside the* Mayflower, *like the Pilgrims on the original ship* Mayflower, *are traveling to settle a new colony in a new world.*

For Bill Lermer, one of the colonists, the decision to leave Earth had been a difficult one. He was leaving his high-school friends and the scout troop in which he had long been active to be with his father, George, who was emigrating with his new wife Molly and her daughter Peggy. With strict weight limits for each traveler, Bill had packed carefully—even going without food so that he could take one unnecessary item. As Bill tells it, "I began to wonder why I was going to all this trouble to hang on to a scout uniform I obviously wasn't going to use."

---

1. **Ganymede** (GAN•uh•meed): the third and largest satellite of Jupiter.

312

When we were fifty-three days out and about a week to go to reach Ganymede, Captain Harkness used the flywheel to precess[2] the ship so that we could see where we were going—so that the passengers could see, that is. It didn't make any difference to his astrogation.[3]

You see, the axis of the *Mayflower* had been pointed pretty much toward Jupiter and the torch had been pointed back at the Sun. Since the view ports were

A *flywheel* is a heavy wheel that helps maintain constant speed.

An *axis* is the straight line around which an object turns.

_____

2. **precess** (PREE•ses): to change the direction of the axis of a rotating body, much like the movement of a spinning top as it loses speed.
3. **astrogation** (AS•truh•GAY•shun): the guiding of a spaceship in space.

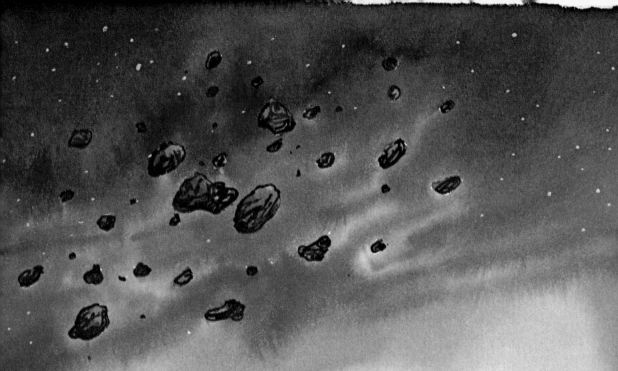

spaced every ninety degrees around the sides, while we had been able to see most of the sky, we hadn't been able to see ahead to Jupiter nor behind to the Sun. Now he tilted the ship over ninety degrees and we were rolling, so to speak, along our line of flight. That way, you could see Jupiter and the Sun both, from any view port, though not both at the same time.

Jupiter was already a tiny, ruddy-orange disc. Some of the boys claimed they could make out the moons. Frankly, I couldn't, not for the first three days after the Captain precessed the ship. But it was mighty fine to be able to see Jupiter.

We hadn't seen Mars on the way out, because Mars happened to be on the far side of the Sun, three hundred million miles away. We hadn't seen anything but the same old stars you can see from Earth. We didn't even see any asteroids.

There was a reason for that. When we took off from the orbit of Supra-New-York, Captain Harkness had not aimed the *Mayflower* straight for where Jupiter

was going to be when we got there; instead he had lifted her north of the ecliptic[4] high enough to give the asteroid[5] belt a wide berth. Now anybody knows that meteors are no real hazard in space. Unless a pilot does deliberately foolish things like driving his ship through the head of a comet it is almost impossible to get yourself hit by a meteor. They are too far between.

A *comet* is a mass of frozen gases, water, and rock material that orbits the sun. It appears to have a long, fiery tail because it reflects sunlight.

On the other hand the asteroid belt has more than its fair share of sky junk. The older power-pile ships used to drive straight through the belt, taking their chances, and none of them was ever hit to amount to anything. But Captain Harkness, having literally all the power in the world, preferred to go around and play it safe. By avoiding the belt there wasn't a chance in a blue moon that the *Mayflower* would be hit.

Well, it must have been a blue moon. We were hit.

---

4. ecliptic (ih•KLIP•tik): the plane, passing through the center of the sun, that contains the earth's orbit.
5. asteroid (AS•tuh•royd): any of several hundred small planets between Mars and Jupiter.

315

It was just after reveille,[6] "A" deck time, and I was standing by my bunk, making it up. I had my Scout uniform in my hands and was about to fold it up and put it under my pillow. I still didn't wear it. None of the others had uniforms to wear to Scout meetings so I didn't wear mine. But I still kept it tucked away in my bunk.

Suddenly I heard the strangest noise I ever heard in my life. It sounded like a rifle going off right by my ear, it sounded like a steel door being slammed, and it sounded like a giant tearing yards and yards of cloth, all at once.

Then I couldn't hear anything but a ringing in my ears and I was dazed. I shook my head and looked down and I was staring at a raw hole in the ship, almost between my feet and nearly as big as my fist. There was scorched <u>insulation</u> around it and in the middle of the hole I could see blackness—then a star whipped past and I realized that I was staring right out into space.

Insulation is material used to keep heat, electricity, sound, or other elements from leaking in or out.

There was a hissing noise.

I don't remember thinking at all. I just wadded up my uniform, squatted down, and stuffed it in the hole. For a moment it seemed as if the suction would pull it on through the hole, then it jammed and stuck and didn't go any further. But we were still losing air. I think that was the point at which I first realized that we *were* losing air and that we might be suffocated in <u>vacuum</u>.

There was somebody yelling and screaming behind me that he was killed and alarm bells were going off all over the place. You couldn't hear yourself think. The

6. **reveille** (RE•vuh•lee): the sounding of a bugle early in the morning to awaken and call together people, usually in a camp or military post.

316

airtight door to our bunk room slid across automatically
and settled into its <u>gaskets</u> and we were locked in.

That scared me to death.

I know it has to be done. I know that it is better to
seal off one compartment and kill the people who are
in it than to let a whole ship die—but, you see, *I* was in
that compartment, personally. I guess I'm just not the
hero type.

A *gasket* is a piece of
rubber, metal, or
another material that
is placed around a
joint to prevent
leakage.

I could feel the pressure sucking away at the plug my uniform made. With one part of my mind I was recalling that it had been advertised as "tropical weave, self-ventilating" and wishing that it had been a solid plastic raincoat instead. I was afraid to stuff it in any harder, for fear it would go all the way through and leave us sitting there, chewing vacuum. I would have passed up desserts for the next ten years for just one rubber patch, the size of my hand.

The screaming had stopped; now it started up again. It was Noisy Edwards, beating on the airtight door and yelling, "Let me out of here! *Get me out of here!*"

On top of that I could hear Captain Harkness's voice coming through the bull horn. He was saying, "H-twelve! Report! H-twelve! Can you hear me?"

On top of that everybody was talking at once.

I yelled: "Quiet!" at the top of my voice—and for a second or so there *was* quiet.

Peewee Brunn, one of my Cubs, was standing in front of me, looking big-eyed. "What happened, Billy?" he said.

I said, "Grab me a pillow off one of the bunks. Jump!"

He gulped and did it. I said, "Peel off the cover, quick!"

He did, making quite a mess of it, and handed it to me—but I didn't have a hand free. I said, "Put it down on top of my hands."

It was the ordinary sort of pillow, soft foam rubber. I snatched one hand out and then the other, and then I was kneeling on it and pressing it down with the heels of my hands. It dimpled a little in the middle and I was scared we were going to have a blowout right through the pillow. But it held. Noisy was screaming again and

Captain Harkness was still asking for somebody, *any-body,* in compartment H-12 to tell him what was going on. I yelled "*Quiet!*" again, and added, "Somebody slug Noisy and shut him up."

That was a popular idea. About three of them jumped to it. Noisy got clipped in the side of the neck, then some-body poked him in the pit of his stomach and they swarmed over him. "Now everybody keep quiet," I said, "and keep on keeping quiet. If Noisy lets out a peep, slug him again." I gasped and tried to take a deep breath and said, "H-twelve, reporting!"

The Captain's voice answered, "What is the situation there?"

"There is a hole in the ship, Captain, but we got it corked up."

"How? And how big a hole?"

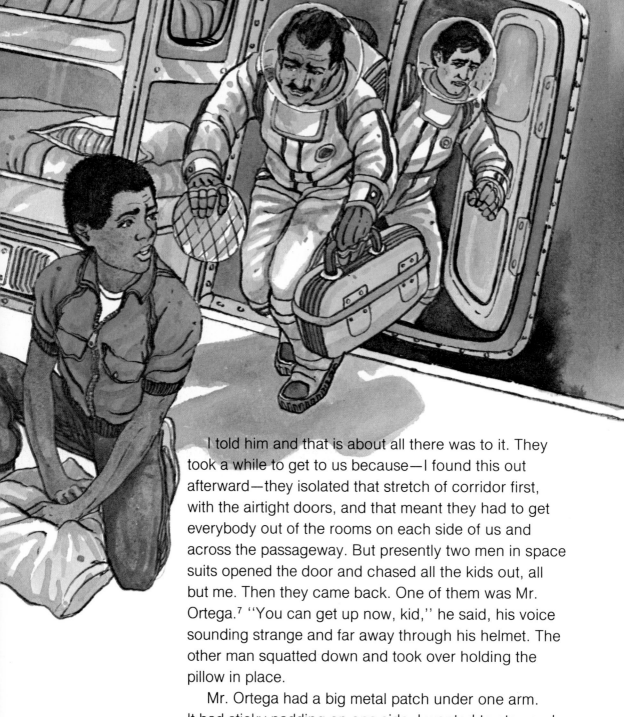

I told him and that is about all there was to it. They took a while to get to us because—I found this out afterward—they isolated that stretch of corridor first, with the airtight doors, and that meant they had to get everybody out of the rooms on each side of us and across the passageway. But presently two men in space suits opened the door and chased all the kids out, all but me. Then they came back. One of them was Mr. Ortega.[7] "You can get up now, kid," he said, his voice sounding strange and far away through his helmet. The other man squatted down and took over holding the pillow in place.

Mr. Ortega had a big metal patch under one arm. It had sticky padding on one side. I wanted to stay and watch him put it on but he chased me out and closed

_____

7. **Ortega** (awr•TAY•guh).

the door. The corridor outside was empty but I banged on the airtight door and they let me through to where the rest were waiting. They wanted to know what was happening but I didn't have any news for them because I had been chased out.

After a while we started feeling light and Captain Harkness announced that spin would be off the ship for a short time. Mr. Ortega and the other man came back and went on up to the control room. Spin was off entirely soon after that and I got very sick. Captain Harkness kept the ship's speaker circuits cut in on his conversations with the men who had gone outside to repair the hole, but I didn't listen. I defy anybody to be interested in anything when he is drop sick.

Then spin came back on and everything was all right and we were allowed to go back into our bunk room. It looked just the same except that there was a plate welded over the place where the meteorite had come in.

Breakfast was two hours late and we didn't have school that morning.

That was how I happened to go up to Captain's mast for the second time. George was there and Molly and my sister Peggy and Dr. Archibald, the Scoutmaster of our deck, and all the fellows from my bunk room and all the ship's officers. The rest of the ship was cut in by visiplate. I wanted to wear my uniform but it was a mess—torn and covered with sticky stuff. I finally cut off the merit badges and put it in the ship's incinerator.

The First Officer shouted, "Captain's Mast for punishments and rewards!" Everybody sort of straightened up and Captain Harkness walked out and faced us. Dad shoved me forward.

The Captain looked at me. "William Lermer?" he said.

I said, "Yessir."

Drop sick refers to motion sickness. The spinning motion of the ship creates artificial gravity. When the motion stopped, people became lighter and some felt ill.

Two metals can be *welded,* or united, by softening them with heat and pressing them together.

A *captain's mast* is a hearing directed by the captain of a ship.

The *visiplate* is a kind of closed-circuit television system.

Scouts receive *merit badges* for achievements in specific areas of interest.

He said, "I will read from yesterday's log: 'On twenty-one August at oh-seven-oh-four system standard, while cruising in free fall according to plan, the ship was broached by a small meteorite. Safety interlocks worked satisfactorily and the punctured volume, compartment H-twelve, was isolated with no serious drop in pressure elsewhere in the ship.

"'Compartment H-twelve is a bunk room and was occupied at the time of the emergency by twenty passengers. One of the passengers, William J. Lermer, contrived a makeshift patch with materials at hand and succeeded in holding sufficient pressure for breathing until a repair party could take over.

"'His quick thinking and immediate action unquestionably saved the lives of all persons in compartment H-twelve.'"

The Captain looked up from the log and went on, "A certified copy of this entry, along with depositions of witnesses, will be sent to Interplanetary Red Cross with recommendation for appropriate action. Another copy will be furnished you. I have no way to reward you except to say that you have my heart-felt gratitude. I know that I speak not only for the officers but for all the passengers and most especially for the parents of your bunkmates."

He paused and waggled a finger for me to come closer. He went on in a low voice, to me alone, "That really was a slick piece of work. You were on your toes. You have a right to feel proud."

I said I guessed I had been lucky.

He said, "Maybe. But that sort of luck comes to the man who is prepared for it."

He waited a moment, then said, "Lermer, have you ever thought of putting in for space training?"

Broached means *punctured.*

Interlocks are devices designed to seal off parts of the ship when something goes wrong.

Makeshift means *serving as a temporary substitute.*

A *certified* copy is imprinted with an official stamp.

I said I suppose I had but I hadn't thought about it very seriously. He said, "Well, Lermer, if you ever do decide to, let me know. You can reach me care of the Pilots' Association, Luna City."

With that, mast was over and we went away, George and I together and Molly and Peggy following along. I heard Peggy saying, "That's *my* brother."

Molly said, "Hush, Peggy. And don't point."

Peggy said, "Why not? He *is* my brother—well, isn't he?"

Molly said, "Yes, but there's no need to embarrass him."

But I wasn't embarrassed.

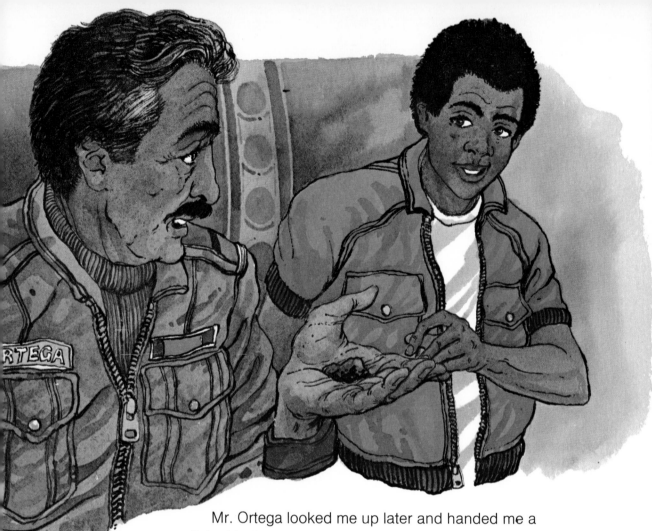

Mr. Ortega looked me up later and handed me a little, black, twisted piece of metal, about as big as a button. "That's all there was left of it," he said, "but I thought you would like to have it—pay you for messing up your Scout suit, so to speak."

I thanked him and said I didn't mind losing the uniform; after all, it had saved my neck, too. I looked at the meteorite. "Mr. Ortega, is there any way to tell where this came from?"

"Not really," he told me, "though you can get the scientific johnnies to cut it up and then express an opinion—if you don't mind them destroying it."

I said no, I'd rather keep it—and I have. I've still got it as a pocket piece.

Discussion Questions *The main character has a conflict with nature. What natural force must he struggle against? (An air vacuum.) How does the struggle end? (Bill contrives a makeshift patch for the hole in the ship.) Bill is described as quick-thinking. What other words describe him? (Possible answers: decisive; brave; a leader.) Why might these characteristics be more important on a spaceship than in everyday situa-* tions on earth? *(Possible answer: accidents can quickly cause death in space.)* **Enriching Activities** *1. Improvisation.* Have groups of students act out the scene in compartment H-twelve. *2. Making signs.* Have each student draw a wordless international sign indicating an action that would be forbidden aboard a space vehicle.

Questions

1. Why did William Lermer wad up his Scout uniform and stuff it in the hole?

2. When the compartment door slid shut, William was scared and said, "I guess I'm just not the hero type." Was he right or wrong about that? Explain.

3. Molly thought that William would be embarrassed when Peggy pointed at him. But William wasn't embarrassed. Why wasn't he?

4. If you had been William, would you have kept the meteorite as a pocket piece or would you have had the scientists analyze it? Explain your choice.

5. The ship's course was set high enough "to give the asteroid belt a wide berth." What is meant by that?
   a. The asteroid belt was really a wide bed.
   b. The ship allowed for a wide space between itself and the asteroid belt.
   c. The ship made its way into a wide dock.

1. Literal/recall
He wanted to stop the air loss in the cabin. (page 316)
2. Interpretive/inference He was wrong. Despite the panic around him, he instinctively plugged the hole and reinforced the covering. (pages 316–318)
3. Interpretive/inference Possible answer: he wasn't embarrassed because he felt proud. (page 323)
4. Critical/relating to experience
Possible answers: I would have wanted to keep it to remember how I handled an emergency; I would have wanted it analyzed to find out where it came from.
5. Vocabulary
b. (page 315)

Activity

Imagine you are aboard the *Mayflower* and another problem arises, this time in *your* compartment. In a report to your captain, describe the scene and what steps you or others took to solve the difficulty.

Interpretive/extrapolation and **Critical/relating to experience** *Writing.* To help students begin, suggest situations such as a power-system failure, a mysterious smell or sound, or a meeting with aliens.

325

Objectives ● To recognize the emotions of a main character. ● To visualize the setting of a story. ● To identify conflicts with nature in a story.

Synopsis of the Story Karana waits to be rescued by the ship that took her people away from their island. When winter comes, she decides to paddle a canoe eastward to the country of her ancestors. One evening Karana slides a heavy canoe into the water and begins her journey. The next day her canoe begins to leak badly, and Karana must make the difficult decision to turn back. A group of dolphins swims beside her, lifting her spirits. The next morning she reaches the island—exhausted but safe.

Background *The Island of the Blue Dolphins* is based on the true story of a Native American woman who was stranded on an island off the coast of California for

Reading Level Average

Dangerous Voyage

A chapter from the novel
Island of the Blue Dolphins by Scott O'Dell
Illustrated by Daniel San Souci

18 years. She was rescued from the island in 1853. The novel won the Newbery Award in 1961 and was on the International Board on Books for Young People (IBBY) Honor List in 1962.

Introducing the Story   *Suppose that, because of some disaster, you found yourself living entirely alone—completely cut off from all human beings. How do you think you would feel? What would you need just to survive? (Food, water, shelter, clothing.) "Dangerous Voyage" is based on a true story of a young woman who found herself alone on an island with little hope of rescue. See how she feels and what she does to try to escape.*

Word to Know

sandspit (sand′·spit): a finger of sandy land that juts into the ocean. (page 331)

Off the coast of California there is an island shaped like a blue dolphin lying on its side, with its tail pointing toward sunrise. For centuries Indians had lived on the island. Then one day a party of sea-otter hunters landed there and tried to cheat the Indians. A bloody battle was fought. When the hunters left the island, only a few Indians remained alive.

The people of the island then shared one fear—that the hunters would return and kill them all. When sailors arrived and offered to carry them to safety, the Indians went aboard—all except six-year-old Ramo, who did not reach the ship in time, and twelve-year-old Karana,[1] who leaped from the ship and swam back to be with her brother. Two days later, Ramo was killed by wild dogs and Karana found herself alone.

As the seasons passed, Karana waited. She hoped for a ship to rescue her. To survive she made her own weapons, built a shelter, and defended herself against her enemies—the wild dogs. But Karana realized that for as long as she was trapped on the island, her worst enemy would be loneliness. In the story that follows, Karana tells her plan for escaping the lonely Island of the Blue Dolphins.

---

1. **Karana** (kuh·RAH·nuh).

Summer is the best time on the Island of the Blue Dolphins. The sun is warm then and the winds blow milder out of the west, sometimes out of the south.

It was during these days that the ship might return and now I spent most of my time on the rock, looking out from the high headland into the east, toward the country where my people had gone, across the sea that was never-ending.

Once while I watched I saw a small object which I took to be the ship, but a stream of water rose from it and I knew that it was a whale spouting. During those summer days I saw nothing else.

The first storm of winter ended my hopes. If the white men's ship were coming for me it would have come during the time of good weather. Now I would have to wait until winter was gone, maybe longer.

The thought of being alone on the island while so many suns rose from the sea and went slowly back into the sea filled my heart with loneliness. I had not felt so lonely before because I was sure that the ship would return as Chief Matasaip had said it would. Now my hopes were dead. Now I was really alone. I could not eat much, nor could I sleep without dreaming terrible dreams.

The storm blew out of the north, sending big waves against the island and winds so strong that I was unable to stay on the rock. I moved my bed to the foot of the rock and for protection kept a fire going throughout the night. I slept there five times. The first night the wild dogs came and stood outside the ring made by the fire. I killed three of them with arrows, but not the leader, and they did not come again.

On the sixth day, when the storm had ended, I
went to the place where my people had hidden their
canoes, filled with supplies, and let myself down over
the cliff. This part of the shore was sheltered from
the wind and I found the canoes just as they had
been left. The dried food was still good, but the
water was stale, so I went back to the spring and
filled a fresh basket.

I had decided during the days of the storm, when
I had given up hope of seeing the ship, that I would
take one of the canoes and go to the country that

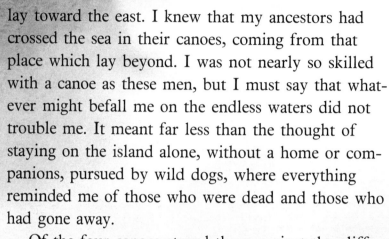

lay toward the east. I knew that my ancestors had crossed the sea in their canoes, coming from that place which lay beyond. I was not nearly so skilled with a canoe as these men, but I must say that whatever might befall me on the endless waters did not trouble me. It meant far less than the thought of staying on the island alone, without a home or companions, pursued by wild dogs, where everything reminded me of those who were dead and those who had gone away.

Of the four canoes stored there against the cliff, I chose the smallest, which was still very heavy because it could carry six people. The task that faced me was to push it down the rocky shore and into the water, a distance four or five times its length.

This I did by first removing all the large rocks
in front of the canoe. I then filled in all these holes
with pebbles and along this path laid down long
strips of <u>kelp</u>, making a slippery bed. The shore was
steep and, once I got the canoe to move with its own
weight, it slid down the path and into the water.

Kelp is a brown
seaweed.

The sun was in the west when I left the shore.
The sea was calm behind the high cliffs. Using the
two-bladed paddle I quickly <u>skirted</u> the south part of
the island. As I reached the <u>sandspit</u> the wind struck.
I was paddling from the back of the canoe because
you can go faster kneeling there, but I could not
handle it in the wind.

Skirted means *moved
along the edge of.*

Kneeling in the middle of the canoe, I paddled hard and did not pause until I had gone through the tides that run fast around the sandspit. There were many small waves and I was soon wet, but as I came out from behind the spit the spray lessened and the waves grew long and rolling. Though it would have been easier to go the way they slanted, this would have taken me in the wrong direction. I therefore kept them on my left hand, as well as the island, which grew smaller and smaller, behind me.

At dusk I looked back. The Island of the Blue Dolphins had disappeared. This was the first time that I felt afraid.

There were only hills and valleys of water around me now. When I was in a valley I could see nothing and when the canoe rose out of it, only the ocean stretching away and away.

Night fell and I drank from the basket. The water cooled my throat.

The sea was black and there was no difference between it and the sky. The waves made no sound among themselves, only faint noises as they went under the canoe or struck against it. Sometimes the noises seemed angry and at other times like people laughing. I was not hungry because of my fear.

The first star made me feel less afraid. It came out low in the sky and it was in front of me, toward the east. Other stars began to appear all around, but it was this one I kept my gaze upon. It was in the figure that we call a serpent, a star which shone green and which I knew. Now and then it was hidden by mist, yet it always came out brightly again.

Without this star I would have been lost, for the waves never changed. They came always from the same direction and in a manner that kept pushing me away from the place I wanted to reach. For this reason the canoe made a path in the black water like a snake. But somehow I kept moving toward the star which shone in the east.

This star rose high and then I kept the North Star on my left hand, the one we call "the star that does not move." The wind grew quiet. Since it always died down when the night was half over, I knew how long I had been traveling and how far away the dawn was.

About this time I found that the canoe was leaking. Before dark I had emptied one of the baskets in
which food was stored and used it to dip out the
water that came over the sides. The water that now
moved around my knees was not from the waves.

I stopped paddling and worked with the basket
until the bottom of the canoe was almost dry. Then I
searched around, feeling in the dark along the smooth
planks, and found the place near the bow where the
water was seeping through a crack as long as my
hand and the width of a finger. Most of the time it
was out of the sea, but it leaked whenever the canoe
dipped forward in the waves.

The places between the planks were filled with
black pitch which we gather along the shore. Lacking

this, I tore a piece of fiber from my skirt and pressed it into the crack, which held back the water.

Dawn broke in a clear sky and as the sun came out of the waves I saw that it was far off on my left. During the night I had drifted south of the place I wished to go, so I changed my direction and paddled along the path made by the rising sun.

There was no wind on this morning and the long waves went quietly under the canoe. I therefore moved faster than during the night.

I was very tired, but more hopeful than I had been since I left the island. If the good weather did not change, I would cover many leagues before dark. Another night and another day might bring me within sight of the shore toward which I was going.

Not long after dawn, while I was thinking of this strange place and what it would look like, the canoe began to leak again. This crack was between the same planks, but was a larger one and close to where I was kneeling.

The fiber I tore from my skirt and pushed into the crack held back most of the water which seeped in whenever the canoe rose and fell with the waves. Yet I could see that the planks were weak from one end to the other, probably from the canoe being stored so long in the sun, and that they might open along their whole length if the waves grew rougher.

It was suddenly clear to me that it was danger-ous to go on. The voyage would take two more days, perhaps longer. By turning back to the island I would not have nearly so far to travel.

Still I could not make up my mind to do so. The sea was calm and I had come far. The thought of turning back after all this labor was more than I could bear. Even greater was the thought of the deserted island I would return to, of living there alone and forgotten. For how many suns and how many moons?

The canoe drifted idly on the calm sea while these thoughts went over and over in my mind, but when I saw the water seeping through the crack again, I picked up the paddle. There was no choice except to turn back toward the island.

I knew that only by the best of fortune would I ever reach it.

The wind did not blow until the sun was overhead. Before that time I covered a good distance, pausing only when it was necessary to dip water from the canoe. With the wind I went more slowly and had to stop more often because of the water spilling over the sides, but the leak did not grow worse.

This was my first good fortune. The next was when a swarm of dolphins appeared. They came swimming out of the west, but as they saw the canoe they turned around in a great circle and began to follow me. They swam up slowly and so close that I could see their eyes, which are large and the color of the ocean. Then they swam on ahead of the canoe, crossing back and forth in front of it, diving in and out, as if they were weaving a piece of cloth with their broad snouts.

Dolphins are animals of good omen. It made me happy to have them swimming around the canoe, and though my hands had begun to bleed from the <u>chafing</u> of the paddle, just watching them made me forget the pain. I was very lonely before they appeared, but now I felt that I had friends with me and did not feel the same.

The blue dolphins left me shortly before dusk. They left as quickly as they had come, going on into the west, but for a long time I could see the last of the sun shining on them. After night fell I could still see them in my thoughts, and it was because of this that I kept on paddling when I wanted to lie down and sleep.

The paddles *chafing,* or *rubbing,* made Karana's hands sore.

More than anything, it was the blue dolphins that took me back home.

Fog came with the night, yet from time to time I could see the star that stands high in the west, the red star called Magat which is part of the figure that looks like a crawfish and is known by that name. The crack in the planks grew wider so I had to stop often to fill it with fiber and to dip out the water.

A *crawfish* is a shellfish that resembles a small lobster.

The night was very long, longer than the night before. Twice I dozed kneeling there in the canoe, though I was more afraid than I had ever been. But the morning broke clear and in front of me lay the dim line of the island like a great fish sunning itself on the sea.

I reached it before the sun was high, the sandspit and its tides that bore me into the shore. My legs were stiff from kneeling and as the canoe struck the sand I fell when I rose to climb out. I crawled through the shallow water and up the beach. There I lay for a long time, hugging the sand in happiness.

Questions

1. The feelings of Karana, the girl who tells the story, are important to what happens in the story. Finish the following sentences to help tell what happens.
   a. Loneliness caused Karana to _____.
   b. Hopefulness caused her to _____.
   c. Fear caused Karana to _____.
   d. Happiness came when she _____.

2. Name three things in nature that Karana might have said were friendly. Then name three things in nature that Karana might have said were unfriendly.

3. In "Dangerous Voyage" Karana makes decisions. She decides to leave the island and later decides to turn back again. What is another decision that she may make in the days ahead?

Activity

Make a pictomap—a map with drawings or pictures—using clues from the story. Show the island, the rock where Karana camped, and the place where the canoes were kept. Show where Karana began her voyage, including the sandspit she passed, where she turned back, and where the dolphins met her. Label those places on your pictomap. You might want to use arrows or dotted lines to trace her journey.

About SCOTT O'DELL

Scott O'Dell was born in Los Angeles when it still had the flavor of a frontier town. His father worked for the railroad, and his family moved a lot. One time they lived on an island in a house on stilts above the ocean. "That is why," he says, "the feel of the frontier and the sound of the sea are in my books."

Scott O'Dell spent his early career as a movie cameraman and as a book editor for a newspaper. Then he began writing adventure stories, first for adults and then for children. His books for children have won many prizes and awards. For each book, Scott O'Dell spends about three or four months doing research and six months writing.

According to Scott O'Dell, *Island of the Blue Dolphins* "is based upon the true story of a girl who was left upon an island near the coast of southern California and lived there for eighteen years, alone." But *Island of the Blue Dolphins* also reflects Scott O'Dell's memories of living on an island. On summer days, he and his friends found big logs and paddled out to sea. The logs were their "proud canoes," taking them wherever they wished to explore.

More Books by Scott O'Dell

The Black Pearl (Houghton Mifflin, 1967)
Sing Down the Moon (Houghton Mifflin, 1970)
Carlota (Houghton Mifflin, 1977)

Song

An Eskimo poem

Translated by Knud Rasmussen

And I think over again
My small adventures
When with a shore wind I drifted out
In my kayak
And thought I was in danger.
My fears,
Those I thought so big,
For all the vital things
I had to get and to reach.

And yet, there is only
One great thing,
The only thing:
To live to see in huts and on journeys
The great day that dawns,
And the light that fills the world.

Illustrated by Christa Keiffer

Sea Calm

A poem by Langston Hughes

Objective ● To interpret the mood of a poem.

Introducing the Poem *Have you ever felt a "still feeling" just before a storm? How did it make you feel? See if this poem gives you the same kind of feeling.*

Discussion Questions *What is the mood of this poem?* (Sad; threatening.) *Why do you think the speaker says "It is not good"?* (Possible answers: the speaker thinks a storm is threatening; a sailboat cannot sail on a calm sea.)

Enriching Activity *Writing.* Have the students write prose or poems telling how some aspect of nature reflects a mood for them.

How still,
How strangely still
The water is today.
It is not good
For water
To be so still that way.

Illustrated by Christa Keiffer

Objectives • To recognize expository writing within a narrative. • To write or diagram step-by-step directions. • To examine the main idea (theme) of a story.

Synopsis of the Story Sam Gribley, the story's narrator, is living alone in the wilds of the Catskill Mountains. One day he hears police sirens, which stop when nearby, then resume and fade away. When Sam returns to his campsite, he finds a sleeping man and assumes he is a criminal. Sam is lonesome, so he talks to the man, whom he calls Bando. Soon Sam learns that Bando is really a vacationing teacher who became lost. As the days pass, the two become friends, each teaching the other how to survive in the wilderness. When Bando leaves, Sam is comforted by his wild friends—a falcon, a weasel, and a raccoon.

Reading Level Average

BANDO

From the novel *My Side of the Mountain*

by Jean Craighead George

Illustrated by Lyle Miller

It was late spring when Sam Gribley left his family's crowded New York City apartment home and set out for some land in the Catskill Mountains that his great-grandfather had once tried to farm. He carried only a penknife, a ball of string, an ax, a flint with steel,[1] and forty dollars. He knew how to fish and build fires, and he figured that was all he needed for a new life.

During his first few days in the wilds, Sam was hungry, cold, and confused. But he learned from his early mistakes, and the mountain soon provided him with food, shelter, and company—Frightful, a baby falcon; The Baron, a weasel; and Jesse C. James, a young raccoon.

Midsummer brought easy living, but also the threat of discovery, as Sam tells it in his diary.

---

1. **flint with steel:** tools used for making sparks to start a fire.

Background In 1960, the novel *My Side of the Mountain* was a Newbery Honor Book and was in "Fanfare," the *Horn Book*'s honor list. It also was on the American Library Association Notable Children's Books list in 1959.

Introducing the Story *If you were to camp in the wilderness for a year, what things would you need?* (Possible answers: clothing; a knife; matches; a tent; food.) *What would you need to know?* (Possible answers: how to build a fire; how to fish; how to find water; which wild plants are edible.) *This story is about a young man who has already spent several months alone in the wilderness. As you read, see how he has learned to survive and what it is he misses most.*

Life was leisurely. I was warm, well fed. One day while I was down the mountain, I returned home by way of the old farmhouse site to check the apple crop. They were summer apples, and were about ready to be picked. I had gathered a pouchful and had sat down under the tree to eat a few and think about how I would dry them for use in the winter when Frightful dug her talons into my shoulder so hard I winced.

"Be gentle, bird!" I said to her.

I got her talons out and put her on a log, where I watched her with some alarm. She was as alert as a high tension wire, her head cocked so that her ears, just membranes under her feathers, were pointed east. She evidently heard a sound that pained her. She opened her beak. Whatever it was, I could hear nothing, though I strained my ears, cupped them, and wished she would speak.

Frightful was my ears as well as my eyes. She could hear things long before I. When she grew tense, I listened or looked. She was scared this time. She turned round and round on the log, looked up in the tree for a perch,

lifted her wings to fly, and then stood still and listened.

Then I heard it. A police siren sounded far down the road. The sound grew louder and louder, and I grew afraid. Then I said, "No, Frightful, if they are after me there won't be a siren. They'll just slip up on me quietly."

No sooner had I said this than the siren wound down, and apparently stopped on the road at the foot of the mountain. I got up to run to my tree, but had not gotten past the walnut before the patrol cars started up and screamed away.

We started home although it was not late in the afternoon. However, it was hot, and thunderheads were building up. I decided to take a swim in the spring and work on the moccasins I had cut out several days before.

With the squad car still on my mind, we slipped quietly into the hemlock forest. Once again Frightful almost sent me through the crown of the forest by digging her talons into my shoulder. I looked at her. She was staring at our home. I looked, too. Then I stopped, for I could make out the form of a man

346

stretched between the sleeping house and the store tree.

Softly, tree by tree, Frightful and I approached him. The man was asleep. I could have left and camped in the gorge, but my enormous desire to see another human being overcame my fear of being discovered.

We stood above the man. He did not move, so Frightful lost interest in my fellow being. She tried to hop to her stump and preen. I grabbed her leash, however, as I wanted to think before awakening him. Frightful flapped. I held her wings to her body as her flapping was noisy to me. Apparently not so to the man. The man did not stir. It is hard to realize that the rustle of a falcon's wings is not much of a noise to a man from the city, because by now, one beat of her wings and I would awaken from a sound sleep as if a shot had gone off. The stranger slept on. I realized how long I'd been in the mountains.

Right at that moment, as I looked into his unshaven face, his close-cropped hair, and his torn clothes, I thought of the police siren, and put two and two together.

"An outlaw!" I said to myself. "Wow!" I had to think what to do with an outlaw before I awoke him.

Would he be troublesome? Would he be mean? Should I go live in the gorge until he moved on? How I wanted to hear his voice, to tell him about The Baron and Jessie C. James, to say words out loud. I really did not want to hide from him; besides, he might be hungry, I thought. Finally I spoke.

"Hi!" I said. I was delighted to see him roll over, open his eyes, and look up. He seemed startled, so I reassured him. "It's all right. They've gone. If you don't tell on me I won't tell on you." When he heard this, he sat up and seemed to relax.

"Oh," he said. Then he leaned against the tree and added, "Thanks." He evidently was thinking this over, for he propped his head on his elbow and studied me closely.

"You're a sight for sore eyes," he said, and smiled. He had a nice smile. In fact, he looked nice and not like an outlaw at all. His eyes were very blue and, although tired, they did not look scared or hunted.

However, I talked quickly before he could get up and run away.

"I don't know anything about you, and I don't want to. You don't know anything about me and don't want to, but you may stay here if you like. No one is going to find you here. Would you like some supper?" It was still early, but he looked hungry.

"Do you have some?"

"Yes, venison or rabbit?"

"Well . . . venison." His eyebrows puckered in question marks. I went to work.

He arose, turned around and around, and looked at his surroundings. He whistled softly when I kindled a spark with the flint and steel. I was now quite quick at this, and had a tidy fire blazing in a very few minutes. I was so used to myself doing this that it had not occurred to me that it would be interesting to a stranger.

"Desdemondia!" he said. I judged this to be some underworld phrase. At this moment Frightful, who had been sitting quietly on her stump, began to preen. The outlaw jumped back, then saw she was tied and said, "And who is this ferocious-looking character?"

"Desdemondia!" (line 8 from the foot of the page) is an exclamation invented by the author.

"That is Frightful; don't be afraid. She's quite wonderful and gentle. She would be glad to catch you a rabbit for supper if you would prefer that to venison."

"Am I dreaming?" said the man. "I go to sleep by a campfire that looked like it was built by a boy scout, and I awaken in the middle of the eighteenth century."

I crawled into the store tree to get the smoked venison and some cattail tubers. When I came out again, he was speechless.

"My storehouse," I explained.

"I see," he answered. From that moment on he did not talk much. He just watched me. I was so busy cooking the best meal that I could possibly get together that I didn't say much either. Later I wrote down that menu, as it was excellent.

"Brown puffballs in deer fat with a little wild garlic, fill pot with water, put venison in, boil. Wrap tubers in leaves and stick in coals. Cut up apples and boil in can with dogtooth violet bulbs. Raspberries to finish meal."

When the meal was ready, I served it to the man in my nicest turtle shell. I had to whittle him a fork out of the crotch of a twig, as Jessie Coon James had gone off with the others. He ate and ate and ate, and when he was done he said, "May I call you Thoreau?"[2]

"That will do nicely," I said. Then I paused—just to let him know that I knew a little bit about him too. I smiled and said, "I will call you Bando."

His eyebrows went up, he cocked his head, shrugged his shoulders and answered, "That's close enough."

With this he sat and thought. I felt I had offended him, so I spoke. "I will be glad to help. I will teach you how to live off the land. It is very easy. No one need find you."

His eyebrows gathered together again. This was characteristic of Bando when he was concerned, and so I was sorry I had mentioned his past. After all, outlaw or no outlaw, he was an adult, and I still felt unsure of myself around adults. I changed the subject.

"Let's get some sleep," I said.

"Where do you sleep?" he asked. All this time sitting and talking with me, and he had not seen the entrance to my tree. I was pleased. Then I beckoned, walked a few feet to the left, pushed back the deer-hide door, and showed Bando my secret.

"Thoreau," he said. "You are quite wonderful." He went in. I lit the turtle candle for him, he explored, tried the bed, came out and shook his head until I thought it would roll off.

We didn't say much more that night. I let him sleep on my bed. His feet hung off, but he was comfortable, he said. I stretched out by the fire. The ground was dry, the night warm, and I could sleep on anything now.

I got up early and had breakfast ready when Bando came stumbling out of the tree. We ate crayfish, and he really honestly seemed to like them. It takes a little time to acquire a taste for wild foods, so Bando surprised me the way he liked the menu. Of course he was hungry, and that helped.

That day we didn't talk much,

---

2. **Henry David Thoreau** (thuh·ROH): an American writer (1817–1862) who lived alone for a time at Walden Pond in Concord, Massachusetts. In his best-known book, *Walden*, Thoreau spoke of going into the woods to live with nature and to learn about life.

just went over the mountain collecting foods. I wanted to dig up the tubers of the Solomon's-seal from a big garden of them on the other side of the gorge. We fished, we swam a little, and I told him I hoped to make a raft pretty soon, so I could float into deeper water and perhaps catch bigger fish.

When Bando heard this, he took my ax and immediately began to cut young trees for this purpose. I watched him and said, "You must have lived on a farm or something."

At that moment a bird sang.

"The wood peewee," said Bando, stopping his work. He stepped into the woods, seeking it. Now I was astonished.

"How would you know about a wood peewee in your business?" I grew bold enough to ask.

"And just what do you think my business is?" he said as I followed him.

"Well, you're not a minister."

"Right!"

"And you're not a doctor or a lawyer."

"Correct."

"You're not a businessman or a sailor."

"No, I am not."

"Nor do you dig ditches."

"I do not."

"Well . . ."

"Guess."

Suddenly I wanted to know for sure. So I said it.

"You are a murderer or a thief or a racketeer, and you are hiding out."

Bando stopped looking for the peewee. He turned and stared at me. At first I was frightened. A bandit might do anything. But he wasn't mad. He was laughing. He had a good deep laugh and it kept coming out of him. I smiled, then grinned and laughed with him.

"What's funny, Bando?" I asked.

"I like that," he finally said. "I like that a lot." The tickle deep inside him kept him chuckling. I had no more to say, so I ground my heel in the dirt while I waited for him to get over the fun and explain it all to me.

"Thoreau, my friend, I am just a college English teacher lost in the Catskills. I came out to hike around the woods, got completely lost yesterday, found your fire, and fell asleep beside it. I was hoping the scoutmaster and his troop would

be back for supper and help me home."

"Oh, no." My comment. Then I laughed. "You see, Bando, before I found you, I heard squad cars screaming up the road. Occasionally you read about bandits that hide out in the forest, and I was just so sure that you were someone they were looking for."

We gave up the peewee and went back to the raft-making, talking very fast now, and laughing a lot. He was fun. Then something sad occurred to me.

"Well, if you're not a bandit, you will have to go home very soon, and there is no point in teaching you how to live on fish and bark and plants."

"I can stay a little while," he said. "This is summer vacation. I must admit I had not planned to eat crayfish on my vacation, but I am rather getting to like it.

"Maybe I can stay until your school opens," he went on. "That's after Labor Day, isn't it?"

I was very still, thinking how to answer that.

Bando sensed this. Then he turned to me with a big grin.

"You really mean you are going to try to winter it out here?"

"I think I can."

"Well!" He sat down, rubbed his forehead in his hands, and looked at me. "Thoreau, I have led a varied life—dishwasher, sax player, teacher. To me it has been an interesting life. Just now it seems very dull." He sat awhile with his head down, then looked up at the mountains and the rocks and trees. I heard him sigh.

"Let's go fish. We can finish this another day."

That is how I came to know Bando. We became very good friends in the week or ten days that he stayed with me, and he helped me a lot. We spent several days gathering white oak acorns and groundnuts, harvesting the blueberry crop and smoking fish.

We flew Frightful every day just for the pleasure of lying on our backs in the meadow and watching her mastery of the sky. I had lots of meat, so what she caught those days was all hers. It was a pleasant time, warm, with occasional thunder showers, some of which we stayed out in. We talked about books. He did know a lot of books, and could quote exciting things from them.

One day Bando went to town and came back with five pounds of sugar.

"I want to make blueberry jam," he announced. "All those excellent berries and no jam."

He worked two days at this. He knew how to make jam. He'd watched his Pa make it in Mississippi, but we got stuck on what to put it in.

I wrote this one night:

"August 29

"The raft is almost done. Bando has promised to stay until we can sail out into the deep fishing holes.

"Bando and I found some clay along the stream bank. It was as slick as ice. Bando thought it would make good pottery. He shaped some jars and lids. They look good—not Wedgwood, he said, but containers. We dried them on the rock in the meadow, and later Bando made a clay oven and baked them in it. He thinks they might hold the blueberry jam he has been making.

"Bando got the fire hot by blowing on it with some home-made bellows that he fashioned from one of my skins that he tied together like a balloon. A reed is the nozzle.

"It was a terribly hot day for Bando to be firing clay jars, but he stuck with it. They look jam-worthy, as he says, and he filled three of them tonight. The jam is good, the pots remind me of crude flower pots without the hole in the bottom. Some of the lids don't fit. Bando says he will go home and read more about pottery-making so that he can do a better job next time.

"We like the jam. We eat it on hard acorn pancakes.

"Later. Bando met The Baron Weasel today for the first time. I don't know where The Baron has been this past week, but suddenly he appeared on the rock, and nearly jumped down Bando's shirt collar. Bando said he liked The Baron best when he was in his hole.

"September 3

"Bando taught me how to make willow whistles today. He and I went to the stream and cut two whistles about eight inches long. He slipped the bark on them. That means he pulled the wood out of the bark, leaving a tube. He made a mouthpiece at one end, cut a hole beneath it, and used the wood to slide up and down like a trombone.

"We played music until the moon came up. Bando could even play jazz on the willow whistles. They are wonderful instruments, sounding much like the wind in the top of the hemlocks. Sad tunes are best suited to willow whistles. When we played 'The Young Voyageur' tears came to our eyes, it was so sad."

There were no more notes for many days. Bando had left me saying: "Good-bye, I'll see you at Christmas." I was so lonely that I kept sewing on my moccasins to keep myself busy. I sewed every free minute for four days, and when they were finished, I began a glove to protect my hand from

Frightful's sharp talons.

One day when I was thinking very hard about being alone, Frightful gave her gentle call of love and contentment. I looked up.

"Bird," I said. "I had almost forgotten how we used to talk." She made tiny movements with her beak and fluffed her feathers. This was a language I had forgotten since Bando came. It meant she was glad to see me and hear me, that she was well fed and content.

I picked her up and squeaked into her neck feathers. She moved her beak, turned her bright head, and bit my nose very gently.

Jessie Coon James came down from the trees for the first time in ten days. He finished my fish dinner. Then just before dusk, The Baron came up on his boulder and scratched and cleaned and played with a fern leaf.

I had the feeling we were all back together again.

Discussion Questions *What did Sam gain by Bando's visit?* (Companionship; new skills; help with projects.) *What did he lose?* (Possible answers: privacy; his special relationship with his animal friends.)
Enriching Activities 1. *Comparing characters.* If the students have read *Dangerous Voyage* on page 326, ask them to list three ways in which the situation of *Bando's* narrator is similar to Karana's, and three ways in which they differ. **2.** *Related reading.* Encourage the students to read the novel *My Side of the Mountain* by Jean Craighead George (E. P. Dutton, 1959) or one of her other books listed on page 359.

1. Literal/recall
Thoreau concluded that Bando was a criminal because he heard a police siren just before discovering him; Bando seemed to be in hiding. (pages 346–348)
2. Interpretive/inference The author wants readers to feel as if they are actually there; details make the story more interesting. (pages 349–350)
3. Literal/recall and **Interpretive/extrapolation**
Possible answers: Sam could teach Bando how to tame a falcon (pages 347, 349), how to build a fire (page 348), how to make a shelter in a tree (page 350). Bando could teach Sam to recognize bird calls (page 351), split logs (page 351), and to make more sophisticated pottery (page 355).
4. Vocabulary
talon—c. (page 346); gorge—a. (page 347); meadow—b. (page 354); preen—d. (page 347).

Questions

1. Sam (the boy called Thoreau) made a wrong conclusion about Bando in this story. What was his wrong conclusion? Why did he make it?

2. Why does the author have Sam tell *how* he fixed dinner instead of just saying, "I fixed dinner"?

3. List three things that Sam could teach Bando about living on the mountain. Then list three things that Sam might *learn* from Bando about living on the mountain.

4. Match each word from the story with its meaning:

   talon   a. a deep, narrow passage between
   gorge   mountains
   meadow   b. grassland
   preen   c. claw
                    d. to smooth or clean feathers

Activity

Critical/relating to experience *Expository writing.* Some students might want to demonstrate their hobbies or skills to the class.

Sam and Bando taught each other different things. What could you teach someone to do? Make a kite? Build a model? Tell a story? Write a paragraph that could teach someone the skill you have. Be sure to include all the important steps. Draw pictures, too, if you wish.

BOOKSHELF

Avalanche! by A. Rutgers van der Loeff. William Morrow, 1958. A deadly avalanche in the Swiss Alps buries the village where Werner and his parents live. Werner and some refugee orphans must try to rescue the people there.
Reading Level Challenging

Children of the Incas by David Mangurian. Four Winds Press, 1979. In this true story, a modern-day boy and his family struggle to survive in the mountains of Peru by raising sheep, knitting sweaters, and harvesting potatoes. **Reading Level** Average

The Cry of the Crow by Jean Craighead George. Harper & Row, 1980. Mandy learns about the nature of wild things when she finds a helpless baby crow in the woods and tames it in secret. **Reading Level** Average

Hawaiian Myths of Earth, Sea and Sky by Vivian L. Thompson. Holiday House, 1966. Pele the volcano goddess, Poliahu the snow goddess, and Maui the trickster-hero are among the mythical people who appear in these retellings of Hawaiian myths. **Reading Level** Challenging

Snowshoe Trek to Otter River by David Budbill. Dial Press, 1976. Three short stories about two boys backpacking in the Vermont woods, learning the skills necessary for enjoyment and survival. **Reading Level** Average

All Upon a Sidewalk by Jean Craighead George. Dutton, 1974. An account of one day in the life of Lasius Flavus, or the yellow ant, who is sent on a food gathering mission by the Queen Ant. **Reading Level** Average

6 From America's Past

Objectives ● To enjoy a historical biography. ● To recognize how a character can influence the lives of others. ● To create a time line for a biography. ● To recognize the effect of a historical figure upon events of the time.

Synopsis of the Story As a young man, Patrick Henry failed as a farmer and as a storekeeper. He then worked in his father-in-law's tavern, where he met many lawyers. He attended court sessions and decided to practice law. After studying on his own, Patrick Henry was issued a law license. His practice was small and his reputation of little note until he won a case for the Virginia colonists against the state's parsons. During the succeeding years, Patrick Henry fought against England's unjust taxation. In 1775, his words ''Give me liberty or give me death'' became the rallying cry for American patriots.

From

Reading Level Challenging

Where Was Patrick Henry on the 29th of May?

An historical biography by Jean Fritz

Illustrated by George Ulrich

Background In 1975, *Where Was Patrick Henry on the 29th of May?* was one of the Library of Congress Children's Books of the Year and was on the American Library Association Notable Children's Books list.

Introducing the Story *Who were some of the important leaders of the American Revolution?* (Possible answers: George Washington; Thomas Jefferson; Benjamin Franklin; Thomas Paine.) *What is each person famous for?* (Possible answers: Washington led the American army and became President; Jefferson wrote the Declaration of Independence; Franklin served as ambassador to France; Paine wrote influential pamphlets.) *These people lived so long ago that they may not seem very real to us. You may feel differently after you read this story about Patrick Henry, one of the leaders of the American Revolution.*

Word to Know
orator: an effective speaker. (page 370)

On the 29th of May, 1736, Patrick Henry had just been born in Hanover County, Virginia. In those days, Virginia was still a colony of England and a wilderness of woodlands, creeks, and rivers. As a boy, Patrick often went off to the woods to hunt or fish. He even developed a good ear for birdcalls.

Patrick wasn't much interested in school or work. It seemed to people who knew him that Patrick had no useful talents except one: he "could send his voice out so that it could be heard clearly at a distance." Patrick's Uncle Langloo also had such a "sending voice"; when he gave a political speech, he could make people's hair stand on end. No one would have guessed that one day Patrick Henry's voice would do even more.

On May 29th, 1752, Patrick Henry became sixteen. He was six feet tall, a lanky, sharp-boned young man with flashing blue eyes, generally dressed in checked breeches and a jumpshirt, generally in his bare feet. He was old enough now to be counted among the men in Virginia and old enough to make his own living. And where was he?

Well, he may have been stretched out on a sack of salt. People claimed this was Patrick's favorite resting place and he rested a good deal. His father

The *Pamunkey* /pu·mung'·ke/ *River* runs through eastern Virginia.

Patrick was *courting* Sarah, which means he was seeking her approval of him as a husband.

had set up his two boys as storekeepers on the Pamunkey River, but William paid little attention to the store and although people came in to pass the time of day, they seldom put down hard cash for the goods they bought. Besides, the store wasn't always open. Come a nice spring day with redbirds calling and Patrick might be at the store and then again he might be down at the river or off in the woods. Or he might be across the county, courting. Patrick was sweet on young Sarah Shelton whose father operated a tavern at Hanover Courthouse.

As it turned out, Patrick's storekeeping was a failure but his courting was a success. When he was eighteen years old, he got rid of the store and married sixteen-year-old Sarah. As a wedding present, Sarah's father gave them three hundred acres of land cut off from his own estate. So Patrick became a tobacco farmer. For three years he went through the business of planting, cultivating, leafing, worming, and curing tobacco, and then his house burned down and he gave up the farm.

He and Sarah moved to Hanover Courthouse and decided to give storekeeping another try, but when they had only twenty-six customers in six months, they quit altogether. Patrick and Sarah had two children now, Martha and John, but they had little else. They lived with Sarah's father at the tavern and Patrick helped take care of the guests, many of them lawyers and their clients doing business at the courthouse across the road. Patrick handed out refreshment, made friends, and sometimes entertained guests with his fiddle.

At the quarter sessions of the court in March, June, September, and December, the most important cases were tried and then every bed in the tavern would be taken. (It cost 75¢ a night for a bed with clean sheets.) Traveling troupes of acrobats and jugglers came to town at that time; peddlers came to sell their wares; there were horse races, cockfights, and wrestling matches. From all over the county people came to see the shows, do their trading, and hear the cases argued.

Patrick attended court as often as possible. He liked to watch a lawyer run his opposition up a tree. He liked to listen to him roll out his words, the way his Uncle Langloo did on Election Day. The more he listened, the more he thought he might like to have a try at it himself. After all, he was twenty-four years old now; he no longer had a farm or a store or even a house. He had to try *something*. So he got a few books and began studying on his own.

This was the winter of 1760, about the same time as young seventeen-year-old Thomas Jefferson met him at a houseparty and was struck by Patrick's "passion for fiddling, dancing and pleasantry." But Patrick read at least two heavy law books that winter and in the middle of April he hung up a sign at John Shelton's tavern. *Patrick Henry,* the sign said, *Attorney at Law.* Patrick had been to Williamsburg, the capital of Virginia; he'd been <u>examined</u> by three prominent lawyers and he'd been issued a license to practice law. (He had also been told that he needed to study some more.)

Here, *examined* means *tested.*

In his first year Patrick represented 60 clients (many of them relatives) in 176 cases, but the cases didn't amount to much and he collected less than half what was owed him. Much of the time he had so little to do, he'd ride into the piney woods for a week or more of hunting—"sleeping under a tent," according to Thomas Jefferson, "wearing the same shirt the whole time." Then likely as not, he'd go directly to court in his greasy leather breeches and a pair of saddle bags on his arm.

What Patrick Henry needed to prove himself as a lawyer was a big case at one of the quarter sessions of court when the whole county would take an interest.

At the December session in 1763 Patrick had his chance. There was an argument between a group of preachers (or parsons, as they were called) and the people, but in one sense it was an argument between the people of Virginia and England. For a long time England had been so busy fighting wars that she had left America relatively free to manage her own affairs. But now the French and Indian War was over, a new king was on the throne, and there were rumors that England had a plan to rule the colonies more strictly. With the Parsons' Case, it looked as if England had already started.

The case went back to a year when the tobacco crop in Virginia failed. Instead of selling for the normal rate of two cents a pound, tobacco was so scarce, it sold for six cents. This should have been good news for the parsons because, according to law, they were paid in tobacco, but this year the people felt they couldn't afford it. So they passed a new law which allowed them to pay the parsons in cash at the two-cent rate. The parsons took their case to the king; the king vetoed the law and now a group of parsons were suing the people for damages and back pay. And Patrick Henry was representing the people.

On the day of the trial Patrick was uneasy. Not only were there more spectators than he'd ever seen at the courthouse, there were two men that he wished were not there. The first was his Uncle Patrick who was one of the parsons. Patrick met his uncle at his carriage when he arrived at the courthouse and asked him if he wouldn't turn his carriage around.

He had never spoken in public, Patrick explained, and his uncle's presence would overawe him. Besides, he might say something about the parsons that his uncle wouldn't like. So wouldn't he please just go home? His uncle complied.

But Patrick couldn't ask the same of his father. Colonel John Henry was the presiding justice of

Vetoed means *did not approve* or *rejected.*

Complied means *did as asked.*

A *presiding justice* is the judge in charge of the court.

the day and all through the trial he'd be sitting on a bench in front of the courtroom, right before Patrick's eyes.

Actually Colonel Henry was as uneasy as his son. He prayed that Patrick, who had failed in so many things, would not be an embarrassment today. But when Patrick stood up to argue the case, he was stooped, awkward, unable to look at the audience. When he spoke, he fumbled for words, halted, started sentences, stopped them as if he'd forgotten where he was going.

Colonel Henry sank down in his chair. He studied his hands. He looked out the window. Patrick's friends in the courtroom stared at the floor. What on earth had Patrick done with his voice, they asked themselves. Why didn't he *send* it?

Then all at once something seemed to come over Patrick. He stopped thinking about the people in the courtroom and about his father looking out the window and he began thinking about the King of England and how he could, if he wanted, change the character of the cheerful, independent world that Patrick lived in. Patrick Henry straightened up, he threw back his head, and sent his voice out in anger. How did the king know how much Virginians could pay their parsons? he asked. What right did he have to interfere?

Patrick was rolling his words out now like his Uncle Langloo. He was doing things with his voice that he had never known he could do—lowering it, raising it not only to fit his emotions but in such a way as to stir the emotions of everyone in the courtroom. The crowd sat <u>transfixed</u>. So did Colonel Henry. And why not? Here was Patrick Henry, a poor country lawyer, turning himself into an <u>orator</u> right before their eyes.

He talked for an hour. What about the parsons? he asked. Were they feeding the hungry and clothing the naked as the Scriptures told them to? No, he said. They were getting the king's permission to grab the last hoecake from the honest farmer, to take the milk cow from the poor widow.

Transfixed means motionless.

When Patrick had finished, the jury took just five minutes to reach a decision. They could not deny the parsons all damages since a previous court had ruled they had to be paid something, but after hearing Patrick, they allowed the parsons so much less than they had asked for that the parsons demanded a <u>retrial</u>. They were refused. *A retrial* is another trial.

The people in the courthouse were beside themselves with excitement at Patrick's success. As soon as court was adjourned, they raised him to their shoulders and carried him around the courtyard, hip-hip-hooraying him all the while. As for Colonel Henry, when asked about his son's performance, he smiled. He'd been pleasantly surprised, he said.

By-your-leave means with your permission.

A *provision* is something that is provided. The act provided for fifty-five conditions under which taxes would be paid.

Treason is disloyalty to one's government. Some people thought that Patrick should be punished for speaking against the king.

A *resolution* is a formal statement of opinion adopted by a governing body.

Spellbinding means *casting a spell.* His powerful words held the audience's attention.

It was a good thing for America, as it turned out, that Patrick Henry became an orator at the same time that England was unfolding her new plan. Taxation was England's next step. Although Americans had always managed their own money, suddenly in 1765 the English government, without any kind of <u>by-your-leave</u> from America, slapped down a stamp tax on the colonies. It had <u>provisions</u> for taxing fifty-five separate items and Patrick Henry was ready to fight every one of them.

On May 29th, 1765, Patrick became twenty-nine years old. He and Sarah had four children now and were living in a four-room house on top of a hill in Louisa County. And on the 29th of May, what was he doing?

Well, he was bawling out the king again. He had become a member of the House of Burgesses, Virginia's governing body, only nine days before and now he was standing up in his buckskin breeches before the finest men of Virginia, using such bold language that at one point there was a cry of "<u>Treason!</u>" But Patrick went right on reeling off resolutions. Later these <u>resolutions</u> were printed and sent out through the colonies, giving other Americans courage to oppose the taxation. Indeed, there was so much opposition to the Stamp Tax that after a year the king repealed it.

But England did not give up the idea of taxation nor did Patrick give up talking. In 1773, when England decided to enforce a tax on tea, Patrick went right to the floor of the House. He was so <u>spellbinding</u> that in the middle of one speech the spectators

rushed from the gallery to the <u>cupola</u> of the capitol
to pull down the English flag. The members of the
House, noticing the commotion, thought there was a
fire and ran for safety.

A *cupola*
/kyōō′·pə·lə/ (line 1) is a
small domelike struc-
ture built on a roof.

Patrick and Sarah had six children now and were back in Hanover County in an eighteen-room house set on a thousand acres. Patrick was a public figure. When he went out, he wore a black suit or perhaps his peach-blossom-colored one, silver buckled shoes, and a tie wig which he was said to twirl around his head when he was excited.

Yet his private life contained much sadness. After the birth of their sixth child, Sarah became seriously ill. Her illness was so severe that, until she died in 1775, she had to be confined to her room. Unfortunately the years of Sarah's illness were also the <u>critical</u> years for the country and again and again Patrick was obliged to leave home. During one of her most severe <u>spells</u>, he was with George Washington in Philadelphia, attending the Continental Congress.

On March 23rd, 1775, just a few weeks after Sarah's death, Patrick delivered his most famous speech at St. John's Church in Richmond, Virginia. By this time everyone knew who Mr. Henry was; they had all heard of his passion for liberty and of the extraordinary quality of his voice. There were those who swore that Patrick Henry could not even announce that it was a cold evening without inspiring awe. So of course on March 23rd St. John's Church was filled to overflowing—people standing in the aisles, in doorways, sitting on window ledges.

Patrick Henry was angry not only at the king who was disregarding America's <u>petitions</u>, insisting on taxation, and preparing for war, but he was also angry at those people in America who still wanted to be friendly to the king and keep peace. Patrick

Critical means dangerous.

Spells are a series of illnesses.

A *petition* is a request or statement of opinion signed by a group of people.

stood up and pushed his glasses back on his head
which was what he did when he was ready to use
his fighting words.

"Gentlemen may cry peace, peace," he thundered,
"but there is no peace . . . Is life so dear or peace
so sweet, as to be purchased at the price of chains
and slavery?" Patrick bowed his body and locked his
hands together as if he, himself, were in chains. Then
suddenly he raised his chained hands over his head.

"Forbid it, Almighty God!" he cried. "I know not what course others may take but as for me—" Patrick dropped his arms, threw back his body and strained against his imaginary chains until the tendons of his neck stood out like whipcords and the chains seemed to break. Then he raised his right hand in which he held an ivory letter opener. "As for me," he cried, "give me liberty or give me death!" And he plunged the letter opener in such a way it looked as if he were plunging it into his heart.

The crowd went wild with excitement. One man, leaning over the balcony, was so aroused that he forgot where he was and spit tobacco juice into the audience below. Another man jumped down from the window ledge and declared that when he died, he wanted to be buried on the very spot that Patrick Henry had delivered those words. (And so he was, twenty-five years later.)

The next year war came and Virginia volunteers marched off to battle with *Liberty or Death* embroidered on their shirtfronts. As for Patrick Henry, the people elected him governor.

On May 29th, 1777, he was elected for the second time. He was forty-one years old now, living in the luxurious palace where the royal governors had lived for fifty-five years. And he was busy, so busy that if a nice spring day came along, he wouldn't even have heard a redbird call.

Discussion Questions *A biography is the story of a person's life. Why is this story called a* historical *biography?* (Because the story is about the life of Patrick Henry, a person who played a part in American history.) *What lesson can be learned from Patrick Henry's life?* (Despite difficulty, a person must keep trying to succeed.)
Enriching Activities 1. *News headlines / stories.* Have the students write newspaper headlines and short articles about important events in Patrick Henry's life. **2.** *Speech writing.* Ask the students to write speeches on issues they feel strongly about. Suggest that they make outlines before writing and rehearse their speeches before presenting them to the class. **3.** *Costume fair.* Ask students to dress as the American hero of their choice. Organize a Great Americans Day parade, ask for brief reports about each character, and have an old-fashioned American picnic lunch.

Questions

1. At the trial of his first big case, Patrick Henry wished two people would *not* be there. Who were these two people? Tell why one of these people went home and why one stayed.

2. Patrick Henry became a great speaker, or *orator.* How did people react when they first heard his speeches? What did his speeches persuade the people of the colonies to do?

3. Why did the crowd become so excited when Patrick Henry cried, "Give me liberty or give me death"?

4. Match these words with their definitions.

   (page 364) client   a. obeyed
   (page 367) attorney   b. revoked
   (page 368) complied   c. lawyer
   (page 372) repealed   d. customer

Literal / recall Making time lines. The students may list any of the dates and events given below:

Activity

The biography of Patrick Henry begins on May 29, 1752. It closes on May 29, 1777. Draw a long line with one of those dates at each end. Find five very important happenings in Patrick Henry's life between those two dates. Write them on the time line you have drawn to show when they happened.

1754—marries Sarah Shelton; 1757—gives up farming; 1761—becomes a lawyer; 1763—wins the Parsons' Case; 1765—member of the House of Burgesses; 1773—speech against tea tax; 1775—"Give me liberty" speech.

1. Literal / recall
His uncle and his father. Patrick asked his uncle to go home and he complied. Patrick's father was the presiding judge so he could not leave. (pages 368–369)
2. Literal / recall and **Interpretive / inference** At first, the people were wild with excitement. Later, Henry's speeches persuaded the jury in the Parsons' Case to give the parsons less restitution; his resolutions against taxation encouraged colonists to oppose taxation; his liberty speech persuaded people to fight for independence. (pages 371–376)
3. Literal / recall and **Interpretive / inference** Possible answer: the crowd was upset about the issue and inspired by Patrick Henry's words. (page 376)
4. Vocabulary
client—d.; attorney—c.; complied—a.; repealed—b.

377

True to Life

A ghillie cap? What's that? And what is a gripsack? Those are two examples of *authentic*, or genuine, details one author used to help her readers picture life in the 1800s. (Read on to find out more about the ghillie cap and gripsack.) You'll find many such details, as well as more important facts, in every good biography you read. Authentic details give a sense of truthfulness to a biography. In a biography, truth and accuracy are essential, for a biography is the history of a person's life.

Writers of biographies may spend months or even years tracking down important facts and details about people and events, times and places. Such research helps biographers make their writings true to life.

Read the following paragraph from the biography *Where Was Patrick Henry on the 29th of May?* by Jean Fritz. Look for authentic details that give you the feeling of the time and place in which Patrick Henry lived.

At the quarter sessions of the court in March, June, September, and December, the most important cases were tried and then every bed in the tavern would be taken. (It cost 75¢ a night for a bed with clean sheets.) Traveling troupes of acrobats and jugglers came to town at that time; peddlers came to sell their wares; there were horse races, cockfights, and wrestling matches. From all over the county people came to see the shows, do their trading, and hear the cases argued.

Illustrations may play an important role in biographies by showing details of how people and things looked at a particular time or in a particular place. Illustrations, then, also need to be accurate. Look closely at the two illustrations on page 379. Can you find one detail that is wrong in each picture?

Objectives ● To recognize the importance of accuracy in biographies. ● To use background material when writing an account of a historic event.

Introducing the Lesson *The word* biography *comes from the ancient Greek word roots* bio, *which means "life," and* graphy, *which means "writing." A biography is a written account of a real person's life.*

Suppose that you were writing a biography of a person who lived in the past. What would you need to know about the person? (Possible answers: dates of birth and death; childhood experiences and important events; family life; friendships; education; accomplishments.) *Writers of biographies often fill in these details to make the person "come alive" for the reader.* (Continued on next page.)

In 1932, Amelia Earhart flew her red Vega monoplane—a single-winged plane—across the Atlantic from Newfoundland to Ireland. She was the first woman, and the second pilot, to make this solo flight.

In 1752, Benjamin Franklin flew a kite in a thunderstorm to prove that lightning is electricity.

(Answers: biplane—a double-winged plane; TV antenna.)

But what about the ghillie cap and gripsack? They belonged to Elizabeth Cochrane who, using the pen name[1] of Nellie Bly, was an American newspaper reporter during the late 1800s. As a reporter for the New York *World*, Nellie Bly became known for her articles exposing some of the terrible living and working conditions of that time. But she became famous for another reason. In 1890, before airplanes or automobiles were invented, Nellie Bly went around the world by train and ship in a little over seventy-two days—faster than anyone else had ever traveled. That's where the ghillie cap and the gripsack came in. On her historic trip around the world, Nellie wore one and carried her belongings in the other.

The pictures on pages 381 to 385 show some events in Nellie Bly's trip around the world. Imagine that you are Nellie Bly's biographer. You are writing a book for people your age about Nellie's trip. Choose one or more of the scenes pictured and describe what is happening. Make each event, and Nellie Bly's part in it, true-to-life and interesting for your readers. You can do this by including authentic details from the pictures as well as the facts given in the text below them. You may also want to include *dialogue,* or conversation, used in a picture, or you may want to add some of your own. Although such conversations are made up, they help to explain what really happened.

---

1. **pen name:** a made-up name an author uses to sign his or her work.

1. Nellie's Plan

Characters: Nellie Bly, a reporter; Julius Chambers—managing editor of the New York *World,* Nellie's employer.
Setting: Julius Chambers's office at the *World* newspaper.
Time: November, 1889
Facts: Few women traveled alone then; main forms of transportation— trains, ships, stagecoaches.

2. Starting Out—New Jersey

Characters: Nellie Bly; Julius Chambers—managing editor of the *World* newspaper; other newspaper editors; steamship-company officials; Nellie's mother.
Setting: Pier in Hoboken, New Jersey.

Time: November 14, 1889.
Facts: Ship was the *Augusta Victoria;* destination—England; articles in Nellie's gripsack included only one other dress and hat, lots of paper and pencils.

3. First Stop—England

Characters: Nellie Bly; London reporter for the *World* newspaper.
Setting: Hotel in London, England.

Facts: Nellie made the trip to Jules Verne's house and wrote a story about it. She didn't miss her boat.

4. At the Market—Singapore

Characters: Nellie Bly; Chinese merchant.
Setting: Singapore.
Facts: Nellie rode in a jinriksha—a small two-wheeled carriage pulled by one or two men. The captain of Nellie's boat considered it bad luck to have a monkey on his ship. Nellie and the captain argued. Nellie kept the monkey.

384

5. Homecoming—New Jersey

Characters: Nellie Bly; Mayor of Jersey City, New Jersey; timekeepers; huge crowd of people.
Setting: Railroad station in Jersey City, New Jersey.
Time: 3:15 P.M. on January 26, 1890.

Facts: All factory whistles in New Jersey blew. Official time recorded by three stopwatches: 72 days, 6 hours, 11 minutes, and 14 seconds. The *World* headlines read: FATHER TIME OUTDONE!

I brought to the New World the gift of devotion

Harriet Tubman was born a slave in Maryland in 1820. She escaped from slavery in 1849. She then began the very dangerous work of acting as a "conductor" on the Underground Railroad, a secret system of helping slaves escape from the South to freedom in the northern United States or Canada. Harriet Tubman risked her life again and again, helping more than three hundred slaves travel the Underground Railroad to freedom. She came to be called the Black Moses because she led so many people out of slavery, just as Moses is said to have led the people of Israel to freedom from the Egyptian pharaoh, many centuries ago.

386

Discussion Question *The poem praises Harriet Tubman's actions. What did she do? (Escaped from slavery; returned to help others escape from slavery.)*

Illustrated by Tim Boxell

I was Harriet Tubman, who would not stay in bondage.
I followed the devious, uncharted trails to the North,
I followed the light of the North Star,
    I ran away to freedom in 1849.
I was Harriet Tubman who could not stay in freedom,
    While her brothers were enslaved.
"Go down, Moses," back into Egypt,
    Back to the land of the bloodhound and the pateroller,
"Tell old Pharaoh, let my people go!"

Everywhere they waited for my coming,
    Tiny treasures hid against my coming—
I was the lone call of an owl in the darkness,
I was the blurred line of a Spiritual under a slave-cabin window,
I was the last, faint tremor of hope upon the wind.
    I was Harriet Tubman,
    Who "never run my train off the track,
    And never lost a passenger."

Enriching Activity
Writing. Have the students choose a person they admire and write a short biographical poem or account.

The poem's last two lines are Harriet Tubman's own words. She is referring to the Underground Railroad.

—Hildegarde Hoyt Swift

SAVED BY A WHISKER

From the novel *By the Great Horn Spoon!* by Sid Fleischman

Illustrated by Willi Baum

Reading Level Challenging

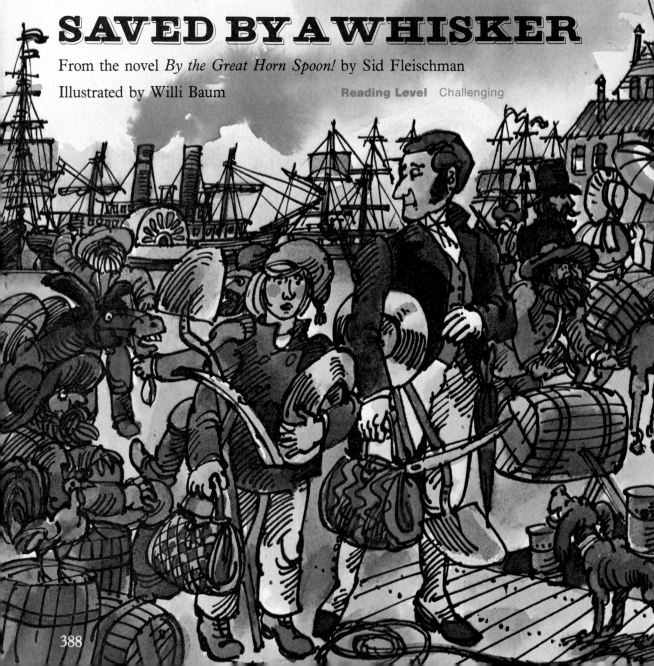

Introducing the Story Display a map of the United States. *In 1848, gold was discovered in the California foothills of the Sierra Mountains, and by 1849 thousands of people from all over the country and the world had come to California to strike it rich. They searched for nuggets or veins of gold in rocks and stream beds. The miners would run water through dirt and rocks to find the gold. (Though dirt would wash away, gold would sink to the bottom of a pan.) This story will give you a good idea of the excitement and confusion in San Francisco during the time of the Gold Rush.*

Word to Know

  quartz: a crystalline mineral in which gold may be found. (page 395)

The year is 1849. Gold has been discovered in California. The scramble for quick fortunes is on. A paddle-wheeled sailing ship churns out of Boston Harbor bound for San Francisco by way of Cape Horn. Below the creaking decks two stowaways hide in potato barrels, while the thief who stole their money travels in comfort above. In one barrel is twelve-year-old Jack Flagg, an orphan on his way to strike it rich so his penniless Aunt Arabella can keep the family mansion. In the other is Praiseworthy, Aunt Arabella's loyal butler.

After a long voyage, during which they cleverly catch the thief, the two gold-seekers arrive in San Francisco—where survival itself requires cleverness.

In his pea jacket and stocking cap Jack felt fourteen years old at least. Maybe fifteen. He stood in the bow of the whale boat and watched the Long Wharf come closer. They bumped against the boat-stairs and Jack was the first out. His heart raced with the excitement of the moment. They had arrived, and he was ready to start digging.

"Not so fast, Master Jack," said Praiseworthy. "Don't forget your pick and shovel."

A *sidewheeler* is a ship that is powered by a huge wheel on its side.

A hilltop telegraph had signaled the arrival of a side-wheeler and now it seemed as if all of San Francisco had turned out. The wharf was alive with men, women and children—not to mention dogs, mules, and chickens. Sea gulls flocked in the air like confetti.

Weighted down with their belongings, Praiseworthy and Jack started along the wharf. There were barrels and boxes piled everywhere. Peddlers and hawkers and hotel runners mixed through the crowd and shouted at the newcomers.

"Welcome, boys! Welcome to the fastest growing city in the world!"

"Flannel shirts for sale! Red flannel shirts, gents! They don't show the dirt!"

"Try the Niantic Hotel. The cleanest beds in town."

A *horn spoon* is a scoop that was used to test gold washings.

"Horn spoons! You'll need 'em at the diggin's. Carved from genuine ox horn!"

"Stay at the Parker House. None better!"

The wharf seemed a mile long and the noisiest place on earth. Beyond, the city rang to the sound of hammers. Buildings were going up everywhere and a sand dredger was pounding the air. Men stood in the doorways of the shops ringing hand bells.

A *dredger* is a ship with a scooping machine used for deepening waterways.

"Auction! Auction going on! Fresh eggs just arrived from Panama!"

"Onions at auction! Fifty bushels just come in from the Sandwich Islands! Also calomel pills, castor oil, and carpet tacks!"

The *Sandwich Islands* are now called the Hawaiian Islands.

Praiseworthy and Jack continued along the boardwalk, which was hammered together mostly out of barrel staves, and reached the United States Hotel. Their ship's captain had recommended it.

Calomel /kal′·ə·mel/ is a white powder used in medicine.

Staves are bent pieces of wood in barrels.

"A fine room, if you please," Praiseworthy said to the hotel clerk. "And I think a tub bath would be in order."

"Very good, sir," replied the clerk. He was a bald-headed man with thin strands of hair combed sideways, from ear to ear. "That'll be ten dollars extra—each."

"What's that?" Praiseworthy scowled. "We don't want to bathe in champagne. Water will do, sir."

"Champagne'd be almost cheaper, gents. Water's a dollar a bucket. Unless you want to wait until next November. Prices come down when it rains."

Diggings is a place where digging or mining is carried on.

The walls were covered with dyed cotton cloth called *calico*.

"We'll wait," said Praiseworthy with decision. In this part of the world, he thought, a man had to strike it rich just to keep his neck clean. He signed the register and Jack gazed at a bearded miner pacing back and forth across the lobby floor. He wore a floppy hat and chestnut hair tumbled out on all sides like mattress stuffing coming loose. He kept glancing at the loud wall clock as if every advancing second might be his last.

Jack couldn't take his eyes off the man. Tucked in his wide leather belt were a revolver, a horn spoon, and a soft buckskin bag. Gold dust! Jack thought. He must have just got in from the mines!

"Ruination!" the miner began to mutter. "Ruination!"

Praiseworthy blotted the register. "How," he asked the clerk, "does one get to the mines?"

"Riverboat leaves every afternoon at four o'clock from the Long Wharf. Fare to Sacramento City is twenty-five dollars. From there you make your way to the <u>diggings</u> by stage, muleback, or foot."

Jack shot a glance at Praiseworthy. Twenty-five dollars—each! Why, they didn't *have* that much money! But the butler didn't so much as raise an eyebrow. "We'll be taking the boat tomorrow," he told the clerk.

"Ruination!" said the miner.

"Come along, Master Jack," said Praiseworthy.

The walls of their room were lined with blood-red <u>calico</u> and there was China matting on the plank floor. The window looked out on the shipping in the bay, the masts as thick as a pine forest. There were not only gold ships, but Navy <u>frigates</u> and Chinese <u>junks</u> and the going and coming of <u>longboats</u>. But Jack wasn't interested in the view.

"*Fifty* dollars just to get to Sacramento City!" he said. "We'll have to walk."

"Good exercise, no doubt, but we haven't time for it." Praiseworthy gazed out at the distant hills across the bay. Sacramento City was more than a hundred miles up river, he had heard, and the diggings in the foothills beyond that. "Let me see. It took us five months to get this far and it will take us another five months to get home. If we are to keep your Aunt Arabella from being sold out—we have two months left. Two months to fill our pockets with <u>nuggets</u>."

Jack found himself pacing back and forth like the miner in the lobby below. "Ruination!" Jack said. "We've come all this way and now—we're no closer."

"Nonsense," said Praiseworthy. There was a pitcher half filled with water on the chest and he poured a small amount into the washpan. "We'll be on tomorrow's riverboat, I promise you. Now then, I suggest we wash up as best we can, Master Jack."

Wash! Jack thought. There wasn't time to wash! "How will we pay the fare?"

"Let me see. We have thirty-eight dollars left. That's a start, isn't it? Of course, we'll have our room and meals to pay. But if I detect one thing in the air—it's opportunity. The sooner you wash, Master Jack, the sooner we can tend to our financial dilemma. Your Aunt Arabella wouldn't allow you abroad on the streets with dirty ears and sea salt in your eyebrows. And don't forget the soap."

A *frigate* is a warship fitted with four-cornered sails.

A *junk* (line 2) is a large, Chinese sailing ship.

A *longboat* (line 2) is a large boat carried aboard a huge sailing ship.

Sometimes gold is formed in lumps, or *nuggets*.

"Ruination," Jack muttered again. He might as well be home in Boston.

They washed and changed into fresh clothes. Then they returned to the lobby. The shaggy miner was still there, pacing and muttering in his dusty beard. He glanced at Jack, a dark sudden glance—and then the butler and the boy went out on the street.

But as they ambled along the boardwalk looking for opportunity, Jack began to realize that the miner was following them. He was still at their heels when the butler and the boy crossed the street. Jack was beginning to feel anxious. Even a little scared. Finally he looked up at Praiseworthy.

"He's following us."

"Who's following us?" asked the butler.

"That miner from the hotel."

"Stuff and nonsense. The streets are free to every-one."

"But he's following us, Praiseworthy."

"Nothing to fear in broad daylight, Master Jack."

They continued along the sandy plaza, still looking for opportunity, and the miner marched right behind them.

"Must be a madman," said Praiseworthy, turning. He stopped and the miner stopped and they stood face to face. "Sir," said the butler. "Are you following us?"

"Ruination! I shore am!"

"I'll thank you to go your way, sir!"

"No offense, gents," the miner said. "Been on the verge of breakin' in on your conversation, but it didn't seem courteous." It was hard to see his mouth for the fullness of his beard. "They call me Quartz Jackson, and I just come in from the diggin's. My fiancée's due in on the stage any minute. Comin' up from the capital at Monterey. We ain't never met, but we writ a lot of letters. And that's just it."

A *fiancée* /fē′·än·sā′/ is a bride-to-be.

"And that's just what?" said Praiseworthy.

"We're supposed to be gettin' married. But *ruination*—when she takes one look at me, she's goin' to think I'm part grizzly bear." He whipped off his floppy hat and his dusty hair fell out on all sides. "She'll get right back on the stage for Monterey. But shucks, I ain't such a badlookin' gent—leastways, I wasn't when I went to the diggin's. I'm just a mite growed over, you might say. Well, I been trampin' every street in town lookin' for a barber, but they all lit out for the mines. Don't seem to be anyone left here but the auctioneers. Anyway, that's why I couldn't help starin' at the lad here."

Leastways means at least.

"Me?" said Jack.

"Why, that yeller hair of yours looks fresh from the barber shop. All cut and trimmed. I figured you must have flushed out a barber and maybe you'd do Quartz Jackson the favor of leadin' me to him."

If Jack had feared the miner for a moment, he couldn't help smiling at him now. He liked the man. "No, sir," he said. "I haven't been to a barber. Unless you mean Praiseworthy."

"Praiseworthy?"

"At your service," said the butler. "It's true, I've been cutting Master Jack's hair, but only out of necessity."

The miner's face—what could be seen of it—broke into a sunny smile. "I'd be much obliged if you'd barber me up, Mr. Praiseworthy. Name your price."

"But I'm not a barber, sir. I'm a butler."

"A what?"

"I couldn't accept any money for merely—"

"Well, now, that's mighty good of you. Tell you what I'll do. I'll let you have all the hair you cut off."

Praiseworthy and Jack exchanged fresh glances. The man was some sort of lunatic after all. What earthly use did they have for the man's <u>shorn</u> <u>locks</u>? But it seemed wise to humor him, and Praiseworthy said, "I'll be glad to help you in your hour of need, sir. Consider it a modest wedding present."

Twenty minutes later the miner was seated on a nail <u>keg</u> in a corner of the hotel porch, and Praiseworthy was snipping away with the shears. Quartz Jackson insisted that every lock be caught as it fell.

Shorn means *cut.* *Locks* are ringlets of hair.

A keg *is a small barrel.*

Jack was kept busy holding a washpan under Praise-worthy's busy scissors. It worried him that time was wasting and they were yet to make their boat fare. But he knew it would have been impossible for Praiseworthy to turn his back on a gentleman in distress—even a peculiar miner like Mr. Quartz Jackson.

"My, ain't the town growed, though," said the miner. "Must be all of four-five thousand folks in the place. You gents figure on goin' to the diggin's?"

"We do indeed," said Praiseworthy.

"I come from Hangtown. The boys have been locatin' a good lot of color up that way."

"Color?"

"The yeller stuff. Gold. If you get up Hangtown way, tell 'em you're a friend of Quartz Jackson. Tell 'em I'll be comin' home with my bride in a couple of weeks. Shore is nice of you to shear me this way. Would you mind trimmin' the beard while you're at it? Always itchin', and I can hardly find my mouth to spit with. Jack, young Jack, a bit of sideburn is gettin' away in the breeze. Wouldn't want you to lose any."

"Yes, sir," said Jack, catching the lock of hair.

Quartz Jackson's face began to appear, snip by snip, like a statue being chipped out of stone. When Praiseworthy had finished the miner turned to look at himself in the hotel windowpane, and he almost jumped out of his jackboots.

Jackboots are high, laceless leather boots.

"By the Great Horn Spoon!" he said. "Is that *me?*" Quartz Jackson was obviously pleased. "Why, I'd forgot I was so young!"

Quartz Jackson was a fine-looking gent at that, Jack thought. He had good teeth and an easy smile. Except for his revolver, his horn spoon, and his red flannel shirt, he hardly seemed the same man. But what did he expect them to do with the hair cuttings? Stuff a mattress?

"Your fiancée will be very pleased," smiled Praiseworthy. "Our congratulations on your forth-coming marriage, sir."

"Much obliged, Praiseworthy. You saved me from certain ruination. The least I can do is learn you how to work a gold pan. Water boy! You there! Fetch us a bucket of dew over here."

Much obliged means thank you.

The miner paid for the water by taking a pinch of fine gold dust from his buckskin pouch. Jack was eager to get the hang of mining and Quartz Jackson, peculiar or not, was clearly an expert.

"Gimme the washpan, Jack, young Jack."

Jack handed over the tin pan, piled high with chestnut whiskers and trimmings. The miner wet them down with fresh water and began to swish the pan around.

"Gold's heavy," he explained. "Nothin' heavier. Even the yeller dust sinks to the bottom if you keep workin' the pan. Like this."

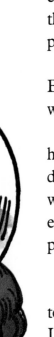

Then he handed the washpan to Jack and taught him the motion. The water turned brown from the dirt and mud that had gathered in Quartz Jackson's whiskers and hair. Finally he poured off everything— everything but a thin <u>residue</u> at the bottom of the pan. Jack's eyes opened like blossoms.

A residue is the part left over.

Gold dust!

"Why, look there!" the miner roared with laughter. "The boy's panned himself some color. I figured I scratched enough pay dirt into my beard to assay out at about $14 an ounce. Since I give you the whiskers and all—the gold is yours!"

Jack had never known a more exciting moment in his life. The grains of dust sparkled like yellow fire—and there was even a flake or two.

Half an hour later, while Quartz Jackson was having a $10 tub bath, Praiseworthy and Jack were plucking opportunity from the air. They put up a sign that said, "FREE HAIRCUTS Miners Only."

Questions

1. Praiseworthy said that he detected opportunity in the air. Why did he say that? What did he mean?

2. Why, at the end of the story, did the sign say "Miners Only"?

3. Do you think that Jack and Praiseworthy struck gold when they got to the foothills beyond Sacramento City? How does the story help you form your opinion?

4. Complete these comparisons that were used in the story. Comparisons that use such terms as *like* or *as* are called *similes*.
   a. "Sea gulls flocked in the air like _____."
   b. The masts in the harbor were "as thick as _____."
   c. Quartz Jackson's face began to show during the barbering "like a _____."

Activity

When you read a story, your mind becomes a camera, showing you pictures of the *setting*—where and when the story takes place. Find a way to show someone what your mind photographed as you read "Saved by a Whisker." Draw a part of the setting, write about it, or find some other way that seems best to you.

About SID FLEISCHMAN

Sid Fleischman is a master of the tall tale. His stories are so outlandish, and his characters so funny, that they make us laugh. Many of his stories are about the American frontier. To gather information, Sid Fleischman reads old books, newspapers, and magazines. His characters often speak in *dialects*, which are special ways of speaking that some groups of people share. The dialects help give the flavor of the time and place he writes about.

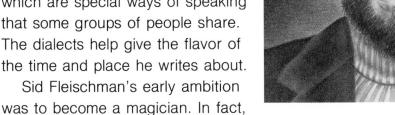

Sid Fleischman's early ambition was to become a magician. In fact, while he was in high school, he and a friend put on magic shows. After he finished college, he worked as a newspaper reporter. Then he began writing books.

Unlike many authors, Sid Fleischman doesn't outline his stories ahead of time. He usually starts with a background, like the California gold rush in *By the Great Horn Spoon!* Then he just writes. "I rarely know what is going to happen next," Sid Fleischman says, "and I have to sit at the typewriter to find out."

More Books by Sid Fleischman

Mr. Mysterious and Company   (Little, Brown & Co., 1962)
The Ghost on Saturday Night   (Little, Brown & Co., 1974)
The Ghost in the Noonday Sun   (Little, Brown & Co., 1965)
McBroom Tells a Lie   (Little, Brown & Co., 1976)
Humbug Mountain   (Little, Brown & Co., 1978)

All Things Are Connected

From a letter by Chief Sealth

Reading Level Average

Objectives ● To para-phrase the main idea of a passage. ● To note poetic word choice and imagery in prose.

In 1855 Chief Sealth[1] of the Duwamish tribe of the State of Washington sent a letter to President Franklin Pierce. The letter was in response to an offer by the government to buy the tribe's land. Here is part of that letter.

---

1. **Sealth** (SELTH).

Introducing the Letter   *Sometimes the writer of a book, an article, or a letter uses language so beautifully that it sounds like poetry. As you read this letter, notice which sentences sound beautiful to you.*

Discussion Questions   *Why did Chief Sealth send this letter?* (He was concerned about how the United States government would treat the land and wildlife.) *Why does the letter still interest us today?* (Possible answer: many people are concerned about preserving the wilderness.) *Read aloud some words or sentences that sounded beautiful to you.* (Possible answers: "sparkle of the water"—line 3; "Every shining pine needle. . . ."—lines 6–9.)

Enriching Activity   *Oral extension/art.* Have each student bring a natural object to class and tell how it is connected to other parts of nature. For example, a shell, shed by an *animal* that lived in the *ocean,* is washed onto land by *waves.* The students could also show the relationships in circular diagrams or pictures.

How can you buy or sell the sky—the warmth of the land? The idea is strange to us. We do not own the freshness of the air or the sparkle of the water. How can you buy them from us?

We will decide in our time. Every part of this earth is sacred to my people. Every shining pine needle, every sandy shore, every mist in the dark woods, every clearing and humming insect is holy in the memory and experience of my people. . . .

If I decide to accept, I will make one condition. The white man must treat the beasts of this land as his brothers. . . . What is man without the beasts? If all the beasts were gone, men would die from a great loneliness of spirit, for whatever happens to the beast also happens to man. All things are connected. Whatever befalls the earth befalls the sons of the earth. . . .

If we sell you our land, love it as we've loved it. Care for it, as we've cared for it. Hold in your mind the memory of the land, as it is when you take it. And with all your strength, with all your might, and with all your heart—preserve it for your children.

Illustrated by Daniel San Souci

405

Oh, My Darling Clementine

A song by P. Montrose

Objectives ● To identify a ballad. ● To identify a ballad's mood.

Introducing the Ballad *A ballad is a song or poem that tells a story. Let's read the unusual story in this ballad.*

Discussion Questions *What is the story in the song?* (A Gold Rush miner's daughter drowns, and her father dies soon after.) *Who is the "I" in the song?* (Clementine's boyfriend; another miner.)

Enriching Activity *Singing.* Have the students sing "Oh, My Darling Clementine."

In the mid-1800s gold had been discovered in California. Soon the small village of San Francisco became a city filled with people with gold dust in their pockets, or with golden dreams in their heads. Tales of new gold discoveries, lost fortunes, and wild mining town doings were on everyone's lips. A few of the stories were true, many were lies, and some became songs to be sung over and over again.

1. In a cav-ern in a can-yon, Ex-ca-va-ting for a

mine, Dwelt a min-er, for-ty-nin-er, And his daugh-ter Cle-men-tine.

Refrain

Oh, my dar-ling, Oh, my dar-ling, Oh, my dar-ling Cle-men-

tine, You are lost and gone for-ev-er, Dread-ful sor-ry, Cle-men-tine.

406

2. Light she was and like a fairy,
   And her shoes were number nine,
   Herring boxes without topses,
   Sandals were for Clementine.

3. Drove her ducklings to the water,
   Every morning just at nine,
   Hit her foot against a splinter,
   Fell into the foaming brine.
   Brine is salt water.

4. Ruby lips above the water,
   Blowing bubbles soft and fine,
   Alas, for me! I was no swimmer,
   So I lost my Clementine.
   A myrtle is a kind of tree.

5. In a churchyard, near the canyon,
   Where the myrtle doth entwine,
   There grow roses and other posies,
   Fertilized by Clementine.
   Entwine means to grow around something.

6. Then the miner, forty-niner,
   Soon began to droop and pine,
   Thought he "oughter jine" his daughter,
   Now he's with his Clementine.
   Pine means long for or mourn.

Illustrated by Michel Allaire

John Henry

A ballad

Objectives ● To identify a ballad. ● To identify the mood of a ballad. ● To recognize that repetition helps people remember ballads.

Introducing the Ballad *John Henry was a steel driver. His job was to drive steel spikes through hard rock and soil with a heavy hammer. The holes that he drilled would then be filled with blasting charges to break ground for a new railroad track. The newly invented steam drill in the song does the same job with a steam engine. John Henry is so proud of his abilities that he challenges the machine to a contest.*

Was John Henry a real flesh and blood man, a steel driver of great strength and grit? To this day people wonder about that. Some say John Henry was an imaginary hero, like Paul Bunyan and his Blue Ox Babe. Others say he really did help build the Big Bend Tunnel for the railroad in West Virginia in the 1870s. But on one thing almost everyone agrees: John Henry is a man worth singing about.

1. When John Hen-ry was a-bout three days old,
Just a-sittin' on his pap-py's knee,
He gave one loud and lone-some cry:
"The_____ ham-mer'll be the death of me,
The_____ ham-mer'll be the death of me."

2. Well, the captain said to John Henry one day:
   "Gonna bring that steam drill 'round,
   Gonna take that steam drill out on the job,
   Gonna whop that steel on down,
   Gonna whop that steel on down."

3. John Henry said to the captain:
   "Well, the next time you go to town
   Just bring me back a twelve-pound hammer
   And I'll beat your steam drill down," etc.

   The last line of each verse should be repeated.

4. John Henry said to the captain:
   "Well, a man ain't nothin' but a man,
   And before I let a steam drill beat me down
   Gonna die with the hammer in my hand."

5. John Henry went to the tunnel,
   And they put him in the lead to drive,
   The rock so tall and John Henry so small,
   He laid down his hammer and he cried.

6. John Henry said to his shaker:
   "Shaker, why don't you sing?
   For I'm swingin' twelve pounds from the
       hips on down,
   Just listen to that cold steel ring."

A *shaker* is the person
who holds the steel
spike in place while
the steel driver
hammers it.

409

Enriching Activities 1. *Listening to music.* Like all folk songs, "John Henry" has many versions because individual singers add their own touches. Play two or more recordings of "John Henry," and have the class discuss the differences. 2. *Singing.* Have the class sing a number of American ballads, such as "The Erie Canal," "Old Smokey," and "Arkansas Traveler." See *Folk Song, U.S.A.*, by John and Alan Lomax (New American Library, 1975), for the music and lyrics. Discuss the tales told in the songs.

7. John Henry told his captain:
   "Look-a yonder what I see—
   Your drill's done broke and your hole's
      done choke',
   And you can't drive steel like me."

8. Well, the man that invented the steam drill,
   He thought he was mighty fine,
   But John Henry drove his fifteen feet,
   And the steam drill only made nine.

9. John Henry looked up at the mountain,
   And his hammer was striking fire,
   Well, he hammered so hard that he broke
      his poor old heart,
   He laid down his hammer and he died.

10. They took John Henry to the graveyard,
    And they laid him in the sand,
    Three men from the east and a woman
       from the west
    Came to see that old steel-drivin' man.

11. They took John Henry to the graveyard,
    And they laid him in the sand,
    And every locomotive comes a-roarin' by
    Says: "There lies a steel-drivin' man."

410

Illustrated by Michel Allaire

Lincoln Monument: Washington

A poem by Langston Hughes

Objectives • To note the effect of repetition in a free-verse poem. • To explore the meaning of a paradox.

Introducing the Poem *Langston Hughes, a Black American, is considered one of America's great poets. This poem is about a visit that Hughes made to the Lincoln Monument.*

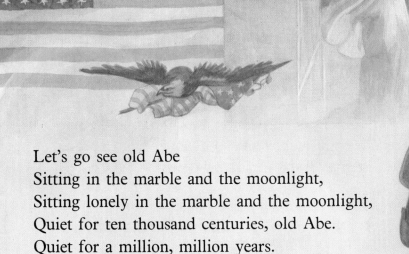

Let's go see old Abe
Sitting in the marble and the moonlight,
Sitting lonely in the marble and the moonlight,
Quiet for ten thousand centuries, old Abe.
Quiet for a million, million years.

Quiet—

And yet a voice forever
Against the
Timeless walls
Of time—
Old Abe.

Discussion Questions *Which words are repeated in this poem?* ("Sitting in the marble and the moonlight"; "quiet"; "million"; "old Abe.") *Why might the poet have repeated these words and phrases?* (Possible answer: to emphasize that it is a statue.) *In this poem Lincoln is both quiet and "a voice forever." How can both be true?* (Possible answer: Lincoln is gone, but his ideas will be remembered forever.)

Enriching Activity *Research.* Have the students prepare short oral reports about famous Americans they admire. Ask them to explain in their reports why these people should always be remembered.

Illustrated by Christa Keiffer

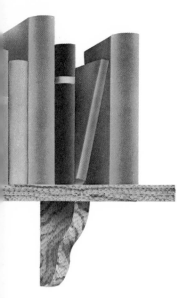

BOOKSHELF

Runaway to Freedom by Barbara Smucker. Harper & Row, 1977. Disguised as boys, Julilly and her friend Liza escape from slavery and manage to reach Canada by way of the Underground Railroad.
Reading Level Challenging

American Tall Tales by Adrien Stoutenburg. Viking Press, 1966. These are eight tough and bold tales about such American folk heroes as Pecos Bill, Mike Fink, Paul Bunyan, and John Henry.
Reading Level Easy

Caddie Woodlawn by Carol Ryrie Brink. Macmillan, 1935. This story of pioneer life, set on the Wisconsin frontier of the 1860s, features the adventures of a courageous eleven-year-old girl and her two brothers.
Reading Level Average

Meet the Real Pilgrims by Robert H. Loeb, Jr. Doubleday, 1979. Through photographs and interviews with the town's inhabitants, the author takes the reader on an actual visit to a working replica of the original Plymouth Plantation as it was in 1627.
Reading Level Average

Sounder by William Armstrong. Harper & Row, 1969. When a sharecropper takes food for his starving family, he is sent to jail. The family's faithful and courageous hound, Sounder, helps them through the difficult years of the father's absence.
Reading Level Average

The Amazing Voyage of the New Orleans by Judith St. George. G. P. Putnam, 1980. This true story of the first steamboat trip from Pittsburgh to New Orleans includes accounts of dangerous floods and a violent earthquake.
Reading Level Easy

GLOSSARY

This glossary gives the meanings of unfamiliar words used in the text of this book. The meanings given here define words only the way they are used in the book. You can find other meanings for these words in a dictionary.

The correct pronunciation of each glossary word is given in the special spelling after that word. The sounds used in these spellings are explained in the following Pronunciation Key. Each symbol, or letter, stands for a sound, a sound you can recognize in the words following it. In addition to these sounds, each glossary pronunciation includes marks to show the kind of force, or stress, with which certain syllables are pronounced. A heavy mark, **′**, shows that the syllable it follows is given the strongest, or primary, stress, as in **sis·ter** (sis′·ter). A lighter mark, ′, shows that the syllable it follows is given a secondary, or lighter, stress, as in **tax·i·cab** (tak′·sē·kab′).

Several abbreviations are used in the glossary: *v.,* verb; *adv.,* adverb; *n.,* noun; *adj.,* adjective; *pl.,* plural.

Pronunciation Key

a	add, map	m	move, seem	u	up, done
ā	ace, rate	n	nice, tin	û(r)	urn, term
â(r)	care, air	ng	ring, song	yo͞o	use, few
ä	palm, father	o	odd, hot	v	vain, eve
b	bat, rub	ō	open, so	w	win, away
ch	check, catch	ô	order, jaw	y	yet, yearn
d	dog, rod	oi	oil, boy	z	zest, muse
e	end, pet	ou	out, now	zh	vision, pleasure
ē	even, tree	o͞o	pool, food	ə	the schwa,
f	fit, half	o͝o	took, full		an unstressed
g	go, log	p	pit, stop		vowel representing
h	hope, hate	r	run, poor		the sound spelled
i	it, give	s	see, pass		a in above
ī	ice, write	sh	sure, rush		e in sicken
j	joy, ledge	t	talk, sit		i in possible
k	cool, take	th	thin, both		o in melon
l	look, rule	t͟h	this, bathe		u in circus

ac·com·plices (ə·kom′·plis·iz) *n., pl.* Helpers or partners, especially in a wrongdoing.

am·bled (am′·bəld) *v.* Walked at a slow and easy pace.

an·ces·tor (an′·ses·tər) *n.* A person from whom one is descended, especially a person further back than a grandparent.

at·ten·dant (ə·ten′·dənt) *adj.* Serving or attending.

au·burn (ô′·bûrn) *adj.* Reddish brown.

auc·tion (ôk′·shən) *n.* A public sale at which each item is sold to the person offering the highest price for it.

bil·lows (bil′·ōz) *n., pl.* Large waves.

blue·bot·tle (bloo′·bot′·əl) *n.* A large fly with a metallic-blue body.

boon (boon) *n.* A blessing.

chiv·al·rous (shiv′·əl·rəs) *adj.* Having to do with the code of life of knights in the Middle Ages—the qualities of gallantry, courtesy, bravery, and kindness.

clar·i·on (klar′·ē·ən) *adj.* Clear and piercing.

co·horts (kō′·hôrts) *n., pl.* Companions or followers.

con·spir·a·to·ri·al·ly (kən·spir′·ə·tôr′·ē·əl·lē) *adv.* Acting in a way that suggests a secret plan to commit an evil or unlawful action.

con·trived (kən·trīvd′) *v.* Figured out; designed or invented.

crum·pets (krum′·pits) *n., pl.* Flat, unsweetened cakes baked on a griddle.

cu·po·la (kyoo′·pə·lə) *n.* A small tower built on a roof, usually having a dome-shaped top.

curt·sy (kûrt′·sē) *n.* A bow made by bending the knees with one foot forward, used by women and girls.

dep·o·si·tions (dep′·ə·zish′·ənz) *n., pl.* Testimonies given by witnesses under oath, especially written testimonies.

de·vi·ous (dē′·vē·əs) *adj.* Not direct or straight.

di·lem·ma (di·lem′·ə) *n.* A situation in which the choices are unpleasant.

dis·cred·it (dis·kred′·it) *v.* To disgrace; to bring dishonor to.

dis·taffs (dis′·tafs) *n., pl.* Sticks holding unspun flax or wool used in spinning.

droll (drōl) *adj.* Amusing in an odd or strange way.

em·bers (em′·bərz) *n., pl.* The glowing remains of a fire.

en·chan·tress (in·chan′·tris) *n.* A woman who practices magic; a sorceress.

ex·ca·vat·ing (eks′·kə·vāt′·ing) *v.* Digging out.

fan·fare (fan′·fâr′) *n.* Music played on trumpets to attract attention.

fend·er (fen′·dər) *n.* A metal guard or frame set in front of a fireplace to keep in sparks or hot coals.

fi·an·cée (fē′·än·sā′) *n.* A woman engaged to be married.

fiends (fēndz) *n., pl.* Cruel or wicked persons.

fi·es·ta (fē·es′·tə) *n.* A festival.

fleeces (flēs·iz) *n., pl.* The coats of

wool covering sheep or similar animals.

fol·ly (fol′·ē) *n.* Foolishness.

gal·lant (gal′·ənt) *adj.* Bold and courageous; brave.

grim·ly (grim′·lē) *adv.* Sternly.

guise (gīz) *n.* A false appearance; a costume.

haz·ard (haz′·ərd) *n.* A danger.

im·pu·dence (im′·pyə·dəns) *n.* Boldness; disrespect.

in·cense (in′·sens) *n.* A substance that gives off a pleasant odor when burned.

in·cin·er·a·tor (in·sin′·ə·rā′·tər) *n.* A furnace for burning rubbish or waste.

in·fec·tious (in·fek′·shəs) *adj.* Likely to spread to other people; catching.

in·trep·id (in·trep′·id) *adj.* Very brave; fearless.

joust·ing (jous′·ting) *n.* A formal combat between two knights armed with lances.

kay·ak (kī′·ak) *n.* An Eskimo canoe made of animal skins stretched over a wood frame with a hole in the center where the paddler sits.

leagues (lēgs) *n., pl.* An old measure of distance. A league was usually equal to three miles on land or sea.

lin·tel (lin′·təl) *n.* The beam across the top of a door frame or window frame.

mal·a·dy (mal′·ə·dē) *n.* A disease, sickness, or illness.

mirth (mûrth) *n.* Great enjoyment, usually expressed by laughter.

mo·men·tum (mō·men′·tum) *n.* Force or strength that keeps growing.

op·por·tu·ni·ty (op′·ər·tōō′·nə·tē) *n.* A right time or occasion.

pa·te·rol·ler, usually patroller (pə·trō′·lər) *n.* During Harriet Tubman's time, patrollers were armed men who hunted runaway slaves, often using bloodhounds.

pen·nons (pen′·ənz) *n., pl.* Small flags ending in a point carried by knights on their lances.

phar·aoh (fâr′·ō) *n.* Any one of the kings of ancient Egypt.

Phil·har·mon·ic (fil′·här·mon′·ik) *n.* A symphony orchestra.

preen (prēn) *v.* To smooth or clean (feathers) with a beak.

prom·i·nent (prom′·ə·nənt) *adj.* Well-known; distinguished.

prow (prou) *n.* The forward part of a ship; the bow.

quest (kwest) *n.* An expedition, as by a knight seeking adventure.

quill (kwil) *n.* A large, stiff feather, sometimes used to make an old-fashioned writing pen.

rec·om·men·da·tion (rek′·ə·men·dā′·shən) *n.* A favorable statement concerning someone's character or qualifications.

reg·u·la·tion (reg′·yə·lā′·shən) *adj.* Made according to certain requirements or rules.

re·mote (ri·mōt′) *adj.* Distant; far away.

res·i·due (rez′·ə·dōō) *n.* What is left after part is taken away; remainder.

scorched (skôrcht) *adj.* Burned slightly on the surface.

sea ur·chins (sē ûr′·chinz) *n., pl.* Small sea animals with round, spiny shells.

seem·ly (sēm′·lē) *adj.* Decent or proper; suitable.

side-wheel·er (sīd′·hwēl′·ər) *n.* A steamboat with its paddle wheel on the side.

smote (smōt) *v.* Hit very hard.

sneered (snērd) *v.* Showed contempt or dislike for in speech or facial expression.

sol·emn (sol′·əm) *adj.* Very serious; earnest.

sor·cer·ess (sôr′·sər·is) *n.* A woman who practices magic, especially with the assistance or control of evil spirits.

spec·ta·tors (spek′·tā·tərz) *n., pl.* People who watch an event.

spin·dle (spin′·dəl) *n.* A stick or rod used in spinning for winding thread.

stow·a·ways (stō′·ə·wāz′) *n., pl.* People who hide aboard a ship or other form of transportation to obtain free passage.

sub·lime (sə·blīm′) *adj.* Noble; supreme.

suf·fo·cat·ed (suf′·ə·kāt·id) *v.* Killed from lack of air.

symp·toms (sim′·təmz) *n., pl.* Signs or indications of something, especially of a disease.

tit·tered (tit′·ərd) *v.* Laughed as if making fun; snickered.

trans·fixed (trans·fikst′) *adj.* Motion-less, as with horror, fear, or admiration.

treach·er·ous (trech′·ər·əs) *adj.* Not as good or safe as it appears; dangerous.

trem·or (trem′·ər) *n.* 1. A quick shaking movement. 2. A nervous or trembling feeling of excitement.

truce (tr o͞o s) *n.* A temporary relief or rest.

tu·tor (t o͞o ′·tər) 1. *n.* A person who teaches another, usually privately. 2. *v.* To give or receive private instruction.

vac·u·um (vak′·y o͞o m) *n.* An empty space where no air or matter exists.

val·or (val′·ər) *n.* Great courage or bravery.

ven·i·son (ven′·ə·sən) *n.* The flesh of the deer, used for food.

verge (vûrj) *n.* 1. The edge of something. 2. The point at which some action or condition is likely to occur.

vi·per (vī′·pər) *n.* Any of a family of various poisonous snakes.

vin·dic·tive (vin·dik′·tiv) *adj.* Revengeful; unforgiving.

vi·tal (vīt′·əl) *adj.* 1. Necessary or essential to life. 2. Important.

wharf (hwôrf) *n.* A structure built along or out from a shore at which boats may tie up and load or unload; a pier.

whim (hwim) *n.* A sudden desire, notion, or idea; an impulse.

wretch·ed (rech′·id) *adj.* Very unhappy; miserable.